The Lost World of Sarala Devi

# The Lost World of Sarala Devi

*Selected Works*

Edited by
Sachidananda Mohanty

OXFORD
UNIVERSITY PRESS

# OXFORD
## UNIVERSITY PRESS

Oxford University Press is a department of the University of Oxford.
It furthers the University's objective of excellence in research, scholarship,
and education by publishing worldwide. Oxford is a registered trademark of
Oxford University Press in the UK and in certain other countries

Published in India by
Oxford University Press
YMCA Library Building, 1 Jai Singh Road, New Delhi 110001, India

ISBN-13: 978-0-19-946667-2
ISBN-10: 0-19-946667-X

Typeset in Goudy Oldstyle Std 11/13.2
by The Graphics Solution, New Delhi 110092
Printed in India by Avantika Printers Pvt Ltd, New Delhi 110065

Dedicated to the memory of Sarala Devi
(1904–1986)

A young Sarala Devi, courtesy:
Estate of Sarala Devi

Sarala Devi with her son
Amitabha Mohapatra,
courtesy: Estate of Sarala Devi

Sarala Devi (lower row, left) at a women's conference in Balasore, 1933, courtesy: Nityananda Mohapatra and Sachidananda Mohanty

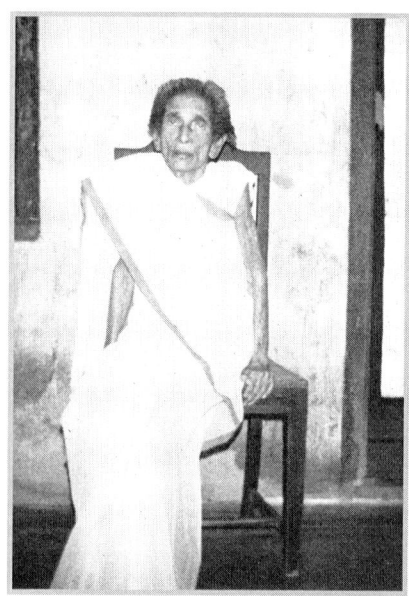

Sarala Devi at a late age, quite close to her death, courtesy: Estate of Sarala Devi

# Contents

## Sisterhood for Empowerment

## Writing for Children

## The Gandhian Vision

## Art and National Life

## Literature and Religion/Spirituality

# Foreword

*The pain and oppression women traditionally suffered for ages are responsible for the flame of rebellion now burning in society.*
—Devi quoted in Mohanty (2005: 154)

Sarala Devi wrote these words in 1934 in '*Narira Dabi*' (The Rights of Women), an essay that chronicled the injustices faced by women throughout the world from ancient to modern times. Directing her attention to India, she censured a society that defined work by gender, denied a woman the right to her body, treasured the double standard as religious doctrine, and used law to render women powerless. However, things had begun to change, she told her readers. All around the world, women were becoming conscious of the injustices they suffered and taking control of their destinies.

These words, echoing two influential feminist documents—Olympe de Gouges's 'Declaration of the Rights of Woman and the Female Citizen' (1791) and Mary Wollstonecraft's 'A Vindication of the Rights of Woman' (1792)—were written by an Odia woman whose name has been omitted from feminist histories and anthologies of women writing in India. Reading Sarala Devi's writings and learning about her activism, one is amazed at what she accomplished and chagrined that historians—including me—are only learning about her in the twenty-first century.

Sarala Devi was one of a number of women Sachidananda Mohanty has called 'Rebati's sisters', a reference to Fakir Mohan Senapati's female character Rebati who resisted conservative society to pursue her education. Born into a zamindar family but raised by her deputy collector uncle Balamukunda Kanungo, Sarala Devi moved with him when he was transferred. Beginning her education in an Odia-medium school, she later studied at Ravenshaw Girls' School in Cuttack, at Crawford Girls' School in Sambalpur, and with tutors. Like so many girls of her generation, she was married soon after puberty—in her case, at 14—and had to leave school. Her husband Bhagirathi Mohapatra was a zamindar like her father, a lawyer by profession, and a man interested in nationalist politics. Although marriage ended the studies of many girls, this was not true for Sarala Devi who read vociferously and acquired the knowledge of someone who had completed a postgraduate degree.

When Sarala Devi was 16 years old, Bhagirathi took her with him in the December of 1920 to the Nagpur meeting of the Indian National Congress (INC). The Nagpur Congress accepted Gandhi's leadership and proclaimed the objective of Swaraj by legitimate and peaceful means. The next year, when Gandhi visited Odisha, he was cared for by the 17-year-old Sarala Devi who also organized a special meeting in Cuttack where he met with about 40 women. 'Gandhiji gave me a new lease on life', Sarala Devi wrote in the essay 'My Idol' (2006: 38). These could have been the words of any one of a number of young women who found Gandhi's message electrifying.

Although calling Gandhi a feminist is unfashionable in today's time, many of the women who joined his movement were attracted by his faith in women's strength and his invitation to them to play a larger role in politics and society. In her article 'Construction and

Reconstruction of Woman in Gandhi', Sujata Patel (1988: 385) argued that Gandhi's ability to help women was hampered by his limited understanding of their oppression, obsession with chastity, and rejection of sexuality. However, Patel's views and those who echo her sentiments seem far removed from the women who knew and loved the Mahatma. Writing after his death in 1948, Sarala Devi (2005: 164) predicted that Gandhi 'would always be revered as the great mentor of the women of India'.

Devoted to Gandhi and the struggle against the British, Sarala Devi convinced her husband to leave the legal profession and devote his attention to the freedom movement. Together they established Alakashram at Jagatsinghpur. Sarala Devi was also deeply concerned with women's issues and organized the Utkal Mahila Sammilani, affiliated with the All India Women's Conference (AIWC), to fight for women's rights.

In 1930, she joined the Salt Satyagraha and broke the salt law at Ganjam. Arrested, she was sent to the prison in Vellore with an illustrious crowd of freedom fighters including Kamaladevi Chattopadhyaya, Durgabai, and Krishnabai Rao. In a cheerful letter to her husband 'Bhagu Babu', written in English, she called it a 'delightful time' and reminded him that 'since I am away from home and will not be back for another period of six months, the responsibilities of bringing up our only child rests upon your shoulders alone' (2005: 161–2).

Sarala Devi's political career was not limited to agitation. The first woman elected to the Odisha Assembly when Odisha became a separate province in 1936, she fought for women's education and property rights, and against early marriage and dowry. After 1947, she 'felt sidelined', Mohanty writes, in both state and national politics. This was a story familiar among women activists who sent Jawaharlal Nehru a manifesto of women's demands before the 1937 election and asked for a list of INC candidates who supported their agenda. Nehru characterized the manifesto as naïve and scolded the women for ignoring the INC's role in achieving social transformation (J. Nehru to Swaminadhan 1936). He promised that the INC would support women running for seats reserved for women but this support was not extended to women who stood for general seats. After Independence, many women activists, including Nehru's cousin Manmohini Zutshi Sahgal, looked forward to claiming a place in the new nation, but like Sarala Devi, they were either denied help outright or given insufficient support to win the election.

A prolific writer—30 books and 300 essays—Sarala Devi discussed a wide array of topics from historical heroines to spiritualism. Mohanty has discussed her writing career in the 'Introduction' and included in the volume examples of Sarala Devi's writing on art and national life, literature and spirituality, and stories for children alongside her feminist and political essays. Mohanty does justice to this complicated woman by his selection from her writings and recognition of changes in her position on certain issues. Sadly, he informs us, she was a neglected woman at the time of her death in 1986.

What is especially interesting and annoying is that it was not until the mid to late 1990s that scholars began to write about Sarala Devi, first in Odia, and then in English. Mohanty's 'Sarala Devi: The Biplabi of Orissa' (1998) was the first article that appeared in English. How do we explain this neglect, and what does it mean for women's history?

Women's history is a branch of social history that aims to transform history and society by recovering the stories of women left out of the dominant narrative. In addition to the problem of archives, the very subjects considered worthy of historical attention seldom meshed with women's lived lives. Women's domain was different—involving the household and children—and, in comparison to men, they were far less likely to have had an education or the leisure to write. Over the years, historians have learned how to read silences, read from the margins, and investigate the material world for clues to women's lives. Difficulties with the archives explain why it is hard to retrieve the stories of subaltern women but not how and why a woman like Sarala Devi—literate, articulate, and fully present in the public sphere—was overlooked. Part of the answer lies in Mohanty's revelation that she was politically sidelined after 1947. In contrast, her friend Durgabai [Deshmukh] became a member of the Constituent Assembly and, in 1953, the first chair of the Central Social Welfare Board. Some loyal women supporters of Gandhi and the Congress were given cabinet positions (Amrit Kaur), ambassadorships (Vijaya Lakshmi Pandit), and governorships (Sucheta Kriplani), while others were left out in the cold. Research that untangles the processes by which Sarala Devi—a feminist, an activist, and an author— lost favour with political leaders or withdrew from politics would help us understand why she has been so long neglected. What her story illustrates is that written history is not what happened at the time but, as George Orwell wrote in *Nineteen Eighty-Four*, an issue of who controls the narrative. Orwell (1949) wrote: "'[He] who controls the past,' ran the Party slogan, "controls the future: who controls the present controls the past.'"

What have we lost by Sarala Devi's absence from the historical record? To begin, the history of the struggle for freedom from colonial rule is incomplete without the inclusion of Odia women's roles. In 1930, women's agitation against the salt laws telegraphed to the world that the nation was behind Gandhi. Women's support of Gandhi was essential to the logistics of the large, peaceful demonstrations that helped wrest moral authority from the British empire.

Secondly, our understanding of the development of Indian feminism is incomplete without Sarala Devi's voice. Her feminism, expressed in her essays and biographies of notable women, developed from her reading and experience. Mohanty informs us that there is no list of what she read, so we do not know if she read Wollstonecraft and other feminist authors or came to these ideas on her own. We can assume her views on child marriage, child widows, property, and women's right to their bodies came from experience, but she also belonged to a circle of women who read, translated, and wrote about their ideas. Her women's organization was affiliated with the powerful and patriotic AIWC with its yearly conferences and dynamic women leaders. Learning about Sarala Devi's ideas can help us understand the vibrant networks women developed in this period.

Finally, we have missed a voice that spoke in Odia to those who did not read English. Women's history began with an agenda—

inserting gender into the dominant narrative—and has often neglected regional accounts that may or may not fit neatly into the picture. To recapture the times, we need to understand how the local was connected to the national agenda and where it diverged. Gerda Lerner, the doyen of women's history, instructed us to both look for what women had done and, at the same time, ponder how leaving them out of history had affected women's lives. Writing long before Lerner became a historian, Sarala Devi knew that unless girls realized there were great women in history, they would accept conventional definitions of female and male roles. Unfortunately, until recently Sarala Devi's story and oeuvre have not been widely available in Odisha. In addition to making selected examples of Sarala Devi's writings available in English, this publication will encourage additional research of value to women's history.

Geraldine Forbes
Distinguished Teaching Professor Emerita
State University of New York at Oswego

# Acknowledgements

I would like to thank the following who contributed to the making of the book: Sarala Devi's family members at Cuttack, in particular, Laxmi Prasad Mahapatra; the translators who spared their valuable time and effort; Professor Jatindra K. Nayak for timely help; the Odisha State Archives, Bhubaneswar; the National Library at Kolkata; the library of the Utkal Sahitya Samaj at Cuttack; the Estate of Sarala Devi, Cuttack, for access to the manuscripts, copyright permission, and the use of photographs; SAGE Publications for the use of translations that had appeared in *A Lost Tradition: Early Women's Writings in Orissa, 1896–1950* (2005); Department of English, University of Hyderabad; and benefactors too numerous to be listed here. I also thank Professor Geraldine Forbes, a distinguished literary feminist for an excellent foreword; the editorial team and others at Oxford University Press who steered this project so ably through various stages of the publication; R. Nagarajan, School of Humanities, University of Hyderabad; my family members at Pondicherry, Bhubaneswar, and Bhadrak; and finally, Simi for her support for a life of the mind.

# Introduction*

There has been welcome attention since the 1970s to Indian women's personal narratives of the earlier era,[1] located in the matrix of gender and the nation. Despite this advancement, however, vital aspects of feminist historiography continue to remain an area of darkness. The main objective of this book is to bridge this gap and bring together some of the best writings of Sarala Devi, an iconic literary feminist and activist of Odisha, who lived and wrote in the first half of the twentieth century, but whose seminal works are completely absent in the public domain today.[2] This work stands at the intersection of gender, translation, and cultural history in the interdisciplinary context and contributes significantly to the making of Indian feminism.

Indeed, few literary women could rival the achievements of Sarala Devi. A multifaceted personality, she was a poet,

---

* All translations of the original texts from Odia into English, unless otherwise stated, are by me.

novelist, short-story writer, critic, translator, and columnist of great distinction. She was also a freedom fighter, a feminist, an activist, a social reformer, and an educationist par excellence. She began as a rebel and a radical in the 1920s, and ended as a critical traditionalist who remained a staunch Gandhian until the end, before passing away in 1986.

## Complex Trajectories

As a part of feminist historiography, this volume attempts to situate the life and work of Sarala Devi in the context of her times; it shows the evolution of her thinking as a literary woman. As explained later in this chapter, the trajectories in Sarala Devi's ideology and politics were complex and, at times, contradictory. The difference is evidenced in the views she expressed in 'Narira Dabi', as well as the nine chapters she wrote in the novel Basanti in 1931, which centre-staged female agency vis-à-vis the memorandum she submitted to the University Grants Commission (UGC) as a member of the Senate of Utkal University regarding the need for a separate system of education for women,[3] a problematic category. Nevertheless, as we shall see, Sarala prefigures some of the best thinking on the subject in a remarkable manner.

Sarala Devi lived between 9 August 1904 and 4 October 1986. Her life and career covered some of the most momentous periods of the twentieth century: the consolidation of the British Empire in India, the national freedom struggle, the two World Wars, the Quit India Movement, the Indian Independence, the euphoria over the creation of the Indian Republic and the subsequent disillusionments, the Cold War, the Vietnam War, and the Sino-India conflict. Her essays record these triumphs and tribulations, hope and despair. Seen as a whole, they provide a vital prism through which we can see the many sides of the Indian experiment during the twentieth century, essentially from a woman's point of view.

## Women as Universal Dependents

Assessing Sarala's position in the Indian feminist thought is an important and challenging project that goes beyond the boundary of an introduction to a critical anthology such as this one. She was a Gandhian feminist and a critical modernist who eschewed exclusive binaries between the home and the public space, the sacred and the secular. It is not known whether she read and was inspired by the earlier narratives such as those of Binodini Dasi (1863–1941), Cornelia Sorabji (1866–1954), Rokeya Sakhawat Hossain (1880–1932), Indira Sahasrabuddhe,[4] Subhadra Kumari Chauhan (1904–1948), and others such as Mahadevi Verma (1907–1987). However, it is likely that she felt attuned to their approach to life and emancipation, albeit with her own caveats to the questions posed. Certainly, she kept herself abreast with the accounts of contemporary critics who spearheaded efforts in this direction. It is time, therefore, that feminist historiography ensured Sarala Devi's rightful place in the Indian feminist thought.[5] Some preliminary reflections in this direction are in order. They would help frame this collection in a certain context.

While Sarala was not a theorist in the conventional sense of the term, her views on feminism were informed by wide readings, critical thinking, and an astute understanding of woman's location in patriarchy; indeed, they appear amazingly close to the views of some contemporary feminists. For instance, while she spoke of women's oppression as a global phenomenon, she was careful to reject the view, as many later feminists did, of 'women as universal dependents' and 'married women as victims of the colonial process'. Similarly, she made a nuanced response to the question of 'women and religious ideologies'. While most Western feminists made sweeping generalizations about the uniformly oppressive nature of religion, especially with regard to Hinduism and Islam, Sarala argued that our critique must be context-specific and be informed by particular histories of women in the given societies and ideologies. Her views on Islam and women, as we shall see in some of the translated texts in this volume, were exceptionally original. While she was against imperialism, she also saw the dangers of an unbridled nativism or linguistic chauvinism. It is important to look at significant aspects of Sarala's writings in terms of the categories a number of Third World feminists such as Chandra Talpade Mohanty, Madhu Kishwar, and Ruth Vanita critiqued. Chandra Mohanty's path-breaking essay 'Under

Western Eyes: Feminist Scholarship and Colonial Discourses' (1997) seems to prefigure in a striking manner many of the insights and seed ideas found in the works of Sarala Devi who strongly advocated the need for grounding Western theory on the Indian soil.

Indeed, contemporary Western feminists such as Geraldine Forbes, with a considerable track record of archival research in India, acknowledge the bias that existed for long in the West regarding the history of the women's movement in India.[6] Forbes cites Miriam Schneir's introduction to the volume entitled *Feminism: The Essential Historical Writings* (1970) as representative of this prejudice: 'No feminist works,' claims Schneir (1970: xiv) sweepingly, 'emerged from behind the Hindu purdah or out of the Moslem harems; centuries of slavery do not provide soil for intellectual development or expression.' As we shall see, Sarala rejected comprehensively this view of woman's automatic subjugation and subordination in Eastern cultures. Her narratives, in *Beera Ramani*, of the heroic women of her land who led emancipated lives despite great odds, amply proves the existence of a vibrant tradition of indigenous feminism. She drew attention to such role models and argued that Indian women could fashion out their lives inspired by such narratives.[7] She contributed significantly to protest literature in the early-twentieth-century India.

Sarala's contribution is noteworthy in at least four areas: first, her critical interventions in building up a modern Odisha in the image of a progressive nation; second, her use of literature, especially essays and speeches, for social critique and social transformation; third, her advocacy of an increasing control of women over their biological and reproductive selves; and finally, her espousal of women's participation in the larger public space.

Important as they are, it would be incorrect to reduce Sarala's writings to the aforementioned four areas alone, for she straddles the worlds of literature, culture, and religion and spirituality with equal felicity and ease. Consequently, the present volume goes beyond social and feminist visions and attempts to bring in representative texts from the domain of religion and spirituality, such as her creative renderings of works such as *Tulasi Das* and *Katha Ramayana* (The Odia Version of the Ramayana). Regrettably, I did not have equal success in accessing her poetry written during the early part of her career. The future editions of her work would hopefully make them more inclusive in this regard.

Sarala came from a conservative zamindar background and studied up to class seven. However, due to her innate intelligence and sheer personal effort, she turned out to be an outstanding littérateur. Although many Odia women excelled in the literary field in the pre- and post-Independence periods, Sarala remains unparalleled as one who combined literary creativity and social activism with remarkable success. Indeed, few women of the region can rival her in terms of the many genres in which she excelled. She scored, above all, as a feminist essayist of rare distinction.

Sarala Devi was the first Odia woman to court imprisonment under Gandhi's satyagraha movement. She was a prolific writer who maintained a high intellectual standard in her works. She was a critical modernist who centre-staged issues such as the importance of mother-tongue education and principles of Gandhian economy that have become articles of faith today. She spoke of women's need to have control over their bodily self and decried the practice of marital rape. Thus she voiced concerns that were far ahead of her times.

Not many critical studies exist on Sarala Devi barring newspaper and magazine articles. Three books (in Odia) are worth mentioning in this context: *Mahiyasai Mahila: Sarala* (Sarala, the Great Woman, 1995) by V. Rajendra Raju, *Sarala Devi* (2009) by Ajay Kumar Mishra, and *Alibha Anala Shikha: Sarala* (Sarala, the Ever-burning Flame, 1999) by Banaj Devi.

Sarala's studies in literary feminism and related areas would rank as some of the best of all times. They were original in approach, insightful, confident in tone, and put forth arguments in a systematic dialogic fashion, backed by wide reading and knowledge of the larger world. Her feminist essay 'Narira Dabi' would remain a classic statement about women's rights that brings to mind the seminal work of Mary Wollstonecraft. Her essay broke free from the conformist feminine discourse of the late nineteenth and early twentieth centuries, much of which eschewed the overtly political in favour of the mystical and devotional. Gandhian in approach, she harmonized in her ideological thinking the contradictions between regionalism and the nascent nationalism that others saw as mutually antagonistic.

In the post-Independence period, she continued writing in order to draw attention to literary and social causes. However, she felt sidelined by the prevalent political and ideological forces in Odisha that made her marginal to the state and national politics as well as the contemporary world of feminism. When she passed away in 1986, she died neglected and unnoticed, and continues to remain so today. Judged from the vantage point of contemporary Indian feminism, Sarala Devi appears to be an avant-garde. Her life and work deserve to be brought to the public domain as an essential part of the feminist archives.

## Life and Times

During the late nineteenth and early twentieth centuries, several factors, including the movement for the preservation of the Odia language, the rise of Odia regional consciousness, the advent of the Brahmo Samaj, the campaign for widow remarriage, the legal abolition of untouchability, and the struggle for national independence, brought the women writers of Odisha into the larger public domain. Writers such as Kokila Devi, Reba Ray, Sailabala Das, Narmada Kar, Pratibha Devi, Kuntala Kumari Sabat, Sita Devi Khadanga, Bidyut Prabha, and others modelled themselves—consciously or unconsciously—after Fakir Mohan Senapati's female protagonist Rebati, who, in the memorable tale under the same title, displays a forbidden desire for learning. Rebati became an icon for female education, a role model for other women to follow. We, therefore, may term these literary women of Odisha as 'Rebati's sisters'. Sarala's writing can be seen in the background of this tradition. It shares interface with many progressive movements in the state such as the rise of female education, trade union movements, and women's participation in various aspects of civic and political life.

Sarala Devi was born into a conservative Karan (Kayastha) family of Narilo village, Balikuda, in the undivided Cuttack district of the erstwhile Odisha. Her parents were Basudeva Kanungo and Padmavati Devi. Raised by her uncle (father's elder brother) Balamukunda Kanungo, who was a deputy collector, and her aunt Hemanta Kumari Devi, Sarala was strongly drawn to education since early childhood. She rebelled against conservative customs and practices prevalent in the household. Though spiritual-minded, she developed strong reservations against orthodox religion when she came across this scriptural indictment: 'Woman is the veritable gateway to hell' (Devi quoted in Raju 1995:14). She expressed similar views in an autobiographical essay entitled 'The Story of My Revolutionary Life': 'The God who does not belong to woman,' she wrote, 'and is only a property of man, the sin in whose committing only woman becomes fallen and a man remains untouched, that religion and that custom gradually became bereft of meaning for me' (Devi quoted in Raju 1995: 14–15).

Sarala studied up to class seven with the help of a tutor and read, by her own efforts, many Bengali books including the works of Bankim Chandra Chatterjee and Sarat Chandra Chattopadhyaya. She also greatly admired Raja Ram Mohan Roy, Keshav Chandra Sen, Dayananda Saraswati, Swami Vivekananda, and Ishwar Chandra Vidyasagar. Much of her formal education, however, came to an end when, at the age of 14, she got married to Bhagirathi Mohapatra of Chatra, Jagatsinghpur, in the undivided Cuttack district in 1918. Educated and a liberal-minded patriot, Bhagirathi practised law under the well-known barrister Madhusudan Das, the architect of modern Odisha.

Bhagirathi and Sarala attended the 35th session of the INC at Nagpur in 1920 along with 14,000 delegates. This marked a turning point in Sarala's life. Soon after the Nagpur session, there was the formation of the Utkal Pradesh Congress Committee (UPCC). When Gandhi visited Odisha in 1921, Sarala looked after him in a cottage on the bank of the river Kathajodi. She played a leading role in organizing a special meeting at Binod Bihari, Cuttack, exclusively for about 40 women. As Sarala (2006: 38) recalled later, 'Gandhiji gave me a new lease of life. He infused into me the flame of a new world and new revolutionary ardor.' She rendered Gandhi's Hindi lecture into English and 'appealed to the women folk to donate liberally in the form of money and jewellery for the "Harijan Fund"'.

Inspired by Gandhi in 1921, Sarala and Bhagirathi Mohapatra set up in their village property the Alakashram on the bank of the historic Alaka river which, in the earlier days, had aided trade activities; they established a school to impart swadeshi education to children. Soon the Alakashram became a well-known centre for nationalist activities. When Gandhi visited Cuttack, and was unable to travel to Jagatsinghpur, he gave a message to the inmates of the Alakashram: 'Lead simple and plain lives. Think of high ideals and thoughts. Do not make your minds so many blotting sheets of Western civilization.' Sarala Devi, Rama Devi, and the latter's daughter Annapurna Maharana were active members of the Alakashram. Following the suggestion of Nabakrushna Choudhury, a monthly journal named *Alaka* was started.

Although the fortunes of the Alakashram declined in due course, it continued to be the centre of nationalist politics and activities. In 1936, Jawaharlal Nehru, the then president of the INC, began his electoral campaign from the Alakashram. Similarly, the ashram was associated with Jayaprakash Narayan during the Quit India Movement (1942) and later, in the 1950s, the Bhoodan Movement of Vinoba Bhave. Thus, an institution that Sarala and Bhagirathi helped create has left a lasting legacy (Patnaik 2006).[8]

Sarala took a leading part in the Non-Cooperation Movement in Odisha. Travelling extensively, she collected money for the Tilak Swaraj Fund. She was assisted in this mission by several writer-activists such as Sailabala Das, Kuntala Kumari Sabat, and Rama Devi. At the initiative of Lavanyavati Devi, the daughter of the eminent Odia lexicographer Gopal Chandra Praharaj, a nationalistic women's association called Mahila Bandhu came into being.

Sarala took part in the Salt Satyagraha at Inchudi in Balasore,[9] following the decision by the UPCC on 16 March 1930. She toured other areas such as Ghumsar and Huma, the latter in Ganjam district. She was imprisoned at Chhatrapur and subsequently spent six months in the Vellore jail in the South in the company of illustrious women freedom fighters such as Durgabai Deshmukh, Lakshmipathy, and Kamaladevi Chattopadhyaya. In a letter dated 23 June 1930 written to her husband from the Presidency Jail for Women, Vellore, Madras Presidency, Sarala describes her eventful life in the jail marked by activities such as spinning and learning of Hindi, English, and music. Her letter, written in chaste English, advises her husband to take care of their little son Tikun in the Alakashram in their village Chatra. She wrote:

> I would like you very much to keep him (Tikun) under special care, and see that he receives at this early age the best possible training, as a child's future always depends upon the manners and environments in which it is brought up. Since I am away from home and shall not be back for another period of six months, the responsibilities of bringing up our only child rests upon your shoulder alone. Before I came away, you made me understand that you would send the little Tikun to the *Alakashram*. If you have not done so, kindly send him as early as you can. Let me suggest that it would be better if you could also reside in the ashram along with the child so that he might not feel lonely. (Mohanty 2005: 165)

After her release from the Vellore jail on 8 December 1930, Sarala returned to Cuttack and was given a triumphant public reception organized by fellow activist Binapani Devi. Sarala joined hands with Kuntala Kumari Sabat, Basanta Kumari Devi (Dei), Sarojini Choudhury, Kokila Devi, and Jahnavi Devi to form the Nikhila Utkal Nari Parishad, with 30 active members and with representatives from Puri, Ganjam, Cuttack, and Balasore. She wrote plays and exhorted women to participate in the freedom struggle in large numbers. As *Utkal Dipika* reported on 7 November 1931, 'She desires to involve Odiya women in her plays. She believes that Odiya women are remaining in the background.

They feel shy to come out. If they can be involved in acting in plays, they will no longer feel different. That is why Sarala is going to many houses on her mission' (Raju 1995: 31). Similarly, she participated in the activities of the Utkal Congress Samyavadi Karmi, a Marxist organization dedicated to the welfare of the peasantry (Raju 1995: 31). It was led by activists such as Bhagabati Charan Panigrahi, Nabakrushna Choudhury, Surendranath Dwivedy, and Malati Choudhury.

Sarala's struggle remained relentless and unabated. She took active part in the Prohibition and Swadeshi movements as well as the movement against untouchability. At the success of the Mahila Bandhu Samiti, Sarala said:

> I feel gratified that my cherished dream of the past has been finally realized. It was truly beyond my expectations that the women of Utkal would one day find recognition. This is a new chapter in the history of Orissa. Which lover of the nation would not be filled with joy in seeing the rise of the woman's voice? There was a ray of hope in the depressed heart. It is worth knowing that the effort might be negligible but that the soul of an institution always remains alive. (Raju 1995: 31)

After Odisha was formed on a linguistic basis on 1 April 1936, Sarala was elected to the assembly as the first woman member. In the assembly, she championed many progressive causes. She piloted a bill related to women's education and welfare, and advocated the use of the mother tongue Odia in all legislative proceedings (Raju 1995: 22). She introduced a bill against the practice of dowry and served as the acting speaker of the assembly on 24 March 1939. She urged that primary education should be free and universal, and that peasants be given interest-free loans by the agricultural cooperative bank.[10] Similarly, for the welfare and protection of women, she advocated the abolition of child marriage and demanded that the house passed the 'Estate Women's Protection Act', following the rape and murder of a 13-year-old girl by a local king who was supported by the British. Sarala participated actively in the Quit India Movement and courted imprisonment along with her husband.

Apart from her activism, Sarala served many organizations with distinction. She was the first woman director of the Cuttack Central Co-operative Bank. She served as an elected member of several educational and cultural organizations of the province, such as the Senate of Utkal University, the local board of Cuttack, the Orissa Pradesh Congress Committee, as well as the standing committee of the AIWC. She was the office-bearer of several organizations, vice president of the Utkal Sahitya Samaj, and secretary of the Cuttack District Congress.

By the early 1950s, Sarala Devi had begun to feel disillusioned by the political developments at the regional and national levels. She found her political aspirations constantly thwarted by vested interests in the Congress Party. In a confidential letter written to Pandit Nehru (dated 1 October 1951), she lamented that the Utkal Congress authorities completely 'ignored the cause of women's representation in Parliament' (Devi quoted in Mohapatra forthcoming). She opposed the policies of successive chief ministers as oppressive and anti-people. As a member of the Utkal Sammilani, she campaigned and courted arrest for the merger of land that she thought justly belonged to the province of Odisha. These included the princely states of Saraikela and Kharsawan[11] that became part of the Singhbhum district of Bihar.

## Literary Works

Sarala Devi's literary works straddle many genres and disciplines.[12] She wrote knowledgeably about issues that are central to the understanding of her life and times.[13] She made wide use of literary forms such as poetry, drama, fiction, essay, letters, and literary criticism. Sadly, her work is no longer in the public domain today. Some of her books were self-published. Despite their radical contents and literary merits, a number of them, in the published form, had limited print runs and editions.[14] The pre-Independence and the pre-Gandhian national imaginary were largely shaped by colonial patriarchy. The Bengal

Renaissance and the subsequent national awakening went
hand in hand with the continued seclusion of women within
the inner chamber of the home. No doubt, as Susie Tharu and
K. Lalitha (1993, 1995) and others show, many aspiring women
broke out of the shackles and taught themselves to read and
write. However, the prevailing society and culture in eastern
India and elsewhere conditioned women in terms of what came
to be known as the conduct books or advice-for-women texts.[15]
In Bengal, such advice-for-women texts include the influential
*Ramanir Kartavya* (Duties of Women), and in pre-Independence
Odisha, Jagabandhu Singh's widely circulated *Grihalakshmi* (The
Lakshmi of the House, 1946 [1940]) that appeared in several
editions is one such text.

Although many Odia women wrote before her, Sarala did
not have the desired role models. For example, Sulakshana Devi
(b. 1829), Suchitra Devi (b. 1881), Annapurna Devi, and others
mostly wrote in the devotional/mystical mode.[16] They were
not concerned, for the most part, with sociopolitical, cultural,
or ideological issues. However, Odia society witnessed major
changes after the arrival of the British in 1803. The introduction
of female education and print culture by the missionary press in
Odisha[17] and the emergence of the native elite, many of whom
wrote in the twin journals *Utkal Dipika* edited by Gourishankar
Ray and *Utkal Sahitya* edited by Biswanath Kar, were the principal
factors that shaped the thinking of male and female writers. The
early Odia novels such as *Padmamali* (1888) by Umesh Chandra
Sarkar and *Bhima Bhuyan* (1908) by Gopal Ballav Das,[18] based
largely on the bedrock of romance and mythology, were replaced
by the social–realistic fiction of Fakir Mohan Senapati. Genres
such as the periodical essay and drama mirrored their Western
counterparts. Sailabala Das (né Hazra), the adopted daughter of
Madhusudan Das and Reba Ray, a distinguished Brahmo poet and
littérateur, were two early literary women who pioneered female
education in the state. Sarala initially followed their footsteps,
but soon she and Kuntala Kumari discovered their own unique
voice and carved out a place for themselves.

## Poetry

Sarala began her literary career early in life. Her first poems were published in a literary magazine called *Paricharika* edited by Basanta Kumari Devi (Dei). She was associated as a co-editor with a handwritten journal called *Alaka*. Some of her pieces also appeared in a Bengali magazine called *Debjani*. Later she published in many leading magazines and journals such as *Nababharata, Utkal Sahitya, Sahakara, Jugabina, Asha Nabina, Prabhat, Asanta Kali, Dagara, Jhankar,* and *Agrani.*

Many of Sarala's early poems published in *Paricharika* were marked by the love of nature, of historical past, devotion to God, and a general philosophical outlook on life. The underlying spiritual and mystical longing is evidenced in a lyrical poem 'Akyansha' (Aspiration) published in *Paricharika*. Similarly, another poem 'Pratiksha'[19] (The Wait) captured the changing mood of women in accordance with the change of seasons. Waiting seems to be endless, for vigil becomes fruitless without the arrival of the beloved. Each of the six Indian seasons has its unique charm and visual appeal. Each has inspired poetry and music capturing seasonal moods. Such memorable nature poems, written in the rhyme scheme, parallel other outputs of Sarala including patriotic compositions such as 'Bharat Mata Ki Jai' (Hail Mother India) published later in life.

Sarala's poetic works are relatively few. Soon she turned to the prose form and concentrated on this genre for the most part of her career. However, her poetry, despite being meagre, was significant. It testifies to her creative self that relied on a spontaneous and original approach to life and literature.

Sarala's literary output includes more than 30 books and 300 essays. Some of her prominent books are *Rabindra Puja* (Homage to Rabindranath, 1941), *Utkal Bharati Kabi Pratibha* (The Poetic Genius of Utkal Bharati, 1940), *Maru Kahani* (Tales of the Desert, 1953), *Pancha Pradipa* (Five Lamps), *Sarala Mahabharatare Nari Chitra* (The Portrayal of Women in Sarala Mahabharata, 1952), *Bharatiya Mahila Prasanga* (About Indian Women, 1935), *Utkalara Nari Samasya* (About the Problems of Odia Women, 1935), *Nari Jagata* (The World of Women, 1936), *Beera Ramani* (Heroic Women),

*Bishwa Biplabini* (Women Revolutionaries of the World, 1958), *Raya Ramananda Kabi* (Ramananda the Poet), *Gopalakrishna Pratibha* (The Genius of Gopalakrishna), *Katha Ramayana*, *Amulyanidhi*, *Narira Dabi*, and others.

## Translations

Sarala devoted her early life to poetry and translation. Initially drawn to the Puranas, she translated into Odia Omkarnath's *Katha Ramayana*. The Odia renderings of the Ramayana are expressed in a simple language and underline the moral significance of the tales. Similarly, she skilfully translated the two plays *Swapnavasavadutta* and Rayaramanada's *Jagannatha Ballava*. Given her creative approach, Sarala's translations appear more like transcreations. The original Sanskrit lines of *Kumara Sambham* are expressed in colloquial Odia. Likewise, Omkarnath's *Sati Dharma* (The Dharma of a Chaste Woman), translated by Sarala, based on the original 13 chapters, underlines the spiritual significance of a concept that was much abused by decadent social practices.[20]

## Short Stories

Sarala wrote many short stories that show a command over this form. For example, the tale 'Kalpita Mrutyu' (Imagined Death), which was published in *Paricharika*, centred on the life of Rama Sahani. The protagonist Sahani is an ideal male character of 60 years who is physically robust and morally upright. He risks his life in order to protect the hapless Alli, the daughter of the milkman Karuna. Sahani is arrested and hanged by the police for killing the cruel and rapacious zamindar Madan Babu. Sahani's manhood is expressed in the remarks he utters before his hanging: 'I was born a man. I died as a man!' Alli immerses the ashes of Rama Sahani in the sacred city of Gaya.

Similarly, Sarala's ghost story 'Dahani Katha' (The Tale of the Witch) is based on a folk tale. Most of her stories are based on animal rights, ideal conjugal conduct, and ethical behaviour. A powerful tale such as 'Gotie Chhabi' (A Portrait) deals with the tragic tale of the widow Rati who is driven out of her home and commits suicide due to illegitimate pregnancy. This story as well as others are born out of a deep desire for social reforms and gender equality.

## Novels

Sarala's sole unnamed novel remains unpublished. However, she wrote nine chapters (Chapters 8, 9, 17, 18, 19, 20, 21, 22, and 27) of the iconic novel *Basanti* that show her unique ability as a novelist. The novel was jointly written by nine leading members of the Sabuja (Romantic) Group, namely Kalindi Charan Panigrahi, Sarat Chandra Mukherjee, Harihar Mohapatra, Annada Shankar Ray, Sarala Devi, Suprabha Devi, Muralidhar Mohanty, Pratibha Devi, and Baishnab Charan Das. Sarala's nine chapters stand out for her ability to sketch powerful women characters and deal with issues integral to feminist concerns. Through the protagonist Basanti, Sarala envisioned her ideal woman: active and intrepid, passionate and independent-minded, ready to chart out untrodden paths.

## Basanti: *A New Novelistic Experiment*

First published in 1931 by New Students' Store, Cuttack, as the second offering by the Sabuja Sahitya Samiti, *Basanti*[21] was reprinted by Pushpita Press, Kazi Bazar, Cuttack, in 1968 and then again in 1986 by Bhikari Charan Dash, New Students' Store. Dedicated to Biswanath Kar, the editor of the celebrated *Utkal Sahitya*, the novel was serialized in the pages of the journal during 1926–7.[22] The prefatory note by Dash outlines the background to the making of this unique book and the copyright agreement signed by 'Kalindi Charan Panigrahi as the Secretary of the Sabuja Sahitya Samiti'. The first edition of the book was published with Sarat Chandra Mukherjee as the editor with the names of 'some women authors left out'. This was the first experiment in collective novel writing in Odisha, and perhaps the last.

## The New Woman: Beyond the Domestic Space

The plot of the novel was outlined in the public for the benefit of would-be writers. The story relates to the family of Deputy Official Balarama Babu, whose untimely death rendered his widow Nirmala and daughter Basanti, living in Cuttack, destitute. Before her illness and demise, Nirmala had offered Basanti's hand in marriage to Debabrata, the carefree son of a wealthy zamindar, a student at the Ravenshaw College, who frequented the family and had become close to them. Romantic, liberal-minded, and honourable, Debabrata got married to Basanti much against the will of his mother Subhadra Dei who lived in their ancestral village in Balasore.

Basanti studied in a girls' school and was a believer in female education. While Debabrata was sympathetic to the woman's cause, he did not favour complete independence of women, for he believed that such independence would come in the way of conjugal love. (This is a refrain found recurrently in the novel.) The relationship between the two gradually soured due to misunderstandings, and Basanti became a near outcast in the immediate family. After much misunderstanding and parting, there was the final union between Debabrata and Basanti at Bardhaman in Bengal.

A careful look at the 30 short chapters of *Basanti* reveals that the 9 contributors to the novel carefully conceptualized and wrote their chapters in accordance with the overall design and the outline suggested at the outset. While a degree of tension may be noticed at a few places between the desire to stick to the given plot and the need to expand and develop parallel issues and secondary/minor characters, overall the novel holds together and seems to evolve organically. The role of the editor is clearly visible with regard to the tight knitting of the narrative and the manner in which the novelistic vision pans out in the 30 chapters, and leads to an effective and credible ending. The novel moves at a moderate-to-fast pace and captures aptly the ethos of its times in a realistic manner. Several issues—both ideological and societal—appear to be at the heart of the novel. These include social reforms, religious conflicts, the need for interfaith dialogue, and problems such as the dowry system, caste hierarchies, and the rural–urban divide. Above all, *Basanti* revolves around the larger question of female education and the need for female emancipation. Not surprisingly, the chapters that are most readable and engrossing are those written by three outstanding women writers of the times, namely Sarala Devi, Pratibha Devi, and Suprabha Devi; the last two were the daughters of Biswanath Kar.

*Basanti* is a political novel in the best sense of the term. Located against the backdrop of India's freedom struggle in the late 1920s, embracing the city and the village, the narrative attempts to find answers to questions that are deeply ideological in nature. Like Rabindranath's *Gora* (1910) that questioned the place of women in politically turbulent times, *Basanti* centre-staged crucial debates of the age. While it was written by nine authors, the three women authors, including Sarala Devi, contributed to the narrative in a distinct feminist tone and tenor.

## Tales for Children

In *Maru Kahani*, Sarala offers a set of fairy tales for children. In the 'Preface', she explains her basic objectives: 'I believe that children are more attracted to fantasy than facts. [The stories offered here] contain moral lessons; they have the twin purpose of delight and instruction.'

The stories are dedicated to women colleagues such as Shakuntala Devi, Radhamani Devi, Sailabala Devi, Debahuti Devi, and Rama Devi. The final tale is dedicated to her son Amitabha Mohapatra. The book contains six tales from different lands: 'The Magic Horse', 'The Tale of the Persian Merchant', 'The Tale of the Sorcerer's Wife', 'The Fisherman's Wit', 'The Ungrateful King', and finally, 'The Land of the Yakshas'.

The gripping tales cross national and cultural frontiers. They focus on universal moral and ethical issues such as loyalty, gratitude, obedience, and generosity. Most stories have alien settings and yet the principal characters in all are Indian. This seems to be a deliberate decision: to guarantee local interest and relevance for the Indian child. The narrator employs an easy, conversational tone, a typically colloquial style characteristic of a grandmother. Even here, one will notice Sarala's unfailing interest in gender and ethical questions. Consider, for instance, the ending of 'The Magic Horse', a story included in this volume: 'As the horse rose into the air, the prince shouted at the sultan, "O Sultan, you, who should have protected the princess who sought your protection, tried to exploit her instead. You humiliated and insulted her. If you wish to marry someone, first learn how to seek her permission."' Here is an advisory for a new conjugal bonding, meant for the socialization of the young.

Similarly, 'The Tale of the Persian Merchant', also inlcuded in this volume, invokes insightful geographical and cultural resonances from far-away Arab and Middle-Eastern regions, bringing in cities such as Cairo, Aleppo, and Damascus and food items such as olives into the discussion. The tale underlines the native wisdom of children in solving issues that are beyond the ken of adults: A group of children engaged in play-acting easily resolved what the Kazi and the Khalifa could not. The story concludes: 'The Khalifa learnt a lesson in law from the young boy: how to bring out the truth through intelligence. He was very pleased with the boy. So he gave the boy 100 gold coins for his wit and bid him farewell.' Here, Islam is not the alien 'other' but part of the lived experience that children of all faiths could empathize with and learn from.

The tales for children are fascinating; they are narrated with wit and humour. Combining delight and instruction, they have retained their freshness and could very well be offered to today's children.

*Essays*

Sarala handled the essay form in an unusually successful manner.[23] She took up a large number of themes for treatment. These ranged from society, culture, philosophy, and nationalism to the plight of the peasantry and other socioeconomic ills. She was particularly drawn to issues of feminist concern. In these essays, Sarala displayed a maturity of vision based on a critique of society and its institutions. A constantly questioning mind led to a defiance of the accepted forms of received wisdom, especially with regard to the social position of women. While personal letters, diary notes, and romances were commonly used by women in colonial Odisha (and India), Sarala was perhaps one of the first Odia women to use the essay form in the third person with logical arguments, facts, and statistics from unusual sources to prove her points. She engaged critically with the works of others and enunciated her own position persuasively with rhetorical flourish. It may, therefore, be correct to state that Sarala innovated the genre and began a new tradition of the feminist essay in colonial Odisha.

Let us consider *Nari Jagata*. The contents of the book speak of the condition of women in several nations such as Turkey, Egypt, Palestine, Spain, Russia, Persia, India, and Afghanistan. It also includes a chapter that deals with the place of women in a resurgent Russia. Sarala provides many other perspectives such as a brief history of women in England and America, agitation of women in China, and progress of women in India. She refers to a very interesting essay 'Does Islam Favor Seclusion' by Khwaja Kamaluddin and draws a contrast between the original tenets of Islam vis-à-vis the later dictates of the mullah based on orthodoxy. She provides a detailed knowledge of the place of women according to the Holy Koran and arrives at the conclusion that indeed Islam has an egalitarian attitude towards women. Under the heading 'Progress of Indian Women', Sarala wrote:

> Many wise men believe that national slavery is the root cause of the backwardness of women. However, it could very well be that the plight of woman could also be a significant cause of the national crisis. Today woman is bleeding herself white and making herself a destitute in society. She adds to the burden of society but there is no way society can pay back this loan.... The woman's agitation today has not been able to reach out to the villages and the country-side. No woman has been born in India to undertake sacrifice or work. Women cannot aspire for liberation so long as the women's movement has not been able to spread its wings among the poor and the illiterate among them. (Raju 1995: 53)

In *Nari Jagata*, Sarala's approach is systematic and analytical. Arguments are backed by comparative statistics from far and near.

For instance, under the title 'Agony of the Widows', she shows us that out of 1,000 women, about 674 happen to be widows. She adds that unfortunately in Odisha, literacy and rote learning are equated with true education. She quotes from the writings of the Englishman Mr Fox who declared that most graduates were full of ignorance and superstition. In this context Sarala brought to the readers' attention the many measures that could spearhead the progress of women. These include education of mothers, introduction of co-education and education through the mother tongue, appointment of female lecturers in institutions where girls are being educated, and increasing the number of training scholars for imparting training to female lecturers (Devi 1936: 30).

Sarala recommends many training programmes for women such as tailoring, binding, jewellery-making, typing, composition of letters in press, knitting, and so forth. Next, she spoke about the problem of prostitution and highlighted the evil role played by pimps: 'Isn't there a role for educated men and women to eradicate this evil,' she asks. 'The Odias,' she suggests, 'ought to resolve to remove this evil.' Advocating the increasing participation of women in politics, she said that women 'do not enjoy their rights since there is no effective women's movement' (1936: 36).

The mental gap between partners grows, she argues, because their relationship is based on artificial constructs. Women think of men as financial or material caretakers of their wives and families. Men, on the other hand, consider women as helpless, dependent beings (Devi 1936: 38). Sarala lists a number of factors that she considers are responsible for the backwardness of women. These include lack of domestic discipline among women, their physical frailty, proneness to superstition, and laziness and indolence (1936: 40–1). Several measures, she suggests, ought to be taken urgently. These include abolition of child marriages and marriages of women to old men and abolition of the purdah system and untouchability. Similarly, there is a need to spread education among women in rural areas to empower them to access their legal rights to annul an unhappy marriage, their right to business enterprise, and an equal right to inheritance of property.

In the book *Bharatiya Mahila Prasanga*, Sarala focuses on several pressing issues which comprise the various chapters of the volume. These include 'The Place of Women in Society', 'Child Marriage', 'Widow Remarriage', 'Purdah System', 'Social Rights', 'Rights to Economic Independence', 'Education for Women', 'Women in the National Freedom Struggle', 'Legal Rights for Indian Women', and 'Domestic Violence'. Sarala puts forth her case with arguments and evidence, including telling statistics. She underlines the need for mutual compatibility in marriage and shows that her views are forward-looking. She observes trenchantly in the book: 'A great many of the educated men in India marry an image (or phantom) of their making. Very few are successful in acquiring an embodiment of this image; the rest get disappointed and after marriage suffer from mental unrest. They lose all interest and attachment for women; at the most, they have compassion for women.'

In the essay 'The Problems of Women in Odisha', included in this volume, Sarala expresses deep distress about the status of women who are currently in an 'impenetrable darkness'. Paradoxically, women themselves seem to be unaware of their problems. She sees several factors responsible for this state of affairs, such as gender discrimination in the field of education and early and untimely marriage of girls. 'The race which chooses to live in the dark in this enlightened age can never rise from its stupor', she observes forcefully. 'Could political change remove the social and cultural factors responsible for the miserable plight of women?' she asks while citing other relevant factors such as higher mortality rates among women. What could be the answer to the presence of a large number of women in Odisha when a great many Odia men are working elsewhere for economic reasons? One answer, she suggests, is that such men could take their wives with them. That way they would 'enjoy domestic happiness and the Odia nation will also be benefitted'. Similarly, the suffering of widows is an area that cries for attention. The plight of widows is uniformly seen across castes in Odisha. Widow remarriage in the province is, therefore, an urgent need of the hour. The situation appears to be particularly bleak in the light of the fact that Indian history, legend, and mythology are replete with instances of able and meritorious women. At the same time, the colonial system of education seems to 'have made women bookish', away from labour. The sooner such a system is abolished, the better it would be for the nation.

Sarala was equally concerned about the place of art and culture in national life. Considering both art and culture as 'twins, born of the same parents', she maintains that 'the artist opens up the first doors to the treasure-house of creation, making any further quest unnecessary'. She says:

> Art was worshipped in every Odia home; every life was touched by it. That is why illiterate housewives embellished their huts with exquisite *muruja*[24] patterns—floral and animal motifs drawn on floors and walls. Such was their sense of proportion in design that no scales or compasses were required to draw the lines. What skills and artistry they showed in producing various handicrafts out of metal, wood, grass, or stalks of paddy, enriching their lives with forms, colours, and odours! Men joined their wives in decorating their homes. Gardens lent elegance to ordinary dwellings. The perfume of flowers carried minds to the world of music and thence to poetry. Folk literature thrived; treasures of human activity were passed on to future generations of Odias.[25]

In her essays, Sarala advances arguments systematically; she invokes facts and figures in a manner unseen in the women's discourse of her time. For instance, she invokes the 17-point resolution of the AIWC dealing with the poor condition of women's education that lays emphasis on the need for gender equality. Similarly, she takes up the problems faced by women labourers and prostitutes. She regrets the shocking manner in which the trafficking of Odia women seems to be taking place in far-away places such as Yangon, Assam, and Kolkata.

Sarala's call for appropriate education for women that would enable them to carry out their domestic responsibilities may not be acceptable to the current exponents of female education, but her call to free education from gender discrimination would strike a sympathetic chord with the enlightened sections of the population.

## Biographies

Sarala distinguished herself as a biographer of eminent women. She tapped unknown sources to bring out narratives of outstanding women who could serve as worthy role models. Two companion volumes are worthy of our attention. They are *Beera Ramani* and *Bishwa Biplabini*. These volumes compare favourably with the literary feminist Ellen Moer's path-breaking *Literary Women* (1977). Prescribed at one time as a high-school textbook in Odisha, *Beera Ramani* has inspiring life stories of heroic women such as Lakshmi Bai, Bundi Mahishi, Karma Devi, Krishna Kumari, and Panna Devi. Through such narratives, Sarala wished Odia women to emulate the examples of contemporary women leaders such as Kamaladevi Chattopadhyaya, Sarala Devi Chaudhurani, Mridu Lakshmi Reddy, and others active on the national scene.

Similarly, Sarala brings to bear on *Bishwa Biplabini* her wide reading and offers the narrative of several women of world stature such as Kalpana Dutta of the undivided Bengal, an associate of the legendary Surya Sen of the famous Chittagong Armoury Raid (1930). There are other accounts like that of Sophia Bardina who fought the oppressive Russian tsar and that of Hazalipij of Romania. Sarala also chronicles the legacy of the Odia princess Suka Devi of Banki and other women such as Lakshmi Bai, Ahilyabai, and Janabai at the national level. As Sarala explains in the 'Preface': 'It is to provide worthy role models for the revolutionary-minded young women in Odisha, that I have published this book.'

More significantly, in *Narira Dabi*, Sarala outlines a manifesto for women's empowerment. What is impressive in this text is her extraordinary knowledge of contemporary history, law, and social life in both India and abroad. In voicing her anger against the subordination of women and marital rape, Sarala distinctly emerges as a revolutionary woman. She begins her essay in a matter-of-fact manner:

> There is much agitation in today's world over the question of women's independence. Both in the West as well as the East, one hears in one voice, the demand that women should become free.

The campaign has made headway in Western countries. In the
East, however, it is still at the stage of inception. Nevertheless,
there is little doubt that the agitation would fructify in near future.
(Devi quoted in Mohanty 2005: 153)

After outlining the status of women from historical times, she
asks indignantly:

Who doesn't know the plight of women? A woman's place, after all,
is in the recesses of the house, in the darkness of the 'Antahapur'.[26]
She has no relationship with the outside world. This world evokes
little interest in her. She has no way of knowing the ongoing
conflicts in the world and the struggle for existence everywhere.
Virtually blind, her sole business is to serve and nurse the menfolk
in the family. Of course, no one is saying that nursing and service
have no value. Isn't it, however, unbecoming of civilized society to
turn out coolie-like females, made to work under duress? To learn
and acquire knowledge, to have pleasure in the place of work—all
these are unfortunately beyond the scope of women today. Her
whole world is confined within the four walls of her household. Her
life revolves around food and toil. Women today are the presiding
deities in the kitchen. Little wonder, then, that whenever we are
reminded of women, our attention is naturally drawn into the dark
corner of houses. (Devi quoted in Mohanty 2005: 155–6)

She quotes favourably some extracts from a judgment given by
a court in Britain, to 'satisfy', she says, 'the worthy of readers'.
Justice Meccard's judgment seems to represent Sarala's avant-
garde thinking on issues such as marital rape and the right of a
woman over her own body and reproductive self:

I maintain that the wife's body can never be owned by her husband.
It's her own property and not her husband's. She can leave her
husband at her will; she can select her business or join the political
party of her choice. She has full rights to decide whether or not
she is going to have a child and at what point of time. No man can
keep a woman under his control on the basis of the fact that he is
married to her. The woman of this country has won independence;
she is a citizen and not a slave. She can turn her wish into action.

One doesn't get the pleasure of married life from codes of rules and regulations. The success of marriage depends on mutual compassion, mutual consideration, mutual forgiveness, mutual sacrifice, and above all, mutually shared morality. (Meccard quoted in Mohanty 2005: 157–8)

Quoting favourably from the writings of women such as Annie Besant and others, Sarala exposes the pernicious hold of patriarchy, the duplicity prevailing in society, and concludes: 'The main cause of the downfall of women of India is the attitude of disrespect shown towards women by our countrymen. Because of this regressive attitude, women of our country are deprived of education today' (Mohanty 2005: 160).

*Literary Criticism*

Sarala's essays on literary topics and her critical works on poets and writers would easily constitute a category in itself. Three works, outstanding in their literary criticism, are worthy of close attention: *Sarala Mahabharatare Nari Chitra, Kuntala Kumarinka Kabi Pratibha* (The Poetic Genius of Kuntala Kumari, 1940), and *Rabindra Puja*. The first edition of *Rabindra Puja* was published by Arunodaya Press, marking the demise of Rabindranath Tagore. Dedicated to Advocate General Bira Kishore Ray who wrote the foreword to this book, the homage to Tagore was read out at the Utkal Sahitya Samaj on 17 August 1941, on the occasion of his *sraddha* (funeral) ceremony. Written in a scholarly yet lucid style, sprinkled with quotations from Tagore's works including *Gora, Ghare Baire* (The Home and the World, 1916), *Char Adhyaya* (Four Chapters, 1934), and poems such as 'The Toiler' and '*Chitrangada*', the long tribute familiarizes the Odia readership with Tagore's outstanding contribution to Indian and world literatures. Sarala points out that a large number of the poet's works had been rendered into Indian languages such as Hindi, Telugu, Marathi, Gujarati, Kannada, Assamese, and others and left a lasting impact on them. Tagore, she says, will be remembered for his lifelong commitment to world unity as well as his deep humanism. She quotes him: 'Age after age, time and again hast thou O' Lord/ sent thy messengers to this pitiless world/ they have left their word.' Citing lines from the poem 'Chitrangada', Sarala declares that perhaps in no other language or literature in India and the world have such a portrayal of woman been given. Chitrangada becomes an effective symbol for the ideal woman of the 1930s epitomized by the poet. Judged against the quest for the new woman of Sarala in the novel *Basanti*, the lines from Tagore assume special significance carrying deeper undertones. She quotes the lines in Bengali:

*Ami Chitrangada!*
*Debi nahi, nahi ami samanya romoni*
*Puja kori rakhibe mathaya, seo ami nahi*
*Obohela kori pushiya rakhibe pichey, shey O ami nohi*
*Jodi pase rakhe more sankatare pathe,*
*Duruha chintar jodi ansa dao,*
*Jodi anumoti koro*
*Kothin broter taba sahaya hoite,*
*Jodi sukha dukhe more koro sahachari*
*Amar paibe tobe porichaya!*

Here is a rough translation of the poem in English:

*I am Chitrangada!*
*I am no goddess! Nor an ordinary woman!*
*None to be worshipped and held high*
*I am no such person!*
*If you hold me close on the path of ordeals*
*Make me part of your deep worry.*
*If you permit me*
*To be your comrade in your trials,*
*Your partner in your sorrows and happiness,*
*Then you will know who I am!*

Sarala closes her discussion of Tagore with *Shesher Kobita* (The Last Poems, 1929) and concludes by stating that 'the only way the Indian literature and the nation could pay back the debt to Rabindranath is by the growth of the national consciousness' (p. 41). The tribute to Rabindranath by Sarala Devi represents one of the most insightful instances in comparative reading.

Apart from these three works, Sarala wrote and published literary critical essays extensively in many journals.[27] These essays, written in a lucid language without self-conscious pedantry, draw our attention to the issues of contemporary language and literature. At the same time, they are not devoid of the concern and ardour that Sarala displays as a feminist and social activist. Such views are visible in essays such as '*Adhunika Sahityare Nari*' (Women in Modern Literature). *Kuntala Kumarinka Kabi Pratibha* constitutes the first major assessment of the poet Kuntala Kumari after her demise in 1938. Presented on the occasion of the first death anniversary of Kuntala on 23 August 1939, the essay was considered the best in its category. It received a cash award of 100 rupees from the famous lexicographer Gopal Chandra Praharaj. Sarala discusses various aspects of Kuntala's poetic genius in an illuminating manner. She compares her to other women writers such as Reba Ray, Annapurna Devi, Aparna Devi, Sarojini Choudhury, and Pitambari Devi. Kuntala's love poetry is shown to have myriad aspects. There is the world of human, passionate love, and there is the love for the almighty God. Indeed, as Sarala shows, Kuntala excels in the field of devotional and mystical poetry.

Kuntala is equally adept in patriotic poetry. Her patriotic verses, expressed in poems such as '*Ahwana*' (The Call), create in us, says Sarala, a revolutionary ardour for the liberation of our motherland. There are very few poetic collections such as *Sphulinga* (The Spark) in India, she contends. Kuntala's empathy and concern for her land and people come out in verses full of deep pathos. Similarly, argues Sarala, Kuntala Kumari's other works such as '*Anjali*', '*Uchhwas*', '*Prema Chintamani*', and '*Odianka Kandana*' (The Cry of the Odias) bear testimony to her poetic achievements, just as her prose works, including the novels, are suggestive of her social and ideological vision. Sarala concludes by saying that Kuntala's poetry can be divided into three main categories: *Bhakti Rasa* (devotional poetry), *Prema Rasa* (poetry of human passion), and *Beera Rasa* (poetry of valour). All three show poetry of the highest order.

Likewise, *Sarala Mahabharatare Nari Chitra*, published by Utkal University, is structured into six chapters. Chapter 1 underlines the social setting and the context. Chapters 2–5 cover the discussion of several characters such as Ganga, Amba, Ambalika, Satyavati, Gandhari, Kunti, and Draupadi. In Chapter 6, she discusses non-mythological characters. The concluding chapter brings into focus several issues such as the ideal of Indian womanhood and the relevance of characters of the earlier age in our own times.

In discussing the women characters of her rendering of the Mahabharata, Sarala's literary gaze is not confined to the past. The significance of the work is to be seen in the literary assessment by Sarala. It must be admitted, however, that the criticism gains significance by her ability to relate the discussion to the contemporary context.

## Plays

Sarala tried her hand in plays as well. Influenced by Kalidasa, she wrote a number of plays. Her *Purba Raga* was based on Puranic themes. She also wrote a historic play called *Bhima Bhuyan* and a social play named *Jajabara*, both of which are unpublished. Two of her plays, *Malavika Agnimitra* and *Swapnavasavadutta*, were influenced by Sanskrit literature. The last one was published in *Utkal Sahitya*.

In all the forms Sarala handled—whether prose, fiction, short story, play, literary criticism, or biography—she brought to bear a rare knowledge of the genre; she wrote with a confidence and ability few of her contemporaries—men or women—could match. That such writings, both critical and creative, came from the pen of someone who had very little formal education and was largely self-taught, must remain one of the paradoxes of a literary genius.

## Complex Discourse

Sarala's advocacy of the woman's cause and female emancipation in *Basanti* needs to be carefully balanced with her views on this issue, especially in the later period of her life and career. The earlier notions underlined in '*Narira Dabi*' were fairly radical and unambiguous: the notion of female agency was considered central and domesticity and motherhood treated as choices women made ideally by themselves independent of social pressure. Religious orthodoxy was decried for acting as the handmaiden for patriarchy.

In the later period, however, Sarala seems to have found westernization destabilizing and threatening the family structure; consequently, she advocated the need for a separate system of women's education in the universities of India. Arguing that a system of learning common to men and women, as practised in India under the influence of the West, would destroy 'Indian values' and 'way of life', she invoked a set of Western thinkers and educationists such as Stanley Hall, Havelock Ellis, Jastrow J., Cyril Burt, and Moor, as well as other psychologists such as Otto Lipmann and G. Heymans who, she claimed, stood for a system of education appropriate to the needs of women. She submitted a 'Memorandum for Women's Education' to the UGC in her capacity as a member of the Senate of Utkal University. Written in English, with corrections in her own handwriting, the memorandum is undated, and the typescript was collected from the Estate of Sarala Devi. An extremely valuable document, it throws light on her views as they developed in the later years. Sarala cited contemporary research in the West that valorized the learning of disciplines such as the sciences, mathematics, and arts based on gender factors, that is, the claim that girls were more attuned to the liberal arts and boys to the hard sciences, mathematics, and engineering because of biological reasons. This is a theory that was prevalent for a long time in the field, and is no longer uncritically accepted by educationists today. Sarala wrote:

xlviii                    INTRODUCTION

The system of education prevalent in India at the secondary and the collegiate stages is not [at] all suited to the culture and civilization of the country. When this system was devised and curricula prepared for it, the women were nowhere in picture. It was meant exclusively for menfolk. So both men and women were required to be educated in one system. That such a system has done havoc to the Western society and the women folk of the Western countries is well known to all the cultured Indians. Due to the mischief done by a single system of education for both men and women, the family ties in those countries have been loosened, people have no home as such and the natural faculties of the children do not develop in the natural way. The wifehood, motherhood of women are not being duly developed. In America the human relationship has become thoroughly mechanized ... After the Independence of India, the eyes of the world have been riveted on her and her spiritual civilization and her ways of life saturated through and through with her innate spiritualism. India has a message of her own to deliver to the world. In this task, the Indian women have to play their role, and [that] is why they have to be properly fitted to the task. (Memorandum n.d.)

The idea that women are the custodians of culture is a notion that is no longer treated as a progressive concept. However, Sarala's thesis that the system of education in India must have indigenous roots, her emphasis on mother-tongue education, and her belief that education must be located in the context of local cultures (Memorandum n.d.: 19–20) are arguments that will find strong resonances in our times of cultural globalization.

## Selection of Texts and the Nature of Translations

It is indeed hard to represent in a single volume the vast range and depth of the writings of an outstanding literary woman like Sarala Devi. All anthologies and selections must finally remain a subjective exercise, though not an arbitrary one. An attempt has been made in this volume to showcase representative texts of Sarala in the translation form for a wider readership within limited space. It is not easy to cover the many genres and areas in which she excelled. What we have here are samples of the many dimensions that go beyond the social vision; they include religion, spirituality, myth, and folklore. Unlike many, Sarala did not see the world in binary terms such as the 'secular' and the 'sacred'. She embraced both with equal felicity and ease. The twin criteria that we have used for our selections are readability of the texts and their contemporaneity.

No effective translation can take place without adequate knowledge of the literary–cultural context and the milieu in which the source texts are located or generated. In Sarala Devi's case, the translators, howsoever able, are restricted by the non-availability of her writings in the public domain. Nor is she present amidst us today. Indeed, if criticism and translation go hand in hand, we have very little of Sarala Devi's studies or Odia women's studies today. As the editor, I have been conscious of such lacunae and, consequently, have worked closely with the translators, acquainting them with Sarala's life history, her fascinating literary and political career, and her evolution as a literary writer and activist over a period of time. We have also looked at similar narratives in the context of other language groups for comparative perspectives. Due care has been taken to retain the cultural specificity in the translated texts rather than opting for an easy English rendering for a so-called pan-Indian readership, glossing over differences in idioms and expressions. If there has been some 'loss' in the renderings (and there must have been), I hope there has been 'gain' too, in terms of the heightened awareness the translators have brought to bear on their translations. This is one way translation could be a mediatrix between the author/text and the readers.

The following texts are included here in the translated form:

(a) Under 'Literary Feminism' we have the following: 'The Rights of Women', 'The Problems of Women in Odisha', 'Basanti', 'The Role of Women in the Freedom Struggle', 'True Womanhood', 'The Awakening of the Women of Odisha', 'Influence of Women on the Lives of Men', 'A Letter from Prison', and finally, 'My Story: Sarala Devi'.

(b)  Under 'Sisterhood for Empowerment', we have the following:
     'World Revolutionaries: Kalpana Dutta', 'World Revolution-
     aries: Sofia Bardina', 'World Revolutionaries: Utkal Bharati
     Kuntala Kumari', and 'Women Revolutionaries during the
     Buddhist Period'.
(c)  Under 'Writing for Children', we present the following:
     'The Magic Horse', 'The Fisherman's Wit', 'The Tale of the
     Persian Merchant', and 'The Tale of the Sorcerer's Wife'.
(d)  Similarly, under 'The Gandhian Vision', we have 'Mahatma
     Gandhi's Message for Indian Women' and 'Mahatma
     Gandhi's Role in My Life'.
(e)  Under 'Art and National Culture', we present 'Art and
     Culture in National Life'.
(f)  Finally, under 'Literature and Religion/Spirituality', we bring
     in 'Katha Ramayana', 'Tulasi Das: A Play', and 'The Portrayal
     of Women in Sarala Mahabharata'.

Hopefully, the translations of these memorable Odia texts,
carried out for the first time for a volume of this kind, will
illuminate our understanding of gender and the nation in the
early-twentieth-century India.

## Notes

1. See, for instance, Jha, Bhatia, and Pandey (2014) and Goyal
(2012–13). The following chapters from Jha, Bhatia, and Pandey (2014)
will be particularly useful in the context of the concerns of Sarala Devi:
'Women, Literature and Culture in India: Multiple Perspectives' by
Malashri Lal and 'Women in India: Terror and Trauma in the Sacred
Space' by Sanjukta Dasgupta.

For early literary women of Odisha, see Mohanty (2005, 2008). The
life and career of Bengali literary women during the colonial era have
been substantially uncovered by feminist scholars such as Malavika
Karlekar and others. Figures such as Jnanadanandini Debi (1850–1941),
Binodini Dasi (1863–1941), Saraladevi Chaudhurani (1872–1945),
Rokeya Sakhawat Hossain (1850–1932), and many others appear in the
excellent volumes edited by Susie Tharu and K. Lalitha (1993, 1995).

For a representative list of critical works on this topic, see 'Bibliography' at the end of this volume.

2. It may be of interest, in this regard, to refer to works like Athavale (1930).

3. It must be added, though, that in the same representation she advocated better nutrition and training of the mind and the body for female students, and mother-tongue and art education for all. See the unpublished memorandum available in the Estate of Sarala Devi.

4. The lifespan for Indira Sahasrabuddhe is not available.

5. See Tharu and Lalita (1993, 1995). The names of Odia literary feminists like Sarala Devi are significantly missing.

6. See Forbes (2014).

7. See Forbes (1996). This book is a welcome addition to the history of the women's movement in modern India. However, notable accounts from Odisha seem to be missing here.

8. I thank Binayak Patnaik, Bholanath Rout, the late Bishnupriya Mohapatra (Sarala's daughter-in-law), and Jagadish Kanungo for valuable information regarding Sarala Devi's early life and upbringing.

9. Gandhi's visit to the historic districts of Balasore and Bhadrak left a lasting impact. An ashram was started at Bhadrak at Gandhi's initiative. It continues until today and carries out many activities including an orphanage.

10. See Pradhan (1988). See also Das (1997).

11. Saraikela–Kharsawan is now part of the state of Jharkhand.

12. For a list of Sarala's works and the genres she dealt in, see Mohanty (2004), Mishra (2004), Raju (1995), and Devi (1999).

13. See the chapters on Sarala Devi in Mohanty (2005, 2008).

14. The relative lack of feminist texts in Odisha during the early twentieth century may be contrasted with the large number of 'advice-for-women' texts by writers such as Jagabandhu Singh.

15. See Walsh (1995).

16. See Mohanty (2005).

17. See the chapter 'English in Colonial Orissa: The Missionary Position' in Mohanty (2008).

18. See Mohanty (2006).

19. Available in the Estate of Sarala Devi.

20. These translations show Sarala's wide reading and scholarship acquired at home.

21. I thank Professor H.S. Mohapatra for providing me with a copy of this rare book.

22. See 'Preface' in Devi (1986 [1931]).

23. Undoubtedly, Sarala was the best essayist of her time to voice feminist concerns. She compares very favourably with her counterparts in the neighbouring Bengal.

24. Powdered rice mixed with colour used in villages to make floral designs on the earthen floor.

25. *Asanta Kali*, 3rd year, no. 9, September. Translated by Bikram K. Das and appears further in this volume.

26. The inner chamber of a house.

27. Some examples are '*Sahitya Prasanga*' (*Asanta Kali*, 2/9 September 1952), '*Bastaba Sahitya*' (*Asanta Kali*, 3/5 May 1953), '*Sanskruta Sahitare Nari*' (*Asanta Kali*, Puja Issue, 1958), '*Nari Kabi Parikrama*' (*Rashtra Deepa*, Puja Issue), and '*Gana Sahitya*' (*Sahakara* 18/4, 1344 Sala).

*Literary Feminism*

# The Rights of Women[*]

There is much agitation in today's world over the question of the independence of women. Both in the West as well as the East, one hears, in one voice, the demand that women should become free. The campaign has made headway in Western countries. In the East, however, it is still at the stage of inception. Nevertheless, there is little doubt that the agitation will bear fruit in the near future.

In India, especially among Hindus, the meaning of women's liberation is being widely discussed. It is difficult to take stock of the divergent opinions of people on this matter. The very existence of serious differences in the points of view on the status

* Originally published as 'Narira Dabi' (Cuttack: Hindustan Granthamala, 1934), the essay later appeared in Early Women's Writings, 1898–1950: A Lost Tradition, Sachidananda Mohanty (ed.) (New Delhi: SAGE Publications, 2005), pp. 153–60. Translated by Sachidananda Mohanty.

of men and women in Hindu society is obviously the basis for the ongoing quarrel.

According to some, the position of women should remain as it was in the ancient Hindu society. For them, there is nothing ignoble in that position. Others argue that formerly, the place of women in society was not high enough, that we must better that position and keep up with the developments in the world. This second line of thinking should, I believe, guide all our deliberations.

In former times, women did not enjoy adequate respect not only in Hindu society but also in other parts of the globe. This is a fact. In order to sing the praises of our ancestors, we might wish to claim that women in those days were accorded favour and respect. This would, in fact, amount to self-deception. The pain and oppression women traditionally suffered for ages are responsible for the flame of rebellion now burning in society. Needless to say, it is clearly the disrespect and neglect shown to women that has led to this calamity. This is the situation not just in our country but elsewhere as well. Such things become possible when society is not civilized. When we analyse history, we see that those periods which lacked civilization betray such attitudes towards women.

Consider the facts. Who does not know that it was Sita's indignity that led to the tragic fate of Ravana? Lanka, the 'Swarnapuri', was ravaged and Ravana's clan wiped out, just as Rama had to face humiliation and lose his wife for insulting Surpanakha! Did not the haughty Duryodhana lose his all by insulting Draupadi? Not only the fall of the Kuru dynasty, but, one might say, it also marked the beginning of the ruin that has come upon the whole country since then. History clearly shows that the abduction of Helen led to the destruction of the city of Troy.

Likewise, the neglect of women during the Roman period becomes amply clear when we analyse history. According to Roman law, women were totally dependent in society. Before a woman married, she had to work very much like a maid within the household. Little was the change after marriage. She had to constantly minister to the needs of everyone within and outside the family, and lead the life of a slave. If the woman offered wine or poison to a man, Roman law permitted the husband to put an end to her life. The Romans were unwilling to accept that wives could be trustworthy. The husband had the right to turn out his wife at his own sweet will. This, of course, is not the situation now. However, the arrangement used to prevail when the Roman society lacked civilization.

The rights of women were particularly neglected in Syria and Phoenicia. Women were treated like beasts of burden. They were regarded essentially as dolls meant to satisfy the carnal desires of men. Women toiled as slaves in the houses of their fathers and husbands. Anyone could own a woman as his wife. They were treated as pawns in a game. The victor could blithely take away someone else's woman and treat her as his slave. Such were the practices when the country was in a state of barbarism.

In China, women were not permitted to enter a temple. They could not worship or touch the deity. In Russia, custom dictated that a discontented husband could beat his wife. Imagine treating a wife as worse than an animal! Only when a mob of ten men killed a woman could the act lead to a charge of murder in the court of law.

A similar situation existed in Japan. Like her counterparts elsewhere, the Japanese woman, too, was not allowed to enter the temple or worship the deity. What a low and ignoble status she had!

What was the situation in Sparta? The husband enjoyed the absolute right to eliminate a weak, 'fallen', or infertile woman. He enjoyed similar rights on flimsy or trivial grounds. A single woman was forced to accept more than one husband quite against her will, and some husbands did not hesitate to loan their wives to other men. It was also fairly customary to mortgage a wife to secure a loan from a moneylender.

The condition of women in Italy was equally bad. It was felt that women, whether quiet or outspoken, had to be controlled like horses using a whip. Women were physically sacrificed at the altar of the deities.

It was even prevalent in Sparta that a householder would engage his wife to show hospitality towards his guests. When a man became old, he used to feel gratified by offering his young spouse to a handsome male. Iranian women, on the other hand, used to be sent to the market to be sold as fruits and flowers. A single man could keep hundreds of women at his disposal to satisfy his lust.

The condition of women in the West has changed a great deal. In the modern age, women in the countries described so far have come to enjoy a position close to that of their male counterparts. In Western society today, the status of men and women is fairly comparable. The rights of women have been adequately enhanced in both the political and social spheres. However, even now, the utterly pathetic condition of women in Hindu society cannot be emphasized enough.

There does not seem to have been much change in the status of women between then and now. After all, don't our scriptures say that 'in childhood, a woman is protected by her father, in youth by her husband, and in old age by her son; she is never independent'. Indeed, a woman is never free; she is always under someone's care. She is meant to be worshipped only as a dependant. On the other hand, the adage 'the gods dwell where a woman is worshipped' does not seem to refer to the independence of women. We find it difficult to believe those who claim that women once enjoyed a very high status and were invariably deified.

Who does not know the plight of women? A woman's place, after all, is in the recesses of her house, in the darkness of the 'Antahpur'. She has no relationship with the outside world; the world has little interest for her. She has no way of knowing the ongoing conflicts in the world and the struggle for existence everywhere. Virtually blind, her sole business is to serve and nurse the menfolk in the family. Of course, no one is claiming that nursing and service have no value. But isn't it unbecoming of a civilized society to turn out coolies made to work under duress? To learn and acquire knowledge, to have pleasure in a place of work—all this is unfortunately beyond the scope of a woman today. Her whole world is confined within the four walls of her household. Her life revolves around food and toil. Women today are the presiding deities in their kitchens. Little wonder, then, that whenever we are reminded of women, our attention is drawn to the dark corners of the house.

The scriptures have always looked upon women with suspicion. It is grossly insulting to promote the view that women, by nature, are disloyal, unchaste, and destructive.

Agreed, the nature of men and women are different. Beauty, softness, and endurance are values associated with women. Similarly, austerity and extraordinary physical strength are generally considered male characteristics. But to use these ideas as a rationale for denying rights to women frankly defies logic. Is it reasonable and fair to make an unwarranted assault on the independence of women based on our perception of what constitutes the basis of female nature? Why should women be denied equal rights wherever they can demonstrate skills and competence matching those of their male counterparts?

It is not necessary that the beauty, softness, patience, shyness, and excellence of women remain confined to the home. With proper care and opportunity, women are capable of making great progress in the outer world. Man's inability to grasp this basic fact has resulted in the serious decline of our national life.

It is surely unreasonable to argue that woman ought to remain subservient to man simply because there are natural differences between the two. Such differences have been used in the past to enchain women in a set of artificial fetters not only in our community, but, towards the end of the eighteenth century, in Europe as well. It has, for instance, been argued that:

(a) In family matters, a woman should always follow in the footsteps of her husband.

(b) Education for women should remain limited. The reason for this is to prevent women from voicing a demand for higher education, which might result in disregarding the authority of their husbands.

(c) A separate code of conduct exists for women. For instance, a term such as 'chaste', which we hear so frequently, seems always to refer to women. Strangely, we never find a corresponding term applicable in the case of men.

(d) Only women are expected to conform to law and social practice. In today's society, such tradition-related laws encompass a vast spectrum, ranging from social customs to laws passed by governments. Such laws act as a deadly noose, suppressing not merely the five senses of fifteen million women, but their sixth sense as well: the mind.

(e) Women are kept economically dependent, from birth till death.

(f) Women need to be protected from the influence of progressive visions and independent thinking relevant to our times. Thanks to such protection, women are made helpless and vulnerable, accepting the conventional codes of the male-dominated society and treating them as the will of God.

(g) If a decent woman from a respected family is unexpectedly assaulted by a beastly rapist, she has no way of expressing the indignity suffered before the world. If she gives up her customary feminine reticence and seeks to punish the wrongdoer, then she has to suffer social opprobrium. Further, she would be belittled in people's eyes. Such instances are so common in nearby Bengal that those who read Bengali newspapers, weeklies, and monthlies regularly can easily ascertain the truth of this statement.

No one can deny that there is a widespread attempt to imprison women through the use of such fetters. Such bonds are surely not the creation of God; they are always man-made. Man has created all such things. Such fetters have effectively turned women into members of the animal kingdom rather than of the human community.

Today the inner self of woman aspires to freedom. She is determined to overcome all the obstacles that stand in the way of liberation. The continued closing in of her inner self can never be accepted. This has become intolerable, especially now. And because it is unbearable now, there is a fire of rebellion. Women are determined to discard all forms of superstitious claptrap and begin their lives anew. Not just in our own country but throughout the world; in the West, there is an effort to seek the total liberation of women.

To satisfy the curiosity of readers, extracts from Justice Meccard's judgment are quoted below:

> I maintain that the wife's body can never be owned by the husband. It is her own property and not her husband's. She can leave her husband at her will; she can choose her business or join the political party of her choice. She has full right to decide whether or not she is going to have a child and at what point of time. No one can keep a woman under his control on the basis of the fact that he is married to her. The women of this country have won independence; they are citizens and not slaves. They can turn their wishes into action. One does not get the pleasures of married life from the codes of rules and regulations. The success of marriage depends on mutual compassion, mutual consideration, mutual forgiveness, mutual sacrifice, and above all, a mutually shared morality.
>
> Anyone who attempts to analyse the causes of unhappy marriages (I, too, have been observing many such marriages) will see that behind all such unhappy marriages, there exists firstly, a lack of the conditions mentioned above; secondly, mutual incompatibility; and thirdly, discordant sex relations. Right now, I do not wish to talk about the friendship between married men and women. This depends to a large extent on human beings and circumstances around them. There is no one who has a stronger dislike for social inequality than me.

Justice Meccard's judgment has created a stir in the whole of the Western world. Though apt and justified, such a progressive attitude is difficult for mankind to accept all of a sudden. Looking at the situation prior to and after World War I, the progress of woman has been like an ascent from the bottom of the pit to the high empyrean. Before the war, the condition of Western women was very much like that of Indian women today. However, the conditions of war completely altered this situation. When millions of men jumped into the battlefield, women were compelled to shoulder all the responsibilities at home. Apart from household work, they were also called upon to earn their livelihood and support their families. Gradually, women developed a faith in themselves and did not think they were in any sense inferior to men. They had the firm faith that, given the time and opportunity, they could stand shoulder to shoulder with men. Further, in mixing with men in the workplace, women lost their sense of diffidence.

Gradually, the situation changed completely. Women were no longer willing to remain the playthings of men. There can be no doubt that this change signals progress for society. Those who do not wish to see liberated women establishing pure friendship with men do not seek social development. It is not a matter of surprise that a healthy interaction between the sexes is always frowned upon by conservative elements in society. Of course, such attraction has nothing to do with sexual desire. Can there be two opinions regarding this? A pure affection that transcends desire brings about the welfare of mankind and makes life pleasurable.

According to Lord Bacon, for instance, love between a man and a woman ought to transcend passion and desire. Western society has tested this and seen that such a relationship between the sexes is perfectly possible. Some people believe that in our own society, too, such ties between men and women existed formerly.

In Hindu society today, men experience a great deal of deprivation by not having women as partners in the outside world. Since half of our society happens to be more or less inert, like a block of wood, the nation naturally cannot stand firm in the battle of life. It is in a state of constant unease. As long as there is no equality and harmony between men and women, it will be difficult to imagine the development of Hindu society. Needless to say, whatever is accorded to a man should be granted to a woman as well. On the other hand, we would share the guilt if we unwisely disallow rights to women out of fear of their possible misuse. One who has the right to commit an error also has the right to realize the truth. Both men and women are liable for punishment; why should punishment be reserved only for women? When men become more humane, they will themselves realize their mistakes. Real womanhood will then blossom. Self-realization will lead to the strengthening of the desire for mutual help and, as a result, there will be all-round social progress.

It is because of the absence of such self-realization in our society today that we have fallen and lost our way. Looking at the misfortune and dependence of Indian women, Annie Besant said:

> Women stand for *shakti*; women are veritable goddesses. Without woman, man can never have a sense of completeness. Woman is an accomplice and not a ruler, a companion and not a rival. This is the true relationship between man and woman. The freedom of women will usher in the independence of the nation, since men and women are the two halves of a single whole. By pooling the energy of both will India achieve her legitimate rights.

Furthermore, the eminent journalist Sant Nihal Singh, a Londoner, has observed:

> India's degeneration, in the main, is to be attributed to our people's inequitable treatment of our women, for a backward mother cannot produce healthy sons and daughters. As long as a woman's life is not made easier, her life continues to be a burden, she has not the time and opportunity to improve her mind and strengthen her body, so long will India's upliftment and regeneration remain unaccomplished and the people backward.

Summing up, the main cause of the downfall of India is the attitude of disrespect shown to the women by our countrymen. Because of this regressive attitude, the women of our country are deprived of education today. An illiterate woman can never raise a developed child. How can the nation hope to grow with children who are underdeveloped, weak, and ill? Even today, the condition of women has not improved adequately; their lives are still a matter of burden. As long as this does not undergo a suitable change and women do not receive enough time and scope to constitute their physical and mental strength, the rise and growth of India will remain a dream. What more can we say beyond this?

# The Problems of Women in Odisha*

I glance in every direction to form an idea of the problems facing women in Odisha. All I see before me is an impenetrable darkness, which is not pierced anywhere by a ray of moonlight. If the status of women in other parts of the world is taken as a standard, one would realize how low the status of women in Odisha is and why it is so. Only those who have studied the situation of women most thoroughly can give a proper answer to this question. Most of the time we depend on inadequate information and insufficient knowledge to form an idea on this issue.

In every sphere of life in this province—educational, economic, and the social and political—one encounters many problems. But the specific problems that women in Odisha face have placed them in a peculiar situation. When I seek to locate the

* Originally titled 'Utkalara Nari Samasya' (Cuttack: Hindustan Granthamala, n.d.), pp. 1–47. Translated by Jatindra K. Nayak.

principal cause of these problems using logic as a weapon, I feel that a national awareness of the need to find a solution to these is lacking. Do men and women in the country ever feel determined to solve problems that can be easily sorted out? Women in Odisha do not know what their problems are, nor do they want to identify them. This is what is responsible for their miserable plight. On account of this attitude, the women of this country have been turned into stone, like Ahalya. Only God knows when a goddess will emerge from this stone.

Women pity men in the family and society. Men, on their part, pity women for their lack of foresight and mental immaturity. Anyone who keeps himself informed about what is happening to women all over the world knows this. I want to ask a question in this connection: Women are portrayed as sentimental. Do they receive the respect they really deserve? In this age of equality, do boys and girls enjoy the same rights in the fields of health, education, and economy?

Do the educational institutions in Odisha have as many girls as they have boys? The faintest noise is made when women raise a demand for opportunities in the job market. Women become unwilling mothers at a young age; this tells us much about their situation. Thus, there can be no two opinions about men being responsible for the plight of women. We should prepare the ground for finding a solution to the problems facing women. The first step towards it would be to end the discrimination between boys and girls in the field of primary education. Educational policy should be formulated before policies relating to economy, polity, society, and family life are crafted. Only an awakened group of women could deal effectively with the problems facing them. A seed decays under the soil if it does not get sunlight and air. Many obstinately entertain the view that women will get spoilt if they receive the benefit of education. In a climate created by such views, a woman can never grow. It is surprising that this has not caused much regret and outrage as it should have.

It is well known that in our society quite a few girls find themselves trapped in marriage before they complete their schooling and are barely able to write letters. Some other girls get so scared at the prospect of getting married that they cannot bring themselves to sit for their examination. Few would like to marry a highly educated girl. The race that chooses to live in the dark in this enlightened age can never rise from its stupor. Could political change remove the social and cultural factors responsible for the miserable plight of women? The solution to our problems lies within our mind. The disease should be dealt with at its very source; dealing only with its symptoms will not do. Our race should develop an attitude that is conducive to the uplift of women. One should do whatever little one can. One may not be in a position to provide lavish hospitality to a visitor, but being courteous to him/her will not cost him anything.

One can mention the names of only a few Odia women who have taken part in a political movement; there are only 30 or 40 women who have graduated from a university. But these cannot provide a solution to the problems facing Odia women. The problems can be solved only through the sympathy and goodwill of the whole Odia race. Unless men adopt the right attitudes towards women, even a ray of light will not pierce the darkness engulfing women.

## Statistical Issues

Out of the population of Odisha numbering a crore and a half, nearly 50 lakh people live in Madras, Madhya Pradesh, and Bengal. Since the provincial government does not carry out a census of Odias living outside Odisha, we do not take them into account when we discuss the situation of the Odia community. Even accurate information about Odias living in the Odisha division and the Gadajats[1] is not easily available. The government has no records relating to the one crore Odias living in the Bihar–Odisha province. For this reason, while writing this essay, one has to depend on whatever information comes one's way. The Odisha division and the Gadajats are home to 9,771,527 Odias.

---

[1] The states in the interior of Odisha composed primarily of the hills and the forest areas.

Of these, 4,745,942 are males and 5,025,585 are females. The women outnumbered men by 279,643. It is clear that for every 1,000 men there are 142 women.... It is to be noted that compared to the other states of India, barring Malabar and Cochin, women outnumbered men in Odisha. The situation relating to women in Odisha is comparable to that obtaining in other countries of the world.

The difference between the number of men and women in the population reveals the following facts:

(a) In Odisha, more girls than boys take birth. According to the 1931 census, 750,729 girls were born in Odisha and the number of boys born during this period is 720,259. This means that the number of girls exceeds that of boys by 30,470.

(b) Every year a large number of men from Odisha have to migrate to Kolkata, Assam, and Rangoon to escape starvation caused by drought and famine. Around three lakh Odias go out of the province to work as coolies elsewhere. More men than women from Odisha migrate to other parts of the country. This is why, in the population, women outnumbered men.

There is something else about the census statistics that deserves attention. The mortality rate of women between 20 and 30 years of age is higher than that of men in the same age group. This is also the situation in the rest of India. The reason for this is not far to see. Many eminent doctors have expressed their opinions on this issue. A census official from Travancore states that the number of deaths per thousand in case of women between 15 and 30 years of age exceeds that pertaining to men by 60. There is no doubt that child marriage leading to early pregnancy is responsible for this high mortality rate among women. Young women become vulnerable to all kinds of diseases because they are made to bear children when they are not ready for it.

Usually, in our society girls get married when they reach the age of 15 and men are married when they are 20 years of age. In Odisha, the number of women above the age of 15 is 2,132,561 while the number of men above the age of 20 is 2,406,871. This shows that married men outnumber married women.

The spread of education among women and the prevention of child marriage will certainly bring down the high mortality rate among women. The women of Cochin have benefited from the law prohibiting child marriage. The spread of education has been accompanied by the changes in circumstances. The mortality rate for women between 15 and 30 years of age has come down perceptibly. This has elicited the following comment from the census commissioner: 'The spread of women's education has resulted in men and women opting for late marriage. The midwifery of old times has given way to modern scientific methods. This has led to safer delivery of children, and the mortality rate for young pregnant women has been considerably reduced.'

This, according to census officials, is responsible for the number of women exceeding that of men in Cochin. However, this does not account for the number of women exceeding that of men in Odisha. The situation here can be explained in terms of men migrating to other parts of the country in search of livelihood.

It is not easy to find a solution to the problem facing women in Odisha. Women who outnumber men in Europe and America are agitating for their rights. However, conditions there are quite different from those obtaining here. This, however, does not mean that the problems facing women would lose their importance. We have to find a solution to our problems keeping in view the local conditions.

In England, the number of women exceeded that of men by 20 lakh. Many tried to find a solution to this problem concerning women. Agitations aiming at improving the condition of women were also launched. Women, on their part, attempted to solve their problems. The observation made by Lady Asquith deserves mention here:

> Women only want to set up their homes. No matter if a woman smokes or dresses up like a man, she wants to get married and many women want to become mothers. But it is a pity that many women fail to fulfil this desire. But in other parts of this British

empire, many men feel desperate because they find it difficult to get women to marry. So there is clearly a need for redistributing the population of the empire. In this age of science a woman living in a colony needn't fear being disadvantaged. They will definitely find suitable occupation to keep them busy. (*Ekalara Dhanadaulat,* Vijaya Kumar Sarkar, p. 92)

According to Miss Sybil Thorndike, 'Women outnumbering men is a good thing. There are many who do not want to get married and they enjoy a kind of freedom. Women can compete on an equal footing with men in every sphere of life.' In Lady Francis's opinion, women always outnumber men and they will continue to do so and will manage to find a solution to their problems.

Nowadays women prefer to take up jobs in thinly populated islands such as Straits Settlement, Niagara, Gold Coast, and so on. Some of them land government jobs, others serve as doctors, and some others work as teachers.

However, it appears impossible to find such solutions to the problems facing women in Odisha today. Here, it may be suggested that men who migrate to Kolkata, Assam, and Rangoon in search of work should take their wives with them. If they do so, they would enjoy domestic happiness and the Odia nation will also be benefited.

## The Sufferings of Widows

The sufferings endured by widows in Odisha are as acute as those undergone by widows in other provinces of the country. The widespread practice of child marriage is responsible for this situation. If we take into account the Hindu and Muslim populations of Puri, Cuttack, and Balasore, we find that out of 1,000 women, 497 are married and 224 are widows. In other words, one-fourth of the entire female population comprises widows.

One is shocked when one comes across five-year-old widows. The condition of women above 40 beggars description. Out of 1,000 women, 634 are widows. The figures given below—relating to the number of widows in some Hindu castes—present a clear picture of the plight of Odia widows.

Out of every 1,000 women:

| Caste | 1921 | 1931 |
| --- | --- | --- |
| Karana | 256 | 258 |
| Brahmin | 268 | 242 |
| Gauda | 183 | 230 |
| Khandayat | 240 | 154 |
| Tanti | 190 | 175 |
| Teli | 185 | 150 |
| Chamar | 159 | 138 |

If we compare the census data of 1921 with that of 1931, it becomes clear that the number of widows in the coastal districts of Puri, Cuttack, and Balasore has come down. This is good news. The number of widows among the higher castes is large.

How long can a race watch helplessly the erosion of its vitality and the loss of its members? How long would it go on listening to the heart-rending cries of helpless widows? The sigh of these widows is going to cause the destruction of this race. A disaster would occur if a solution to this problem is not found soon.

These days no one needs to exert oneself to convince people in Odisha of the propriety of widow remarriage. Of course, this is a desirable development. In some places of Odisha, widow remarriage is taking place but the number of such marriages is still very small. Unless reform-minded people become more active, the suffering of widows will cause society to decay.

## Problems Affecting the Education System

*Educate a man and you educate an individual;*
*educate a woman you educate a family.* (Lord of Avebury)

Many societies in Europe witnessed great upheavals due to the First World War (1914–1918). One is amazed to see how the sphere of women's work has undergone a revolutionary change.

Women have understood the importance of the role they have to play in society. Society cannot make any progress until women are able to stand on their own feet. Women are now convinced that if they get the right opportunities, they will be able to give a good account of themselves in every sphere of life. Everyone has realized that the progress of society depends on the uplift of women and the achievements in various spheres of activities, both in the East and the West, no longer cause anyone any surprise. Everybody now sincerely wants women to develop their potential and is helping them achieve this goal. Women are actively working towards the all-round development of society. They are constantly striving to make their mark in the social and political spheres. The progress of a race depends on the improvement in the condition of its mothers. Not giving women proper education and rendering them unfit for the struggle for survival not only does them harm but also causes harm to all classes of society.

If we go through accounts of the life led by Aryans in ancient times, we find that they were not uneducated. We have little information regarding the educational level attained by women from the lower castes. It appears that Brahmin and Kshatriya women were educated.

In the Vedic age, the condition of women was not as degraded as it is today. In that age, women could perform yajnas alongside their husbands and were allowed to read the Vedas and compose verses. Many *suktas* (spiritual hymns) of the Vedas have been authored by women such as Bag Devi, Lomasa, Lopamudra, Sarparanji, Juhu, Saswati, Biswabara, Jyotsna, Surya, Buddha, Jami, and Shraddha. Some of these such as Biswabara had won fame by composing rigs and performing yajnas. Biswabara was an organizer of yajnas. Instances like this can be multiplied.

And later, Khana achieved fame for her contribution to the science of astrology, and Lilavati became famous as a mathematician. A great scholar like Sankaracharya was defeated in a scholarly dispute by the wife of Mandan Mishra.

Debahuti, the mother of Kapila, who established the Sankhya school of philosophy, was a great scholar. Gargi and Maitreyi provided solutions to profound philosophical problems in the court of King Janaka.

In the age of the Puranas, Prahlada's mother was a devout and scholarly woman. Savitri, the daughter of Aswapati, was not only devoted to her husband but was also a learned woman. Another erudite woman ascetic Sulabha explained the theory of moksha to King Janaka. It is needless to mention that women such as Sita, Kunti, and Draupadi possessed every virtue and great learning.

In the Buddhist era, women were known to be educated. In this age, one comes across learned women such as Sukanya, Kshama, and Kashi.

It is clear that everyone appreciated the importance of education. Education was not only considered a means of earning money but also a way of improving oneself.

However, the education people receive these days seems to be dominated by economic considerations. The education system that has been put in place in India today differs significantly from the one prevalent in ancient India. The present education system has more shortcomings than strengths. This system does not lead to physical, moral, and spiritual development of boys and girls. If anything, it is likely to harm them.

Opinions regarding the meaning and purpose of education differ widely. In the ultimate analysis, education consists in an attempt to ensure physical, mental, and spiritual development of a human being. This view advanced by Plato has found acceptance among many people today. However, with the passage of time, changes should be introduced in the system of education. Change and evolution determine every activity in the world. In the days gone by, people thought that their village constituted the world. However, this attitude has undergone a change with the advancement of knowledge. People have realized that their village would not be able to fulfil all their aspirations and they try to move in step with a wider world. They constantly strive to expand the sphere of their activities. In these circumstances, it would be impossible for a human being to live in social isolation. He will benefit himself and will also do society good. It is education which instils in a human being a sense of his rights and duties. It, therefore, goes without saying that education should be recognized as an important means of gaining knowledge and developing oneself. The main objective of education is to equip human beings with the ability to cope with the struggle for survival.

The kind of education that is imparted in India today is not at all suitable to bring about personal and social development. Until an education system that is in harmony with our culture and our climate is introduced, the nation will never be able to make progress.

We can never receive education in the true sense of the term as long as the aim of the education system is to perpetuate the British rule over India. The existing education system encourages Indians to despise Indian civilization and culture and to adore British culture. Lord Macaulay advocated the introduction of an education system in India that would make Indians forget their glorious ancestors and dissuade them from imitating them. His dream has been realized today. Indians, as a race, have become effete. There is no reason why one should feel surprised at this.

The kind of education that is being imparted today does not teach anything meaningful to students. There is something extremely harmful about this education. No one really becomes educated by memorizing dozens of books and neglecting one's health and by the acquisition of knowledge. This book-centred learning prevalent in India led an author to make the following observation: 'This bookishness has turned Indian women away from labour. They think that marriage is the ultimate aim of their life. The sooner such an education system is completely abolished, the better for the nation.'

Women should get the education which would train them to be good mothers, good citizens, and become self-reliant. Today's girl students do not realize that they bear the future of India in their wombs. Unless men and women cooperate with each other, family, society, and the nation will not be able to achieve progress.

Everybody knows how neglected women's education in Odisha is. Whatever has been done for the spread of women's education in Odisha with the help of the government is deplorably meagre in comparison with other states. Again, this education consists in mere literacy and an ability to recite a few literary texts such as the *Laxmi Purana, Bedhabula*, and the *Bhagabata*. The knowledge which makes human beings understand the nature of things is beyond the reach of Odia women. This knowledge would have come to their rescue in their hour of distress. However, the nation has deprived them of this and has made them lead a cursed life. Not only the government but the municipality and the local board also neglect women's education. The report of the Department of Mass Education, Odisha Division, relating to the period 1927–32 shows that women's education has progressed at a slow pace. In 1926–7, 34,861 girls were enrolled in schools, but in 1931–2, the number of girl students was 32,543. This indicates that 2,318 have dropped out. In 1926–7, for every 1,000 people, there were 73 boys and 13 girls going to school. In 1931–2, for the same number of people, there were 12 girls and 66 boys at school. It seems that there are now fewer girls' schools than before. Only Ravenshaw Girls' School has somehow survived as an inspiring symbol of women's education.

It is easy to imagine how much progress women's education has achieved in Odisha under such circumstances. Out of 50 lakh Odia women, nearly 34,000 are literate. In other words, seven out of every 1,000 women know how to read and write.... That only 1,440 among 50 lakh Odia women know English is a matter of great regret. This situation has resulted due to the negligence of the government.... There is no need to dwell on this topic any longer. Only a handful of them receive college education. One should not expect that by receiving the kind of education that is imparted in India today, a student can gain in any way. Many great men have expressed the view that those who have obtained BA and MA degrees are incapable of making their way in the world. Of such degree holders it may be said that they do not possess knowledge about ordinary everyday matters. Everybody should pay close attention to what Mr Fawcus, Director of Education, Bihar and Odisha, said in 1927:

Last year, I had an opportunity to put questions on general knowledge to some graduates. The answers which 55 out of them gave shocked me. The answer to what the population of Odisha and Bihar was, was given by only four students and the figures they mentioned was 20 lakh less than the actual figure. Others, in answering this question, gave figures such as one lakh, three crore, and forty-five thousand. To the question when this province was formed, they mentioned years from 1894 to 1917. One-fourth of the examinees gave figures which missed the correct answer by one year. Many were unable to give correct answers to the question 'What is prohibition?' and some defined prohibition as protection. One of them thought it meant inter-caste marriage. To the question as to what should be done when one is bitten by a snake, 15 examinees said that one should save the victim's life through talismans and mantras. One of them wrote that people in villages bitten by snakes were saved through mantras, whereas such people in the city have no option but to go to hospitals. When I asked them to name industries other than agriculture in the state, they said that there were no industries worth mentioning. And those who answered this question correctly didn't mention the coal fields. Six of them could not state when the World War had begun. Nineteen of the examinees could not tell me when the war came to an end.

This clearly shows the direction in which the prevailing education system is leading our country. Especially, when one takes into account the educational attainment of women in comparison with men's, one is rendered speechless. An education that is so shallow cannot enable people to contribute anything significant to the glory of their nation. Unless this system is transformed, human mind will not develop and a disaster will occur.

The resolution taken at an All India Conference relating to this poor condition of women's education is given below:

(a)  The conference is of the opinion that education should mean a process whereby a child or an adult can fully develop his potential to serve mankind. The system of education should, therefore, aim at bringing about the physical, mental, and spiritual development of a citizen. Such an education system should ensure that the personality of an individual should be in harmony with what the country and the community expect of him.

(b)  A lot of attention should be paid to girls in the education system and they should be taught the ideals of motherhood and the skills required to make the household an attractive place.

(c)  Girls and boys should be given good physical education at school. They should be given facilities for playing in an open field.

(d)  Women inspectors should be appointed to inspect girls' schools.

(e)  School buildings should be properly ventilated and should have large open fields, or a building with such facilities should be chosen as the school building.

(f)  Every province should have a department of information, which would educate people about the nutritional value of food items produced there.

(g)  The government should not extend any assistance to a community which wants to establish a particular type of school. Boys and girls belonging to their community should study where students from other communities are enrolled.

(h)  In areas inhabited by a lot of poor people, the school should make provisions for giving midday meals to children from poor families. In such areas, the initiative should be taken by women.

(i)  The school's medium of instruction should be the language of that province. English should be taught as a compulsory second language. Hindi and other languages should be taught at school.

(j)  Competent teachers should teach students about eugenics at school and colleges.

(k)  In colleges where girls receive education, women lecturers should be appointed.

(l)  In all education boards and textbook committees, a large number of women members should be appointed.

(m) No schools should be allowed to be set up on a communal basis.

(n) Hindi should be accepted as the national language to facilitate communication among all provinces of India. The examinations conducted by Indian Women's University set up in Pune should be recognized by the government and other organizations.

Moreover, women teachers should teach students in all the primary schools of the country.

A large number of training schools for women teachers are needed for the spread of women's education in the country. Women trained here would open night schools in mofussil areas and educate married women.

The rules laid down by the district board related to establishing girls' or boys' schools have to be completely changed. Instead of spending 1,250 rupees on setting up one school, 1,200 hundred schools should be set up in mofussil areas. With 1,250 rupees, one can build only one or two pucca rooms. However, kutcha schoolrooms with gardens can be built with the same amount. Of course to do this, one needs to organize and motivate villagers on a massive scale. The women teachers who would run this school should be patriotic and committed to the cause of women's education. They should spurn grants amounting to 1,215 or 1,220 rupees and be willing to accept a salary of 4 or 5 rupees given to them by the villagers or the board. They should also learn how to survive on the food and clothes produced in villages. If this does not happen to women's education, even men's education will remain an unfulfilled dream. It would be even beyond God to change the existing system and lead the country in a new direction.

The practice of purdah presents the chief obstacles to the spread of education. Unless the middle and the upper classes get rid of this practice, ordinary people will not be able to defy this custom and light the lamp of education in the women's quarters of their houses. Purdah is the worst enemy of women who want to improve their condition. It leads to social corruption. Personal commitment is needed to uproot this custom. It is the symbol of moral degradation. Everyone should be keen to get rid of this.

## Problems Faced by Women Labourers

Earning a livelihood presents a serious problem to women in Odisha. They do not find many opportunities for earning money. They, therefore, face a lot of hardship in their family lives. Ten lakh out of 50 lakh women are able to make a living and support themselves through the money they earn. However, 40 lakh women depend on men for their survival. Seven lakh women work in the field of agriculture. About four lakh women serve commercial and industrial establishments. The number of women who earn their livelihood working in other fields is negligible. We cannot believe that women can live a comfortable and happy life as long as they are not able to be self-reliant and support their families with the money they earn themselves. They should also be taught how to earn money without damaging their health and engaging in futile labour. Until this happens, poverty will continue to plague the country.

There are many activities which would give women, if they are trained, the opportunity to earn a little money even in the present situation. Some of these are mentioned below:

(a)  To spin cotton thread with a charkha. Spinning tussar threads with charkha makes one earn more.
(b)  To make pickles, jams, soaps, perfumed oils, stationary goods, and snacks.
(c)  To roll bidis, leaf plates, and leaf packets.
(d)  To make ornaments. Women in goldsmith families in our country help their husbands in making ornaments and setting precious stones in them.
(e)  To do the job of a tailor and embroider dresses.
(f)  To engage in photography, enlarging, oil and water painting, drawing cartoons, and making puppets.
(g)  To weave mats.
(h)  To knit vests and socks.

(i)   To learn how to bind books and notebooks.

(j)   To learn typing.

(k)   To weave and dye clothes. (Our weaver women prepare all the items needed for weaving for their husband, but they do not know how to work a loom.)

(l)   To weave cane baskets, containers, and bags.

(m)  To work as a compositor in a printing press.

(n)   To learn the rudiments of homoeopathy and Ayurveda and treat children and women.

(o)   To make bedcovers, pillows, and pillow covers.

(p)   To prepare sweets.

(q)   To make moulds for ornaments.

Even today there are many such ways of generating income which women can adopt to make a little money if they receive some sympathy from the society and their families.

## Problem of Prostitution

Like other provinces, Odisha has a problem related to prostitution. Although our countrymen ridicule the rise of women in a civilized country, they cannot deny that the laws of these countries have been able to prohibit prostitution as a business. In Madras, the deputy president of the council has made the proposal for making the eradication of prostitution into a law by setting up a vigilance committee. Our provinces should take a similar initiative. One feels that unless women agitate to introduce a law to solve this problem they face, nothing meaningful will happen. Another thing is that even if such strict laws are introduced, serious problems will confront this family-oriented race. In my opinion, prostitutes should organize themselves and society should take steps to get their daughters married. Many would find such a proposal ridiculous, but there seems to be no other way out. We have to pay the price to improve the condition of a fallen woman. No other alternative exists. The daughters of prostitutes are not allowed to enrol themselves in government schools. This restriction should be completely removed. The government and society should set up special hostels for these innocent girls and provide them education and training. Or else, this problem will remain unsolved forever and will be considered one of the chief reasons for the decline of the nation.

Many who became prostitutes by choice and under compulsion (from the point of society) are now living in places such as Rangoon, Assam, and Kolkata. No one with a heart can bear to read or hear the accounts of the hardships and humiliation they endure. If one visits the colonies they live in and see the life they lead, one would easily understand how a degrading occupation reduces human beings to beasts. One would be shocked to find out how pimps have grown rich and how women plying in this trade are turned into witches. The miseries these prostitutes face when they pass their prime would fill a volume. Should only such women suffer for their sins? Should not the educated people and the government feel responsible for them? Many families are ruined under their influence; the lives of many women and children are destroyed by hunger and disease because of these women; they ruin the lives of many virtuous young men who could have brought glory to the nation. Can no one see this terrible calamity?

I appeal to the Odia race to be committed to enabling these miserable, unfortunate, and neglected women escape their terrible situation.

## Odia Women in Politics

Only a few women participate in the political process in Odisha. If the conservative mentality of women in the villages and towns of Odisha has ever received any shock and if their static tradition-bound life has ever been slightly unsettled, the credit must go to these women. Women have not been able to enjoy the rights they are entitled to owing to the absence of a vigorous women's movement. In this age, everyone knows that there is no need to elaborate on women's rights. Efforts should be made to ensure that in every department of the administration, such as the municipality, district board, and the legislature, women get the same opportunities and enjoy the same rights as men. It is a pity that until now Odia women have not been given any role in the provincial administration of Bihar and Odisha. Everyone should realize the great harm denying women these rights does to the nation. We hope that the province of Utkal will set an example in this regard for the whole of India.

The problems women face in Odisha are more or less similar to those faced by women in the other provinces of India. However, the situation of Odisha cannot be compared to that obtaining in the other provinces on account of the peculiar problems here such as poverty resulting from lack of women's education and its natural location. There are some problems which are peculiar to women and which afflict them not only in India but also everywhere in the world. God knows when these problems came to oppress women and how these can be solved in the future.

In our country, modern educated men marry according to traditional customs prevailing in society. They try to visualize an attractive image of their cherished brides. However, very few are lucky enough to find such a woman and the majority is disappointed. For this reason, they fall prey to depression a few days after marriage. They no longer feel respect, attachment, or affection for women. All they end up feeling for them is pity. For whatever they think, read, or do, they do not receive any support from their wives. The life of a young girl's husband often takes the form of a tragedy. In no sphere of life—be it physical strength and the power of judgement, intelligence, analysis, memory, and finer feelings—does a young man receive support from his wife. The world a husband inhabits thus becomes completely separate from that of his wife. No harmony exists between the parlour and the women's quarter of a house. The painful and terrible gulf separating the two escapes everybody's notice. Though this gulf presents no problems to anyone, the greatest problem facing women is to be found here. The man of the parlour comes to the woman wearing a disguise and speaking lies. A woman does not get the opportunity to see his real self. The accumulated misunderstandings resulting from this lead to disaster and reduce life to a cremation ground. Husbands and wives do not know, understand, or recognize each other. Women think that men have been created to earn money and support family. Men think women are the embodiments of frailty and God has created them to satisfy some of men's biological urges and to assist them in running families. Act after act of a tragedy unfolds in this way. Imperceptibly, worldly ties—children, marriage, life, death, joys, sorrows, good fortune, and misfortune—weave themselves into a braid.

The happiness of family life depends on both men and women. Some contribute more to it, others less. Since time immemorial, men have become extremely selfish, consolidated their own position, and laid all kinds of blames on women. Women are weak, so they have to bear all this injustice meekly.

It is not as if women cannot contribute to the happiness of families, in spite of the difficulties and deprivation they face. They can live happily and display their talents even in the face of all kinds of hardships. However, they felt to do this due to a lack of clarity in their mind. In a few cases, some unforgivable mistakes committed by women lead to strife in families.

Women render themselves weaker because of certain shortcomings. It is true that she finds in her tears the means for keeping restless men under control. However, without her faults, there is no doubt that she could have heaven in hell.

The following shortcomings are responsible for making women weak and impeding the development of their families.

### Inefficiency in, and Ignorance of, Housekeeping on the Part of Women

Our women lack the skill and the experience to manage a household. They are not aware of the ways in which family life can be led happily and peacefully. Everyone would agree that performing all the household chores in a neat and disciplined way is an important duty. Who does not know the harm caused to families if this duty is not performed properly?

### Excessive Soft-heartedness

Generally speaking, an excess of soft-heartedness takes away their courage to fulfil any tough task. It also reduces their mental and physical strength.

## Proneness to Superstitious Beliefs

Women espouse a lot of blind belief which places obstacles in the way of their mental and material development. They entertain several superstitions regarding ghosts, witches, she-demons, finding cures for diseases through sorcery, food taboos, and auspicious moments for beginning a journey. This is not to say that men do not have these shortcomings, but as compared to women, they are much less prone to superstitious beliefs.

## Tendency to be Imitative

Women display a strong tendency to imitate others. Men also tend to imitate others but they are not as deeply affected by this tendency as women. The desire to imitate does not allow women's originality to express itself.

## Laziness

One notices that those who are slightly better off consider idleness a comfortable state. However, they never realize how much damage idleness causes them. They not only harm themselves but also harm society.

## The Dominance of Negative Feelings

Jealousy is one of the defining characteristics of women, which leads to envy, slander, intolerance, and so on. These prevent women from reaching the highest level of development. Had women striven to get rid of these evil tendencies, they would have certainly occupied the highest place in the world.

Many such bad qualities pollute women's lives. If they try to get rid of these, then their lives will be filled with peace and happiness and their houses will turn into temples for goddesses.

The problems besetting women in Odisha are the same as those facing women in India. I cannot do better than presenting the gist of the lecture Pandit Nehru delivered at Mahila Vidyapith in Prayag:

People are of the view, which I also share, that the education system meant for women should be different from that for men. Women should be trained and prepared for discharging the duties of a housewife and the profession of marriage. I can never accept this narrow view of the aim of women's education. I firmly believe that women should be given the best possible education to make them fit for every sphere of human activity. They should acquire the ability and power to excel in all fields and all professions.

One can never say that women have achieved freedom in any form as long as marriage is regarded as a profession and the chief source of income for women. In politics, too, freedom depends on one's economic situation. If a woman is not economically independent and cannot choose a profession on her own, she will have no option but to depend on her husband or some other person. This life of dependence can never be regarded as freedom. The relationship between men and women should be based on complete independence and complete cooperation.

How long will you go on beating trodden paths relying on precedents and old examples and not exercise your own judgement? Why should you not reject whatever is not good and whatever impedes progress. Why should you not assert your true identity based on your ability and education, disdaining and rejecting the polluting environment that surrounds you?

Who is not aware of the evil effects of the practice of purdah? Purdah survives as a symbol of a barbaric age and continues to imprison the bodies and minds of many of our sisters. Why shouldn't you tear the purdah to pieces and burn it up? Untouchability and casteism degrade human beings and enable one class to plunder another. Why shouldn't you launch a campaign against these and destroy them? Why won't you spread the message of equality in this country and promote egalitarian values? The rules governing the institution of marriage in our country and obsolete customs place obstacles on our way forward. These have crushed the spirit of women. Why don't you fight against these with all the weapons at your disposal to make these conform to the circumstances of the modern world? Why don't you oppose these with a firmness of purpose? If these difficulties are removed, our sisters will be able to develop their minds and bodies by breathing the air of freedom. Strong, healthy, and beautiful women will give birth to children who will bring glory to the nation.

Why shouldn't you actively participate in the struggle for the liberation of our country which has been going on for such a long time? ... I would like to entrust you with the task of keeping the flame of liberty burning forever. I sincerely hope you will undertake this task and make this flame illuminate in every corner of India.

In conclusion, I would like to appeal to the educated women of the country to throw themselves wholeheartedly into the task of helping thousands of their helpless and ignorant sisters. There are many ways in which they can help them. They should do whatever they are capable of doing. They should try to make women exert themselves actively in all spheres of activity—political, social, and economic—and build a bright future for the nation. As long as we knowingly blindfold ourselves, our problems will never be solved. If we come forward to perform our duties, our well-wishers among men will never hesitate to assist us. If we have faith in ourselves and step into the world of action with noble purposes, the misery, the misfortune, and the agony endured by our nation will disappear in no time.

I appeal to the women of our country to keep the following tasks in mind when they enter the sphere of public life:

## The Social Sphere

(a)  To ensure a higher place for women in society.
(b)  To eradicate evils such as child marriage, promote widow marriage, and raise the age of marriage for girls, and to ensure that importance is given to a girl's opinion in a marriage.
(c)  To abolish purdah.
(d)  To eradicate untouchability.
(e)  To spread education by setting up special schools for girls and adult women and take steps to ensure that women remain in charge of primary education for boys and girls.
(f)  To try to improve the health of women and make arrangements for spreading education related to reproductive health.
(g)  To agitate to give women the right to divorce which is now enjoyed only by men.
(h)  To abolish prostitution.

*The Economic Sphere*

(a) To try to popularize cottage industries in every family.
(b) To persuade women to engage independently in business activities and improve their financial conditions.
(c) To launch a campaign to enable women to have an equal share of their parental property like their brothers.
(d) To lead a campaign to ensure that the sale of homegrown products far exceeds that of foreign goods.
(e) To set up an industrial workshop to provide women with training.

*The Political Sphere*

(a) To start a movement to encourage women to play their role in the freedom struggle.
(b) To launch an agitation to make sure that the share of women in the administrative system of the nation is not reduced.

It goes without saying that a strong organization is needed to accomplish all these tasks. I am confident that work in this direction can begin if my sisters in the country establish a women's organization. For the whole of Odisha, a central organization should be set up with its branches in different parts of the province. With the help of women volunteers the goals of the organization can be achieved.

I hope that my educated sisters, and my brothers who wish women well, will pay close attention to this.

# Basanti*

Despite being constantly buffeted by life's struggles and bogged down in mundane chores, Debabrata never let himself forget that his most important duty was to ensure that Basanti was happy to take care of him. How could he forget this, when she was a ray of moonlight in his life? How could he ever forget, when he had accepted to risk his bright future and almost everything he held dear? This sacrifice had brought him joy. His heart's beloved—with whom his youthful soul had envisioned a blissful union, enveloped in the magical qualities of a dream—was now at his side, in flesh and blood. Had he ever

---

* Extracted from Chapter 9 of the novel *Basanti*, serialized in *Utkal Sahitya* during 1924–6 and published as a book in 1931 by Sabuja Sahitya Samiti. It is one of the nine chapters Sarala Devi wrote in the novel. The English translation by Himansu S. Mohapatra and Paul St. Pierre uses the chapter from the revised edition of *Basanti* (New Students' Store, Cuttack, 1968), pp. 54–62.

for a moment imagined that his sacrifice would yield results so quickly? At first, he had been astonished that his beloved had so easily become his. Innocent in the ways of the world, he had no idea how a young man should behave towards such a precious object. He had not expected to receive God's favour so soon, and suddenly gaining the object of his love had—because he lacked confidence—overwhelmed him with fear and misgiving. Would he have the strength to take good care of this person he had so desired? Would he be able to cherish his beloved for all eternity, be able to provide her with all she deserved? He was not able to satisfy himself; the ease with which he had won a creature as rarefied as Basanti had planted in his mind the seeds of doubt.

At first when Basanti came to his house, Debabrata did everything he could to make her feel at home. He did not want her to be sad and miss her mother, or think she had been forsaken and become an orphan, or consider her fate was now to be one of perpetual slight. He did not know how far he had succeeded in this.

Fifteen days had passed since she had come to Similipur. Debabrata was seated on the rooftop terrace, with a book in hand. He could not remember when his gaze shifted from the book to the sky above as he went over the chain of events leading from the death of Nirmala Devi to the present moment. His life seemed to have dramatically changed in the twinkling of an eye, almost like scenes quickly shifting on a stage. Was he still the same Debabrata? Why did he feel the same life force coursing through him as it did when he was a student? Why did he feel the same joy bubbling up within him, the same torrents of thoughts and imagination racing through him? Yet, he truly was still the same person! Why had his poetic soul become mute, why did he feel so dispirited? He must surely have changed. He realized that under the barrage of onslaughts from the outside world, his soul had been crushed. He heaved a long sigh of despair and wondered if he was doing right to Basanti. A feeling of deep self-loathing came over him; he was unable to forgive himself.

He looked within himself once again, and could see there all the feelings he had for Basanti. What was he doing wrong, then?

Maybe there was something missing somewhere in him, and that was making her unhappy. There seemed to be no reason as such for his mental turmoil. Maybe it was his mother's hostile behaviour and the spiteful attitude of neighbours, relatives, and friends that had disturbed his equilibrium. He felt distanced from everybody—a stranger, a rank outsider who had been cornered like an animal. He was a man after all, an educated man of means, but he felt undone by this subtle feeling of exclusion within his family, which affected him more than the external social pressure.

The beams of the *shukla ekadasi*[1] moon bathed the terrace floor in a flood of silvery light. The dew-drenched flowers in the pots lined up in rows smiled radiantly. The stars seemed dim in the moonlight. The blue sky, peaceful and beautiful, seemed to empathize with Debabrata's grieving heart. The strong breeze, blowing in from afar, troubled the smooth mop of his curly hair. While rearranging it, he caught sight of a blurred figure standing behind the window in the room at the top of the stairs. Who could that be?

Acting nonchalant, he moved towards the landing. Suddenly he grabbed the bunch of keys tied to the end of the sari the shadowy figure was wearing. Peals of laughter rang out from a woman standing some distance away on the staircase. They dissolved into the air along with the sound of her footsteps as she ran down the stairs.

'Oh! What are you doing?' The words were followed by a feeble entreaty from the familiar creature. 'Please let me go. Let me go down and give Ma a massage.'

'Don't try to trick me,' Debabrata answered. 'Why were you hiding? Were you afraid to come closer?'

Basanti was caught off guard. 'Please forgive me. I'll make sure I won't be caught again.'

'Fine. You've admitted your guilt; now get ready for your punishment.'

'Whatever Your Lordship wishes. Any punishment you decide upon will be most respectfully accepted.'

---

[1] A holy day meant for fasting according to the Hindu calendar.

'That's good. Now come and sit. Let's talk.'

Letting a light smile crease her crimson lips, Basanti sat on the mattress.

Debabrata asked, 'Who ran away laughing when I caught you?'

'Nisa and I came up to the roof to stretch our legs. Dhania had told me you had gone out on your bicycle. When I saw you, I told Nisa that we should stand absolutely still and that she should make sure her bangles didn't jingle. When you turned towards us, she knew you'd play that prank, but the imp didn't warn me. So she ran off laughing when I got caught. Will she spare me now? She's going to tease me to death,' said Basanti.

'Serves you right! Now you're going to get it from both sides, from my sister and also from me. Your just desserts! I haven't come up to the roof to lie down for quite some time. I found it hot down below. Anyway, why don't you ever come up here? Look at the beautiful moonlight! Feel the cool breeze! It seems like you're too caught up in your domestic chores,' said Debabrata.

'Well, what else would you expect, now that I have a house to look after? Maybe you think that because I don't come up to the roof I'm languishing in the heat. You think that while you're enjoying yourself here, we're frying down below. Well, you're wrong. My room also gets the breeze, and your sister and I read and gossip. You may be lying here like the ever forgetful Bholanath, with nothing to do, but I have a lot on my hands, from household chores to my own work,' said Basanti.

'What work is that? I know you are caught up in the drudgery of housework day and night. You won't listen to me. When you were at your place, you used to go for a stroll every day; unfortunately, you can't do that here. Otherwise, what work do you have?'

'Oh, I forgot that for you reading books and writing for the newspaper doesn't count. Well, I used to go out for a walk when I had the chance. Now I don't; it's not possible, but I don't mind.'

Basanti kept silent after smiling wanly. Debabrata was cut to the quick when he understood his wife's innermost desire. A heart-rending sigh issued from his anguished heart and melted into the night air. Resting Basanti's head on his shoulder, he said: 'Do you think, Basa, that pretending not to see your situation

makes me happy? Don't you think I understand that after leaving
your home in Cuttack for mine, you've constantly been at odds
with your principles, your values, and your happiness—and all
because of me? Hasn't your "Debabhai" seen how you used to get
angry with your mother when she forbade you from going to the
riverbank for a stroll? Doesn't he know what your pastimes are—
reading, knitting, and making carpets—and that you would spend
your leisure time with your companion Boula? These eyes of mine
have witnessed all this, haven't they?'

Basanti saw how troubled her husband was and, to ease his
feelings, said in mock anger: 'All cheesy stuff and molasses nonsense
you're speaking now, raking up stories from the ancient past as if
you've nothing better to do! I'm quite happy, quite satisfied. How
could I possibly be sad? This is of your own invention, whatever
it is. I don't remember things that happened ages ago. You only
know how to unravel a whole spool to find a single thread.'

Debabrata knew what Basanti was trying to get at. 'No, Basa,
no! Do you think I'm such a hopeless good-for-nothing? Don't
you think I know how much you have had to sacrifice to adjust
to these new surroundings? And all that just to make one person
happy!'

Basanti said, 'You'll never change, no matter how hard one
tries.'

Drawing Basanti even closer, Debabrata said, 'Basa, I don't care
about myself. My regret is that I haven't been able to make you as
happy as I wanted. It's difficult for me to imagine that my hopes
for us will reach full bloom at some happy time in the future.'

Basanti felt warm teardrops fall on her forehead. She looked
up and saw that Debabrata's large chest was inundated by streams
of tears. She fondly wiped them away with the end of her sari.
'What's this!' she exclaimed. 'Are you crazy? Since when have you
made crying a pastime?' She tried to laugh but could not. Tears
streamed from her doe-like eyes like a spring in the Himalayas,
giving an outlet to the storm of pain raging inside her heart.

What earnest attempts Debabrata was making for her happiness
and comfort, Basanti thought. This living proof of how deep his
feelings for her were made Basanti brim with a sense of glory,

gratification, and immeasurable happiness born of love. Deeply moved, she encircled Debabrata's neck and spoke with great tenderness, 'Listen, you're the same Debabhai I knew before, but my arrival was like a stumbling block in your way. Because of me you've come into bitter conflict with society and your mother. Before getting married, you hadn't actually thought much about whether you'd be able to come to terms with it. On finding yourself in a hostile situation, you must have felt bitter towards me. That's what I used to think when I saw how depressed you were. But now I see I was being unfair to you and wronging you by thinking such thoughts. Now I ask myself if God will resent the good fortune of a helpless woman like me, so singularly blessed with so much affection and tenderness. Deprived of a secure haven from the very start of my life, I now depend on you. Very often I'm afraid that this security will also elude me, that one day my wretched life will be without your life-giving affection. No, no, I couldn't live without your love. I don't have the strength.'

Debabrata was completely engrossed in the soulful and passionate utterances of the darling of his heart. He felt as if an angel had descended from heaven and poured ambrosia into his ears out of pity for his shattered, feeble, and persecuted mind. It was as if the Mandakini was surging through him, banishing all forms of weakness. The ambrosial touch made his youth return; he felt reborn in the lost realm of youth known to him in his student days, discarding the feebleness of the present. Embracing his beloved in an excess of emotion, Debabrata said, 'I'm so fortunate to have you; because of you my life is a success. Even if you feel you're lucky with a hapless fellow like me, I still think I'm luckier, because my youthful dream has come true and all the obstacles and troubles have been overcome. I'm beginning to believe this more and more today. I know that immediately after our marriage there was discord in our conjugal life; it was like a barrier in the path of our complete union. It is clear to me now that this was why my life felt dull and weak. The indomitable power and strength a man gets from doing something noble has always eluded me. I wanted to feel this through a deliberate effort of the will. For that, I have fought hard with myself but have not been able to get rid of this half-heartedness. This has made you apprehensive. My indifference and absent-mindedness have caused you terrible pain.'

A hint of smile lighted up for an instant Basanti's *bimba*-like lips before fading away. Debabrata said, 'Neither of us tried to understand the other. This lack of communication has not actually crippled our union but has constrained it. That is why I felt myself to be devoid of strength, lost self-confidence, and was full of self-reproach. I felt I was being accused of some unknown crime by society and my mother. Now it is clear to me that my listlessness and passivity were the result of not having made you my own, earnestly and fully. Please forgive me, Basanti.'

Pressing her tender arms in an access of deep remorse, Debabrata went on, 'Will you please pardon my unforgivable crime? In not controlling my mind I haven't done the right thing, even if I didn't understand that. I may not have failed in my duty towards you, but my regret is that I haven't tried hard enough to bridge the gap between us and reach an understanding. Please tell me whether you'll forgive me for the hurt my dilemma has caused you?'

Basanti broke into a smile. 'If I had had an inkling of the momentous discovery you'd make, I'd never have let you catch me. There's nothing in my mind that says you have hurt me. What am I to do if you work yourself into such a pitiable state and ask for my forgiveness? You express your regret to me for some presumed offence you've caused me, but I've never thought about you in this way. Whom shall I forgive then? Please know this: you stand forever forgiven in my eyes, come what may.'

'Please tell me plainly that you've forgiven me,' Debabrata persisted.

Basanti continued, 'You're talking as if you've killed a cow and are desperate to be pardoned.' In a state of elation, Debabrata suddenly kissed her. Blushing deeply and her eyes lowered, Basanti darted downstairs, not heeding Debabrata's plea to wait. She went down and started to massage her mother-in-law.

The relationship between Debabrata and Basanti had become whole under the open sky; this moment had become auspicious. They realized how close they were to each other and felt this new-found intimacy could stand up to any outside force. Their attraction to each other had grown, and their reliance on each other was now based on an even more solid ground. Not a trace of conflict troubled their souls.

Basanti was like the wild current of a river—fast, fresh, and flowing. Nothing that was bland and broken had any place in her life. She was a child of nature; her soul had been conceived in freedom, in the freedom of a woman. From the very beginning, her life had unfolded under this aspect. She had her sights set on higher things; her loving and desiring mind knew no limits. But this did not mean she was aggressive. No. Restraint was an important part of her nature. She never had to struggle to impose control on herself, since by nature she was remarkably self-controlled. The instrument in the deep recesses of her heart rang out new melodies in new rhythms every day and resonated through her daily life of cares and duties. She was never tired of her many chores—from work in the house, to writing, reading, looking after her mother-in-law, to other work. Like the ever-smiling sephali flower in autumn, she was always cheerful, basking in the radiance of her own being.

Since coming to Debabrata's house as his wife, Basanti had carried on a quiet battle against all sorts of odds. She had endured outmoded customs silently, putting on a cheerful face and doing as she was directed. Not that this left her indifferent. She wondered why she bent to her mother-in-law's every whim, when doing so clearly went against her own likes, thoughts, and desires. She was not intimidated by her mother-in-law; she only wanted to spare Debabrata pain. And even that would not have counted for much if their relationship were based on impurity, falsehood, and convenience. Her love for her dearest was deep; if he felt so much as the prick of a tender blade of grass, it was as if she herself were struck by a stone. She always strove to make Debabrata happy, to flood his being with the soothing splendour of peace, even if that meant sacrificing her high ideals. What sacrifices had he not made for her! When, after the marriage, Debabrata's family had invited their relatives to a feast in Similipur, and they had refused to come because the bride was from a lower caste and had cut all ties with his family, Debabrata had boldly replied: 'Our house is not going to be swept away if no one comes. I'm at nobody's mercy, and I'll not flatter anyone. Let's see who's cutting off whom.' Hadn't her husband accepted the punishment completely and without complaint? Hadn't he tolerated all kinds of harsh words from his mother, keeping silent only for her sake? Weren't there more important problems to be surmounted in trying to serve respectfully a person like him, who took his conscience as his inspiration and who was so dedicated to his duty? She never wanted to come across as someone who could endure far less than her husband just because she was personally affected. As a woman she was expected to show greater openness and tolerance than a man, she thought, and, buoyed by this, she went on performing her duty with pleasure.

Subhadra, however, bore a grudge against Basanti, not only for having taken away her son but also for the torment this caused her. Her anger rained down in torrents on her poor and innocent daughter-in-law.

Through sheer willpower, Basanti endured her mother-in-law's hostility and the hurtful and vile words that accompanied it, and went on about her work in silence. She did not think of herself as weak or lowly; rather, she felt she was strong and that by tolerating the abuse she became worthy of her husband. This gave her great joy.

And precisely for this reason, Debabrata began to harbour misgivings. He began to smart under the ill treatment Basanti was receiving from his mother. He was quick to realize that Basanti was enduring everything only for the sake of his own peace and well-being.

Debabrata did not, of course, fully understand that behind Basanti's calm exterior lay a tumult that rocked her mind from time to time, a tumult arising from her desire to efface herself, to brutally repress her deepest feelings. He could guess and imagine what lay concealed in her heart. Her suffering was truly unbearable to him. The more she tolerated and sacrificed, the more restless and impatient he grew, and the more he began to reproach himself out of an anguished sense of his utter inadequacy.

# The Role of Women in the Freedom Struggle*

Twenty or thirty years ago, women's participation in politics was unheard of. Inspired by Annie Besant, who had dedicated her life to the uplift of women in our country, many women took part in the struggle for Independence. The struggle went on for 15 years under the leadership of Gandhi. Indian women came out of their seclusion, sacrificed their wealth, even their lives, to carry this struggle forward. They remain active in the public sphere even today. Sarojini Naidu emerged as a highly esteemed leader of the Indian National Congress. In future, more and more women will certainly be part of various organizations of national repute. If this does not happen, there will be a distinct decline in the position of women. When the issue of the honour and dignity of the nation will be raised,

* Extracted from *Bharatiya Mahila Prasanga* (Cuttack: Hindustan Sahitya Mandira, 1935), pp. 49–58. Translated by Jayaprakash Paramaguru.

the silence and indifference of women will constitute a source of painful embarrassment. They should always deem it their duty to contribute to the overall development of the nation.

It is a matter of great satisfaction that Sarojini Naidu, Saraladevi Chaudhurani, Mridulaxmi Reddy, Srimati Subrayan, and others have provided leadership to Indian women. This is most encouraging. One is confident that if women follow their example and attain their rights, many of the problems faced by the nation will disappear.

For women in India, the road to liberation is full of obstacles. Their condition will never improve unless they work selflessly and with energy and dedication. As long as a feeling of solidarity is not aroused in the hearts of women, their condition will remain as miserable as ever. The obstacles on the path to freedom will be removed when the hearts of women are filled with self-confidence. The hardship they face will disappear. They should overcome their feeling of inferiority and perform their duties. There is every reason to believe that the future of the movement for the upliftment of women going on in India at present is very bright. Let me quote here an extract from Sarojini Naidu's speech, which will enable the people of our country to understand the problems of women more completely:

> Women are no longer tools and toys of men. Women today are fired with new enthusiasm. We do not want our rights to oppress anybody, but we want them in order to carry out our responsibilities. Women today are suffering from various legal disabilities. We want to work for the political, moral, and economic uplift of the country shoulder to shoulder with men. We do not want to be a dead weight around their neck. (From a speech at New Delhi, delivered on 2 March 1935)

Several women's organizations have been set up in India to realize the goals defined in the aforementioned extract. Whatever they have managed to achieve in this short span of time makes us feel optimistic about the future.

The task performed by the Indian Association for Women founded by Annie Besant during the Home Rule agitation in

1917 fills our hearts with hope. Within a period of 17–18 years, the association has done a lot for women. It has successfully drawn the attention of the government and the public to issues such as the right to vote, girl's education, welfare of mothers, and eradication of prostitution. The association is active in different parts of the country and it has as many as 4,000 members. In a short time, 120 branches of the association have been established in the country. In every province, a provincial conference is organized. The association has focused on bringing about social reform and promoting women's education. It includes members from all sections of society, people supporting and opposing the government. Lady Irwin College in Delhi is the outcome of tireless efforts made by this association. The college provides special instruction related to home science. The impact of All India Women's Educational Conference held in 1927 and chaired by the Queen of Baroda—organized especially for the development of Indian women—could be easily felt. The same year, as many as 30 women's conferences were organized in different parts of the country.

The eminent Parsi social reformer Behramji Malabari set up a *seva sadan* (a place of service) in 1908 and opened another branch at Pune in 1909. This seva sadan provides education to hundreds of women. The sadan has earned the gratitude of the nation by performing tasks such as providing care to the ailing, bringing relief to the poor, and offering shelter to orphans. A women's university has been established as a result of exertions made by famous scholar D.P. Karve. Over the last 17–18 years, about 500 women have received education from this institution. About four colleges, fifteen high schools, three middle English schools, seven normal schools, and a training school function under the auspices of this university. The fame of this university is spreading throughout the country, and there is no doubt that this will soon emerge as one of the foremost centres of learning in the world. In a short time, the Sarojini Nalini Organization of Bengal has taken long strides in the field of education. Every year hundreds of girls receive instruction from the institution set up by this organization. The organization set up by Sir Gangaram of

Lahore, a man famous for his charity and passion for social reform, is working hard to ameliorate the condition of widows. Many widows have remarried with the support of this organization. Its area of operation is expanding gradually.

Besides the aforementioned organizations, many others, large and small, are active in different parts of the country. Some short-lived organizations also appear from time to time. Although these do not function in a disciplined manner, no one can deny that they are making a significant contribution to the well-being of the nation.

## Odia Women of the Future

Ever since Indian women came under the influence of Western culture and education, a conflict has ensued between the indigenous culture and its Western counterpart. This situation has given rise to divergent responses. It is true that Indian women have not adapted themselves to Western culture as aggressively as Indian men have. This usually happens when a society finds itself being influenced by renaissance. When we consider the conflict between the conservatives and modernists, we feel like accepting Gandhi and Rabindranath Tagore's middle course, as avoiding extremes is always desirable. When we take a close look at women in India, we notice that they have adopted the middle course. Everyone would agree that the number of Indian women who have come heavily under the influence of Western culture and grown away from their own is small.

Here Western education has been comprehensively defeated. Our women have not been able to receive the essence of Western education and, therefore, have not been able to contribute much to the development of their country. This convinces us that what they learn from the West has little to offer to their own world. Had it been otherwise, the Western-educated society ladies would have been able to solve the hundreds of problems afflicting our nation. We notice that such women have grown impossibly conceited. Of course, there are a few exceptions that empathize with the poor and miserable of their country, but one must admit that Western education promotes extravagance, hedonism, greed, and selfishness. As a result, women with Western education have not been able to alleviate the misery oppressing the women and children of the country. Therefore, when visionaries and intellectuals seek to promote women's education, the poor and the deprived hold up the undesirable products of Western education and denounce women's education. For this reason, the life of women in future will be full of responsibilities. These women will have to forget completely how their predecessors blindly imitated the Western ways. They must take upon themselves the task of building the nation. Their education should not be bookish and should be responsive to the needs of their nation and the demands of the new age. India is a predominantly agrarian country. Here millions live in unhygienic conditions in the villages and fall prey to epidemics. Heavy taxes make people of this land spend sleepless nights. The misery endured by the boys and girls of this country who are deprived of education beggars description. Many villages in India do not have wells, and people contract all kinds of diseases by drinking water from hyacinth-choked malarial marshes. Women in this country do not know how to raise children. Many women die in unhygienic lying-in rooms tended by inexperienced midwives. Some women, who have received no education, find it difficult to earn their living, leave home, and commit suicide. Many of them do not even have a spare sari to wear and are unable to cope with the elements, and fall ill. God knows who will bring an end to their misery. I think this responsibility must be shouldered by women who have been educated in the true sense of the term.

If, in the future, the educated women in Odisha and India fail to be moved by the condition of the nation and society as a whole on account of their narrow-minded selfishness, this poor country will have every right to despise their educational attainments. India will not feel proud of educated women who are devoid of a sense of duty towards the nation and society.

There is no doubt that the nation will pay homage to women and realize the importance and utility of their education if women are inspired by the noble ideal of service to the people.

The nation has every right to expect something from doctors and teachers who have received their education at girls' schools set up in the past. While treating their jobs as a means of making money, these professional women could have formed associations and served the nation in an important way. However, this has not happened. If those who earned more than 100 rupees donated 10 rupees for bringing about improvements in the field of education, health, and literature, the nation would have remained eternally indebted to them. However, women have not been able to do so due to their greed and extravagance. The misery of Mother Utkal will come to an end if women will acquire a new outlook and respond to the call of duty.

# True Womanhood*

Today members of the Western race boast that no one in the world pays more respect to women (in their community) than they do. However, perhaps no other race despised women as intensely as they did in the past. In the religious conference held in AD 578, it was agreed that women do not have souls. Any thoughtful person can see why such a belief gained ground if one takes into account the way men have treated women since time immemorial. What a pity that the authors of scriptures, which women revere so deeply, make them appear so utterly contemptible. Religion which holds women responsible for all kinds of degradation is taken for truth by everyone. Consequently,

* Originally titled 'Naritwara Prathistha', this essay first appeared in Utkal Sahitya, No. 25/8, 1329 Sala, pp. 268–80, and later appeared in Sarala Devi: Lekhika, Sanskarika, Biplabini, Sachidananda Mohanty (ed.) (Cuttack: Agraduta Publications, 2004), pp. 55–70. Translated by Akhtar Jamal Khan.

no one treats women with respect or affection. A woman will be cherished only to the extent that she serves someone's self-interest. Women will never receive more love or rights from men than this even if they demand it desperately banging their heads against a wall, because they are weaker than men. Here strength means brute force or physical strength. A Chinese saying goes like this: Knowledge suits men as ignorance suits women. What help can women expect from men if they truly believe in this saying.

It would be futile to ask why *Brihadaranyakopanishad* describes the lives of Yajnavalkya and Maitreyi, Yajnavalkya and Gargi, and as to why Sage Kanva, King Asvapati, and King Janaka educated their daughters Sakuntala, Savitri, and Sita. Six thousand years ago, when Egypt was a civilized country, its influence on Roman society led to an improvement in the condition of women there. On the rights women enjoyed in those days, Maspara says the following: She is her husband's privileged guest; she inherits equally with her brothers; she is the mistress of the house and, judicially, is the equal of men; she has the same rights as men and is treated in the same fashion. Henry Mein, in his book *Ancient Law*, explains why such pagan laws had no influence on modern laws.

Although European laws were deeply influenced by those of ancient Rome, the harsh Hebraic prescriptions found greater acceptance in Europe because these are in consonance with what men want women to be. At first sight, the system based on these prescriptions appears natural because it has close links with religion. However, close scrutiny reveals that it appears natural not because of its links with religion but because men like it. However, the influence of religion cannot be denied. Jesus Christ said many things but nothing about the oppression endured by women.

St Paul expressed the view that, unlike men, women cannot ask questions related to religion, that women are subordinate to men because God created them for the benefit of men. He also stated that under no circumstances could a woman teach a man anything. Women are embodiments of slavery. She is doomed to be consigned to hell for eternity and can never be redeemed. What a wonderful view St Paul espouses! What an easy way he suggests for the salvation of women! We get to know this when we read any religious texts of the English people. In Indian Puranas, too, women are considered important because they bear children and men are advised to take a wife to have a son. In religious texts all over the world, one comes across such attitudes to women. On her own, a woman amounts to nothing; her worth depends on her ability to produce a male child. To men, this is the only aim of a woman's life. Nothing else is expected of a woman in the world. She is respected only when she becomes the mother of a child. For example, Mayadevi, Mary, Yashoda, Kunti, Madri, and Kaushalya were considered blessed because they had given birth to Buddha, Jesus, Krishna, the Pandavas, and Rama respectively. This is the reason why praise is lavished on modern women too, but it is nothing more than rhetoric.

Our scriptures sanction having children through the procedure known as *kshetraja*. Kunti gave birth to the Pandavas and Ambika and Ambalika gave birth to Pandu and Dhritarashtra by adopting this procedure. However, for a chaste woman to have children in this manner is not honourable. In the ancient Zeus community, a childless widow had to marry her husband's younger brother in the hope of bearing a male child. Even today in Odisha, young widows belonging to Chasa (tillers), Keuta (fishermen), and Gauda (milkmen) castes marry their husbands' younger brothers or other men. Our scriptures consider childlessness a terrible sin. So the way women are valued can be easily understood. Women matter because they serve men's interest and function as a child-producing machine. This is why they are respected and valued. The truth of this observation can be established by referring to thousands of social aberrations. It would be no exaggeration to say that men have always tyrannized over and humiliated women. Men understand this very well but women do not. It seems women do not try or want to understand this. Engrossed in the small pleasures of life, how could she realize that the man she worships as a god is not her well-wisher? How could a daughter in the presence of a father think that the latter is not her friend but her enemy? In fact, taking individual cases into account, it is impossible for women to realize this unpleasant truth.

However, taking the totality of women's joys and sorrows, and their good fortunes and misfortunes into consideration, one finds the truth shining through the attitudes and behaviour of their fathers, brothers, and husbands.

When some special rule is established in our country, it does not find full expression in a day; it develops fully over time. Those who enforce it do so with the help of the rights they enjoy as men and not as someone's father, husband, or son. Those whom the rule targets are not related to the men who frame the rules; they are women and nothing else. While framing these rules, men do not think that they, too, have a girl child at home. They only worry about the welfare of men. They only think of the ways in which they can derive satisfaction and pleasure from women. Then sages such as Manu and Parashara arrive on the scene, compose slokas, and author scriptures. Self-interest assumes the disguise of religion and acquires the right to rule over society with an iron hand. Men are like Sage Vyasa and the authors of scriptures are like the pot-bellied Lord Ganesha. The scriptures of our country came to be written in this way. When the time comes to perform one's religious duty or share one's personal joys and sorrows, love and affection get swept away like blades of grass in a tide. The world is aware of the practice of sati observed in our country and even more cruel practices in other countries.

The Jews never hesitated to sacrifice their children before their deities. Their holy texts are replete with instances of parents offering their own children as sacrificial victims. In Mexico, parents experienced no scruples while sacrificing their beloved daughters in order to earn religious merit. Like Karna, famous for his boundless charity, many kings must have killed their own sons. The king of Mewar did so. The king of Carthage sacrificed his daughter to a deity. In ancient times, in many countries parents killed their children in the name of religion. Does this mean that these parents did not love their children? No, they certainly did. Then where did this filial affection disappear when they committed these cruel deeds? When customs take the form of religion, no act of cruelty appears impossible. In fact the more brutal and heinous an act, the more virtuous it appears to be. While committing such deeds, parents turn their gaze away from their children's faces, for they do not want to be deterred by feelings of affection. When men give a custom the dignity of a religion to serve their collective interest, an individual father finds it impossible to defy it when it comes to sacrificing his children. Experience bears this out in all ages.

When a young girl is married to a 50-year-old man, her father must be feeling miserable, but he finds himself helpless. He is scared that society would ridicule and ostracize him. The custom which he has sanctioned as a member of society makes him wipe his tears with the back of one hand and offer another young daughter to an old man with the other. Feelings of affection would not give him the courage to desist from committing this cruel deed. It is seen that in spite of being kind and affectionate, people can harm others and cause pain to those who depend on them for their survival. In their eagerness to adhere to customs, they become devoid of all affection and find peace of mind by taking shelter in religion. However, on close scrutiny one would find that these customs are rooted in boundless self-interest. However, it would be difficult for a father and his daughter to realize this. When human beings lose themselves in a maze of rites and customs, they fail to distinguish between right and wrong, humanity and beastliness. Who could see the injustice in sacrificing countless animals in the Vedic age? However, Lord Buddha could make human beings realize how unjust this practice was. Sati has been abolished, but one shudders when one recalls this terrible custom. The cruelty of throwing children into the river Ganges would now persuade people to praise the British law that prohibited it.

However, one cannot be sure that the people of our country have learnt anything from this. We know how many people called Raja Ram Mohan Roy, the greatest well-wisher of India, an enemy of religion because he wanted to lead society away from licence to virtue. His crime was that he sincerely looked for proper solutions to human problems, thought that men and women are equal, and tried to promote equality among them.

Even today, when someone returns from Britain we rush to the pundits of Sanskrit *tols* and Muktimandapa in Puri to find solutions to the strange social problems arising from a person's visit to Europe. We want them to tell us what is right and what is wrong because we consider them authorities on scriptures. However, no one cares to think that they know only the slokas of the scriptures and nothing else. Does it occur to anyone that knowledge has no meaning at all if it fails to broaden one's heart and mind? If someone asks these pundits at what age a girl should get married, they will reel off a few slokas. If one asks them if widows should remarry, they would open a holy text and try to find out what it says on this issue. Scriptures have blurred their vision. A layperson who is ignorant of scriptures will use his intellect when confronted with a question whereas an authority on scriptures will not do so. The latter will find it impossible to cross the limits set by the scriptures and mistake memory for intelligence. A well-known pundit once told me that anyone who could memorize a 100 slokas would be considered a pundit. What a wonderful argument! This may not be to the liking of many but this is something worth thinking about and acting on. As far as the histories of our country and of other nations, scriptures, and study of nature are concerned, the knowledge of many people will surpass that of mine. However, no amount of scholarship can persuade me to reject what I consider to be true, based on the experiences I have had since my childhood.

Who in our society should be responsible for providing a solution to social problems? Let those who have been taking this responsibility go on doing so. We should not object to their deciding when to stop cooking before a lunar eclipse, how much water mixed with cow dung should be given to drink to someone who has returned from England, and which abbot would go to hell if he takes a wife. However, they should not be allowed to take decisions related to the welfare of society and ways of modernizing it. Only those whose minds have been broadened by education should be entrusted with this task, not pundits. These pundits do not know the difference between the age described by the scriptures and the present age. Discussions on these things do not take place in Sanskrit tols of *chaupadhis* (traditional seats of learning). Everything outside their little group is impure for these people.

They are convinced that the opinions and conducts of others are inferior to theirs. Everyone except them is less than human. They fail to realize that rules and customs change with the passage of time. Even the mere mention of a movement aiming at changing these rules makes them burn with anger. The leaders of society also follow their examples. It is difficult to believe that these pundits really follow the prescriptions of the scriptures themselves. Would they now approve of ancient customs such as asura marriage and the kshetraja way of having children? When it suits them, they cite a number of precedents.

*Jadyapi siddham lokabirudham nadaraniyam namaraniyam.* In other words, these customs are part of *desachar* (national customs), not *kulachar* (family customs). However, if someone else dares violate these customs, the pundits drag them to the Muktimandapa. Men never accept a scripture if its prescriptions go against their vested interests. Even if God Himself descends on earth and sanctions those prescriptions, they would not listen to Him. However, the case of women is entirely different. They have to accept what the scriptures prescribe for them whether they like it or not. In Western countries, too, such a situation prevailed. A law now no longer in force there went like this: If a wife hates her husband and says 'Thou art not my husband', into the river they shall throw her. Another law was as follows: If a husband says 'Thou art not my wife' to his wife, half a mina of silver he shall weigh out to her and let her go. How generous men are to women! I don't know how much half a mina of silver amounts to, but we can never compare having to pay half a mina of silver with drowning a woman in a river. What strange justice!

I have never seen men paying respect to women in scriptures or public lectures. If a woman achieves something in our society, she does so only through her own hard work and sincere efforts and in spite of opposition from men. Such efforts by women in ancient Egypt and their influence spread as far as Rome. These initiatives were also taken in India. Here women aspired to compose the Vedas, but later they were forbidden to touch these texts.

Many men—almost everyone—seek to make sure that child widows and the newly widowed remain under society's control.

However, sometimes some of them go astray. The number of women who go astray keeps increasing. Widows are tempted to go astray. So men try to find ways to keep the newly widowed and child widows occupied with rights, religious rituals, and festivals and keep them under control so that they remain busy and pose no threat to society. Men are oppressed by the fear that women are eager to leave the confines of home if they are not kept under proper control. Some say *strisu rajakulesu cha biswasa naiba kartabya*. Others go a step further and say *anke sthitapi yubati parishankaniya*.

Finding these two mild, some others declare that *striya charitan purusasya bhagyam debo na janati kuteh manusya*. Some assert that *stri budhim pralayankari strina budhis chaturguna*.

Needless to say, all these statements do not enhance the dignity of women. Do the scriptures prescribe something equally harsh for men? I am not raising the issue of widow remarriage here. However, if people want widows to remarry to keep them from straying from the path of virtue, then, in my opinion, widows should not be remarried. Men may consider this to be self-evident. However, is it true that widows are always keen to get out of the confines of domesticity? While declaring such views about women and presenting these as firm beliefs, do men ever pause and think? What a terrible allegation they bring against guiltless women! A famous British philosopher had once stated that slavery is the sum of villainy and prostitution is the sum of degradation. Does this reflect a woman's true nature? Carried away by their brute strength, men may say yes, but a closer investigation would prove them wrong.

In the province of Bengal, a gentleman carried out a survey to ascertain how many women had been cast out of the community. He collected brief accounts of the lives of more than 1,000 wretched women living in different districts in Bengal. His report contained the names, addresses, caste affiliations, and the regions from where they were excommunicated. His report informs us that 70 per cent of those cast out of the community were married women, and only 30 per cent of them were widows. The report also mentions the reason why these women had left their homes.

These included unbearable poverty and intolerable ill treatment inflicted on the women. Most of the married women belonged to the lower castes, and most of the widows came from higher castes. Low-caste married women revealed that they had left their homes because they were not given anything during the day and were beaten up by their husbands at night. High-caste widows informed the gentleman that they had taken the step of leaving the community because they found the behaviour of their brothers-in-law, sisters-in-law, and parents-in-law intolerable. If one takes all these into account and considers everything carefully, one would feel that they are stating the facts. High-caste widows are rendered helpless by the death of their husbands. Women from lower castes find themselves equally helpless even when their husbands are alive. If one takes a close look at the lives of wage earners in Odisha and that of people from the higher castes, such as Karanas and Brahmins, one would realize the truth of this statement. However, one feels that the condition of widows belonging to the lower castes is relatively better, because they do not have to fear anyone and live a more or less independent life. They go to markets and make a living by pounding paddy. If need be, they work as maidservants. So they find it easy to survive by earning money through honest means and they do not have to transgress the limits imposed by the community. However, these options are not available to the married women of their community. If their husbands are alive, they are not allowed to work for a living, and yet their poor husbands are unable to provide them with food and clothes. They keep them under control by beating them within the house. The conditions of upper-caste widows resemble those of married women from the lower castes. They are not permitted to make a living by doing physical labour because this would bring disgrace to their parents or husbands. Everyone knows how miserable the condition of widows who stay confined within their houses is. So it is generally seen that 70 out of 100 such wretched women find themselves compelled to leave home to escape hunger and ill treatment from their relatives. Widowhood does not force them to do so, but without getting to the root of the issue, men have jumped to the conclusion that only widows leave home. So, they take every possible measure to keep widows under their control through all kinds of rights and restrictions. Men are not willing to accept that a majority of women who run away from home do so to escape their oppressive husbands or because their husbands have rejected them. On the one hand, a woman's husband abuses her nature by inflicting poverty and tyranny on her; on the other, a man who lures a woman away from home holds out false promises to her and destroys her life. Should we, then, blame a woman for the calamity that befalls her? Are those who apply epithets such as 'frail', 'fickle', and 'unable to defend herself' to women and try to display their intellect in doing so, entitled to describe women as fallen? Men have nothing to fear. They can enjoy themselves to their heart's content and still return to their families and communities. They withdraw to a corner of the house appearing penitent. Overjoyed by their return, their kith and kin melt out of pity and comfort them saying, 'Never mind, this is how men behave. There is nothing surprising about this. Forget what you have done. Show us your face once more.' Men feel very happy and step out into the open and, assuming the role of the custodians of morality, declare, 'Under no circumstances can a woman's moral lapses be tolerated.' Once a woman strays from the path of virtue, no matter what the reason, the orthodox Hindu society would throw her out of the community's fold and refuse to accept even water from her. Gradually, when lapses are given the form of a sin, she loses her identity as a woman and is regarded as a witch. Even so, the custodians of society find her indispensable and want her presence in family festivals and temples. Overwhelmed by feelings of devotion, people gave Lord Krishna a hundred names and Lord Rama a thousand.

In Sanskrit literature, prostitutes have been lovingly mentioned thousands of times. Among the gods in heaven, divine courtesans are the most respected and adored. This makes it amply clear who is more selfish and sinful, who should be the target of harsh prescriptions of scriptures in order to get rid of sin in society, who—men or women—should be kept under a close watch and punished. Why should society refuse to forgive even minor lapses on the part of women and overlook terrible sins committed by men? The answer lies in man's possession of brute strength.

If someone criticizes a man's lapses or his looks, society would raise its head and protest. 'After all, they are men. Do men ever face ostracization anywhere in the world? Do people bother about their looks or conduct? Looks are essential for a girl. If a young man is ugly or bad, would it be difficult for him to find a bride? The case of a girl is different.' So on and so forth. These sayings have entered the marrow of society and even women, through their contact with men, parrot these. One day I had an argument with an educated elderly woman about this opinion of mine. She told me, 'We can't think of the large world that lies outside our little one. We share the opinions held by our fathers, brothers, husbands, and sons. We don't express our views when we differ from them for fear that they might feel hurt. We do as they say and somehow survive. We don't think of anything that does not concern our household affairs and our family life. We have grown used to this.' I told her, 'Tell me more; I would like to take it down. Men who want to write essays on society will find much material from this.'

'Such and such task is despicable.' This makes men hate women. They are given the right to hate and are exercising that right. A woman is not given this right. However despicable a man may be, he is her 'husband'. How could she hate her husband? The scriptures have taught her that her husband, however bad he may be, is her adorable lord. When the lord dies, she should put his lotus feet on her lap and burn herself in his funeral pyre. In this age, a woman need not die when her husband dies; she can fulfil her existence by doing something heroic by becoming a living corpse. If she dies, everything will be over at one stroke. So her heroism depends on silently enduring the torture society and her family inflict on her all her life.

Some people cite scientific evidence to say that if one takes the welfare of the progeny into account, a woman's lapses cause greater damage to the family. Doctors know how many wives fall prey to terrible diseases because of their husband's misdeeds and how many children take birth afflicted with diseases that ruin their whole lives. They have to expiate the sins committed by their fathers and grandfathers. However, the scriptures say very little about this, customs are quiet about this, and society chooses to be silent. In fact, the sayings of scriptures are empty like the sound of guns not loaded with bullets, but what really matters is what men want and this shapes social customs. Manu, Parashara, and Harita are nothing but figments of fancy. Men will go on committing sins in full public view, and women keep quiet to appear chaste. Women would even allow men to transmit their terrible diseases to their bodies. What can be more humiliating for women than this? However, someone versed in scriptures would raise his eyebrows and say, 'Sita and Rama are an ideal couple. Rama made Sita undergo the ordeal of fire several times to establish her physical purity and banished her into the forest to placate his subjects. Sita shed tears thinking of her husband's lotus feet. In spite of the intense agony she suffered, she blamed only her fate, not Rama. Doing this didn't diminish, but enhanced Sita's glory.' Did Rama do justice to Sita by banishing her, especially when we think of him as an avatar, an ideal human being? When Rama made Sita undergo the ordeal of fire again and again, didn't she reach the end of her patience? Could she remain confined within social conventions? Sita's ideals show that women have no other option but to sacrifice themselves for society and men. In all ages, more or less, this has been happening, but can anyone assert that God has created women to become slaves to men and satisfy their animal desires? Let the matter rest there.

In other countries, the law sanctions divorce. So women there have some options. However, our country, which is God's own country and whose scriptures and religion have no parallels, offers women no options at all. In this country, men tie up women like animals and beat them with a stick. If they fail to get what they want from women, they beat them so hard that they bleed, and women endure all this meekly. For this reason, men boast to others, 'See, in no other country, will you find women who bear pain so uncomplainingly.' Who doesn't know this? But why should men feel proud of this? If a newspaper in a foreign country publishes news of someone filing a case to divorce their spouse, our editors here feel elated and declare in big headlines full of exclamation marks: 'See, how flawed Western civilization is!' They believe that their virtues will be easily manifested if they advertise the faults of others. Women in the West understand that divorce is not desirable but they cannot keep quiet when they are beaten up and sometimes return the blows. When couples hit each other, people outside get to know and their enemies get the chance to laugh heartily at their expense. If someone asks Hindus whether causes which lead to divorce cases in the West are absent in their families, even the most shameless among them would find it difficult to give an honest reply. If they cannot, what right have they got to laugh at Western couples? Should divorce cases be more important than the factors which cause them? In Europe, in the past marriages were indissoluble. This is why one comes across the following observation in *The Ethic of Free Thought*: the church's irrational rigidity as regards divorce tended to foster disorder and shame.

No one should get the impression that I support divorce. Of course, no one wants violent conflicts in society. However, when social customs in India approve of husbands abandoning their wives, why shouldn't one accept wives leaving their husbands? Why shouldn't women in India enjoy rights that their counterparts in other countries are entitled to? No convincing answer to this question can be offered by men, who will only burst out angrily: 'What a stupid thing to say! How can one introduce something into our social world which was never there?' The fact is that if women are made equal to men, the latter would lose their liberty to commit crimes with impunity. So no man—especially an Indian man—would like a woman to be his equal. It is but natural that men who are cowards, who derive pleasure from oppressing the weak and the helpless, would humiliate women and will not recognize their dignity. They may die but will not part with even a fraction of their privileges. It is well known that men would quote from the scriptures, swear in the name of science, cite precedents relating to social practices, and pretend to be custodians of morality in this moribund society. However, women have awakened and acquired the ability to understand things. It is time they devote all their God-given energies to achieving the task of restoring their lost womanhood. They should strive tirelessly to show men that womanhood is in no way inferior to manhood. They should reject the scriptures that say *pathi nari bibarjita* to suit the interest of men who, intoxicated by power, refuse to protect women from other men in public places. I think the things I say may not appear palatable to men, and they would not want these to reach women in the inner wings of their houses. However, I have no doubt that one day women who are being oppressed and tortured daily by men would demand an explanation from them. Outraged men may try to exterminate women; they may find this demand distasteful but truth will come to prevail in the fullness of time. Men have no power to resist the inevitable. Once Napoleon Bonaparte said to Madame Condorcet, 'I don't like women to meddle with things.' Madame's reply to this was: 'You are right, General, but in a country where it is the custom to cut off the heads of women, it is natural that they should wish to know the reason why.'

# The Awakening of the Women of Odisha*

In the last century, a Bengali poet wrote: 'Unless women of India awaken, India cannot achieve progress.' Although the civilization and culture of Odisha have a distinctiveness of their own, they are not disconnected from Indian civilization and the Vedic tradition. So, if we look at the extent to which women have been awakened in the other provinces of India, it appears that we do not lag far behind.

In Odisha, the foundation of women's education was laid during the last part of the nineteenth century. From the early years of the twentieth century, it kept advancing as a part of the gradual process of development and remained largely unnoticed. The irresistible

* First appeared in *Asanta Kali*, 9th Year, December 1959, and later in *Sarala Devi: Lekhika, Sanskarika, Biplabini*, Sachidanada Mohanty (ed.) (Cuttack: Agraduta Publications, 2004), pp. 89–94. Translated by Sangram Jena.

call of Mahatma Gandhi aroused a national spirit in the hearts of millions in India belonging to all classes of society. The women of Odisha came under its influence. The political struggle in those days stirred the Odia society. Inspired by the clarion call of the national movement, women broke the restrictions of purdah and poured into the streets shattering the fetters of age-old traditions. The illiterate, neglected, and oppressed women in those days felt agitated by the admonitions voiced by their soul. They tried to assess their situation and became conscious of their contribution to society and the nation, of which they formed an inalienable part.

The day the women of Utkal participated in the political life of the province, the story of their awakening began. They were aroused by the spirit of the national movement. They felt that they should no longer allow themselves to fall victim to the hatred and negligence of other people. As members of society, they deserved to be treated as equals of men.

Living under foreign rule for hundreds of years, the people of India believed that they were inferior to the British and incompetent in all respects. The derogatory and patronizing views of the British made them suspect their own ability and wisdom and undermined their confidence. Similarly, the women of Utkal thought themselves to be unqualified, insignificant, and unfit for every task. Even they thought that their foolishness and the prevalent purdah system were ordained by God. Living as they did in conditions of bondage, they were afraid of welcoming education and enlightenment. They lacked the necessary mental energy and physical strength to march ahead along the path of life. Their everyday life was spent performing domestic chores and rearing children within the narrow confines of their houses. They could not assess their own potential. Burdened with the responsibilities imposed on them by others in society, they passed their days enjoying an irresponsible life living at the mercy of others.

This way of life was not peculiar to the women in Odisha. This tragedy in women's life was a serious social problem in all provinces of colonial India and it went largely unnoticed.

At long last, people threw off the shackles that had bound them. The deep darkness was dispelled. The country woke up from centuries of slumber. In that new dawn, hundreds of women's lives bloomed and filled the country with fragrance. With a new consciousness, women discovered their soul and society. The mists that blurred their sight slowly disappeared. They became conscious of social and economic opportunities. They realized that their position in society was in no way inferior to that of men; in fact, it is much higher. Since they carry the burden of creating life, they have a rightful demand on society. They are, therefore, expected to play a more vital role in society. They are not born to be slaves to society or victims of neglect and ridicule living at the mercy of others. They are entitled to their wishes and opinions, views and thoughts.

As this feeling grew and they asserted themselves, new laws were enacted to ensure their self-development and protection of their rights. Today the presence of women in every sphere of social and national activities in Odisha is clearly visible.

Women in rural Odisha, whom even the sunrays could not touch, are now engaged in a struggle for living a better life as they have become socially conscious, aware of their rights and responsibilities. Of course, these women earned their livelihood by doing physical labour and were part of the struggle for survival in all ages. However, now it is observed that not only those classes of women labourers but women from middle-class families also are facing the hard and complex challenges of life arising out of social changes and diversification of economy with courage. Coming from the remote corners of Odisha, the women have crowded these paths of struggle for existence. Their numbers are steadily on the rise. A woman's mind is now free of all doubts and hesitations. They are now participating in the affairs of the nation effectively, and their place in our national life has been recognized.

The demand of women for securing their personal freedom is heard no more. They are now capable of earning their livelihood through employment in government and private offices, schools and colleges, courts and factories, theatres and industries, hospitals and hotels, and houses and tea shops. In the past, it was unthinkable on the part of women to learn Hindi in Hindi schools and sit for examinations. Now female students are far more interested in, and serious about, their studies than their male counterparts.

After the awakening occurred, the small number of women in various spheres of activity is not reflective of their desire to remain backward. The low level of their participation in the public sphere is the outcome of the absence of an effective support system composed of various institutions and the government.

As primary education is not compulsory in our province and there are few government girls' schools in rural areas, the expected growth in women's education has not been achieved. Some social welfare organizations want to support women in their efforts for development. Even that has not yielded the desired results because of financial constraints that restrict the scope of vocational training for women.

Nowadays women in Odisha are going to educational institutes to study engineering, science and technology, and medicine, but their number is small compared to that in the other developed countries of the world. They lack the required physical strength because of malnutrition, and have fallen victim to an artificial urban lifestyle. In spite of their poor health, they have achieved tremendous mental development. In the past, women were not used to discussing literature. We now find hundreds of women writers in Odisha. They are now frequently addressing meetings. They are engaged in many occupations to earn wages. Women from the remotest corners of Odisha are today engaged in delicate works of art, which was once the monopoly of urban women workers.

Women's awakening in Odisha can lead to better results if it gets adequate support from institutions and the government. Today the soul of women in Odisha has been stirred. The buds have appeared in every house. It looks for the right kind of manure, air, water, and light. Hundreds of flowers of women's lives will bloom and spread their fragrance, if properly nurtured.

In this age, the women of Odisha have failed to discharge the duties entrusted to them. They do not have the capabilities required for the purpose. They have the mental strength but have failed to utilize it due to adverse circumstances. Along with other rights, women have secured their right to property too.

However, they are unable to protect and manage their property. Women have not yet performed their role at the national level. Courage and intelligence are still wanting in our women. They will acquire these qualities gradually through the process of development. Looking at the level of awakening among the women of Odisha, I am quite confident of such change taking place.

Under the influence of Western education, our women have moved away from Eastern traditions, culture, and modes of living. Everything that was vital in the past is slowly vanishing, but nothing fills the void. This is a dangerous and critical phase in our social life. Due to changes in our national policies and social norms, an impasse has been created in their lives not only in Odisha but also in the other provinces of India. Outwardly, a lot of progress has been made in their financial condition, but the other side of their life is darkened by sorrows and despair. The tradition that provided them with ample opportunities to introspect, and the age-old practices that influenced their ways of living, are now termed superstitions, ignorance, and blind beliefs by modern people. So now women no more subscribe to the noble aspects of our ancient culture. They neither value our worship, festivals, and ceremonies nor the spiritual and moral principles of life as before. The life of the awakened women of Odisha has become materialistic under the influence of Western education, science, and philosophy. So the awakened women are now completely alienated from our traditional Vedic value system. However, they alone are not to blame for such a state of affairs. It is said that the king always sets the rules. Today states and politics determine the social system. Earlier people used to decide the principles of administration, institutions, social norms, popular culture, and practices, but with the interference of the state, we find a change in the political, social, and cultural practices of the people in the contemporary period. This has considerably influenced the life and living of the women of our province.

To build a classless and casteless society without any discrimination based on colour and creed, a society free from exploitation, is our cherished goal. To achieve these goals, women should give up a materialistic outlook on life.

# Influence of Women on the Lives of Men[*]

In the newspaper it is printed:
500,000 women to be unveiled
at King Jog's order.

King Jog's order for half a million Albanian women to cast aside the
veils worn for centuries in accordance with Mohammedan custom was
inspired by his future wife, Countess Hannah Mikes of Hungary.

—Srimati Sarala Devi, MLA

[*] Originally titled 'Purusha Jibanare Nari Prabhava', this essay
first appeared in Sahakara, Jyestha, 18th Section, 2nd Issue, 1937,
pp. 160–4 and later appeared in Early Women's Writings, 1898–1950:
A Lost Tradition, Sachidananda Mohanty (ed.) (New Delhi: SAGE
Publications, 2005), pp. 167–71. Translated by Priyadarshi Patnaik.

Countess Hannah has made the abolition of Mohammedan restrictions
on women a condition of becoming the queen of Albania. She also
insists on obligatory monogamy in Albania.

—*Illustrated India*, 5 April 1937

The gist of the above English passage is this: a feature
has come out in *Illustrated India* that five lakh women
of Albania will be free of the Muslim tradition of veils
(purdah). The king of Albania, Jog, has proposed to Countess
Hannah Mikes of Hungary. Princess Hannah has kept a condition
for her marriage—the tradition of veils for Muslim women be
abolished and it be made obligatory for men to be monogamous.
Only then would she marry the king. As per her terms, the king
has given an order that the women should cast their veils aside.

The feature has come out briefly, but is it possible not to bow to
that extraordinary personality and womanhood of the Hungarian
princess who has made the termination of an age-old tradition of
veils and polygamy a condition for marriage to her betrothed, the
king of Albania, and sent such a message to him?

Woman's power, since time immemorial, has achieved
impossible feats. Since the birth of civilization, it would not be
inappropriate to say that woman's force has nurtured and reared it
from childhood. If we leave apart the ladies of the inner palaces of
Europe, forget Queen Victoria who was known for her compassion
and benevolence to her people, and examine closely our own
motherland, then what do we see? Influenced by the spirit of
women of this county, kings and emperors have done impossible
deeds and brought about radical changes in the monotonous
pages of history. The influence of women of this country has had
a deep impact on the likes of Sri Chaitanya, Raya Ramananda,
Nityananda, Raghunatha, and other such holy saints and their
followers. Starting from saints, holy men, yogis, to ordinary men
who rose to do immortal deeds, in the inner sanctum of everyone's
heart lies the inspiration of women. In ancient times, in Utkal,
the Hindu emperor who dug Jain caves for the queen's puja and
his own meditation created Ranihansapur—at its root one finds
woman's inspiration. Influenced by Queen Singhapatha Jhusi—

the princess of Uttara Patha—her induction to, and acceptance of Jainism, the emperor also accepted Jainism and spread its message throughout Utkal.

Very often the kings who ruled over Utkal have been inspired by the religious beliefs of their wives. They have constructed and named many palaces, sites, and cities after them. Women such as Draupadi, Kunti, Satyabhama, Sita, and so on, of the Puranic times have inspired their husbands and sons and have been the central force behind their good deeds. Starting from establishing kingdoms to building temples, pools, wells, and so on, many such creditable achievements have been made possible in the world because of such virtuous women.

The influence of women has been great in the lives of great poets, idealists, dramatists, and also artists. If one goes through the biographies of poets and writers such as Dante, Tolstoy, Shelley, Shakespeare, Rabindranath, Kalidasa, Vyasa, Valmiki, Vidyapati, Chandidasa, and so on, one can see and judge the inspiration and motivation that they received from their beloveds.

During the Muslim rule, many gardens, springs, tombs, mosques, and Taj Mahals were constructed for the begums and queens. In contemporary times also, in the lives of poets and eminent statesmen, well-known dramatists and novelists, the influence of women can be felt. In the life of Edward the Eighth and Amanulla, this was distinctive. If the reformation proposed by Queen Suraiya had been rejected or if Lady Simpson had been given up, these kings would not have had to renounce their kingships. Sri Ramakrishna Paramhamsa's spiritual realization was possible only due to his wife. He saw the reflection of the Ultimate Shakti in his wife. The way Radha is inseparable from Krishna, Laxmi from Narayana, and Sita from Ramachandra, similarly, in the sacred sanctum of the hearts of thousands of Hindus, their wives reside inseparably. The devoted Padmavati has been immortalized in the poems of her husband Sri Jayadeva who shared her devotion. Gandhi and Napoleon are the creations of their mothers. Since ages, the influence of women has been felt on men. It is only woman's tenderness that has leant beauty to the austere male self. Man is the creator, and woman the mother of such creation.

Where has man succeeded in his creation without the support of woman? History gives no such evidence. In a nutshell, it is only woman who has inspired creation, self-expression, self-control, and the spiritual quest in man. The men in whose life there is no touch of women, who have rejected women, neglected them, and gone on spiritual quest, only in rare cases have they succeeded. The failure and ignominy in the life of a millionaire are illustrated repeatedly in the history of men and in day-to-day life as well. Woman is not the creation of man. On the other hand, it is only because of woman that man has come into being. With family, at home, in society and country, at workplace, and in spiritual endeavour, it is only woman who is the solace-giver, companion, and fellow worker. This essay is not written to praise women; to show how they influence the busy and responsibility-ridden lives of men is its chief intention.

Along with these, if one looks in the opposite direction, what does one see? Due to women, many bad things have also happened in this world. And even now there is no end to this.

I have already said that man is the creation of woman. Where man is all powerful, where man's good is the only objective of woman, there man is no longer an ordinary man and has to be measured by the yardstick of a superman. However, that is only one in a lakh or a crore. On all the occasions, for everything, their examples are not apt.

There is an intrinsic link between the Christian civilization of the West and its relation to women, the way the fate of Muslim women and the Muslim civilization are closely related. In the same way, it cannot be denied that women had a certain influence on the Aryan tradition of the Middle Ages, the civilization of the Hindus and the Buddhists.

Today in India, it would be appropriate to say that we have been influenced strongly by the Western materialistic civilization. Men and women, all suffer the same fate! Still, if the lamp of the house of the Indian householder is still burning strong, who is it other than the Indian woman? Because of the dismal state of statesmanship, the Indian man has lost his spine. He is forced to tell lies, be dishonest, steal, and commit crime and violence. For his very survival, like a lost traveller, he is wandering bewildered. Deluded by the glamour and illusions of the Western civilization, he has drifted far away from his ancient and rich civilization—into the infinite middle of an endless ocean. To struggle against this endless futility—one no longer sees that courage, that inner force in the Indian woman anymore. She is putting the noose of defeat, dependence, and servitude around her neck and wrapping the same knot around the neck of her man. What a humiliating defeat? What ridicule of God with fate! What sad state of Indian cultural life! Any self-respecting person—man or woman—would his heart not rend to pieces on seeing such things?

And what does one see if one stretches one's sight towards Utkal? One sees an unhappy wife of a lawyer. Why? Because the lawyer has taken less money from the poor client. If the husband cannot earn something extra by taking bribe, then he is considered an unworthy husband by the wife.

One sees the doctor's wife who challenges her husband's worth if he doesn't take a heavy fee from the poor patient, or else for the virtue of his kindness, he has to feel ashamed before the wife. One sees situations where the landlord is considered unworthy of his position by the wife if he cannot get back the principal as well as interest from the poor tenant by making him sell his very utensils. In that case, there is no end to his humiliation. One finds the wife angry because the businessman makes less profit from his customers.

One finds the wife of the careerist, engineer, deputy, clerk, peon, constable, policeman, examiner, teacher, publisher, writer, railway officer, priest, industrialist, and government servant, all suffering from the same fate! Through job or bribe, whichever way, we want money—need ornaments like our rich neighbour's wife, need mahogany furniture, oil paintings, horse-driven carriages, and motorcars. We need Banarasi sari, voil and silk sari, blouse, wristwatch, fountain pen, shoes, broaches, dark glasses, and houses! In equal proportion we need useful and useless things for our children! Thirst, material things, goods, money! Nothing behind, nothing ahead either—the whole world is dark! Running after glamour, gold, and money, all activities centred around desire, crores of greedy tongues, only chasing the fire of lust, to find where it all ends. The lamp of life suddenly blows out—everything becomes dark. This is life—this is the ugly naked shape of modernity! In this golden palace of the ogres, the woman of the twentieth century is a prisoner! Fiery thirst! To the adventure of pleasure, today's woman is drawn. She has lost her very self. Can such a woman influence man with her gesture, sign, or words? The queen is today dressed as a destitute, a beggar! With what offering will man today worship this woman? Today the goddess is hungry for blood. Unless she drinks the blood of crores of men, puts the smear of blood (tilak) on her forehead, and turns the earth into a funeral ground, she is not fulfilled. She has created, but she has achieved. Today's lust and desire have intoxicated and destabilized her. She is the fallen woman of the same creation of which she is the mother.

Since those days, man in this country has had to experience the agonies of a fate-less life. Woman can no longer motivate man to change things. She motivates, she influences only towards destruction and killing—that fire into which she has sacrificed thousands, including herself as well.

Today, on seeing the news clip about the terms set by the countess of Hungary, I remember the ancient history. The Kshetriya princesses of North India used to bet on the conduct of their husbands. Today's queen, in order to eliminate bad conventions and rites, is trying to influence her would-be husband. It is likely that had the would-be husband not loved his would-be wife immensely, the possibility of such a condition would not have arisen. However that may be, if women try to influence men in this way, there is no limit to the great benefit for the country and the community that they could achieve. Because man loves woman, respects her, admires her. It is natural for an educated, cultured woman to lead her husband along the fair path. However, it is because she is leading her man along the selfish, evil way that the world is in such a dire state today.

# A Letter from Prison[*]

23-6-30, Vellore
The Presidency Jail for Women
Raj Vellore
(Madras Presidency)

Dear Bhagu Babu!

I am glad to tell you that I am having the most delightful time here in the company of other political prisoners. Most of us except three or four belong to the B-class prisoners. However, there is no distinction between A- and B-class politicals. Our food is the same, and by the kind courtesy of the jail superintendent, we have started our own kitchen in a small tin shed especially erected

* Editor's note: Written originally in English; only a few spelling mistakes have been corrected. This letter first appeared in *Early Women's Writings, 1898–1950: A Lost Tradition*, Sachidananda Mohanty (ed.) (New Delhi: SAGE Publications, 2005), pp. 161–3.

for our purpose. Major Khan, the superintendent, is charmingly delightful in his manners and comes around to our quarters every morning to enquire after us—whether we are happy and whether our comforts are being attended to.

Among our company, which mostly consists of Andhra ladies, are two elderly widows, both of whom have been sentenced to six months SI.

You may perhaps be under the notion that I am idling much of my time. I am busy with the study of English. The others also are as busy like me with the study of Hindi and English. Some also spin and others practise music. Regular classes in both English and Hindi are being conducted, the former by my friend Mrs Lakshmipathy BA and the latter by my dearest friend Durgabai who is very clever, pretty, and an active young Andhra lady and who was a dictator of the satyagraha campaign in Madras.

From the morning till evening until we go into the lock-up, each one of us does her works regularly, and it looks as though everything is being done in a clock-like manner. In the morning soon after our 'chotahazrey', some of us sit together to study the Bhagavadgita, and I occasionally attend when I feel like going there. I have another friend Kamala Devi who also is an Andhra lady and who speaks Bengali beautifully.

During the Puja holidays, I want you to come here with Tikun as I am dreadfully longing to see both you and Tikun, who, I trust, has been put to school and his comforts carefully looked after. I would like you to very much keep him under your special care and see that he receives at this early age the best possible training, as a child's future always depends upon the manners and environments in which it is brought up. Since I am away from home and shall not be back for another period of six months, the responsibility of bringing up our only child rests on your shoulder alone. Before I went away, you made me understand that you would send the little Tikun to the Alakashram. If you have not done so, kindly send him as early as you can. Let me also suggest you that it would be better if you could also reside in the ashram along with the child so that he might not feel lonely.

I have received [the letters] at Jagatsinghpur when I went to attend Chain's marriage ceremony, but I have not received the subsequent numbers. I wonder what has happened to them. Kindly ascertain from the postmaster of your place whether he received them.

Give me all the news about Bapa and Maa, also about my Banku Bhai, Joti, Nani, Mira, Tima, Rini, Shanty, and Hari, and Bapa Bou, and my uncles and aunts. What about Gopa Babu's family? Alakashram? Write to me as early as you can because I am eager to know all about my home and Utkal.

I am looking somewhat fresh and pretty and strong, but as the food consists mostly of chillies, I do not relish it. To compensate for the food which is not so much to my taste, the superintendent has sanctioned me an egg daily.

You remember that some years ago I lent B. Nayak a sum of 100 rupees which he had promised to pay back; the letter of his must be with you and before the (time) expires I want you to sue him in the court and realize the money from him. Please pay back 15 rupees to B. Das (advocate) which I borrowed from him long ago.

I want half a dozen of Javakusum oil and three thick exercise books. Kindly send them if possible. Please write to Radhamohan, the brother of Niranjan, that he should send the books of Rabindranath Tagore which I left at their house and write to Banshu Ratha, the manager of Utkal Khadi department, to send a thick woven, nice-coloured khadi blanket for me. All my saris are torn. Send me some khaddars from my box. Durga wants to see you. My love to Tikun. Please write me something, the daily routine of Tikun. With namaskar ...

Yours
Sarala Devi

# My Story: Sarala Devi*

You have asked me to send a contribution for your 'Souvenir'. I have so many things to say, but without bringing up weighty topics, I will write a few things simple and straight. I am very happy to know that you are organizing a women's conference after all these years. It is heartening to note that you have mustered the required confidence to hold this conference at Balasore after the bitter experiences of the Utkal Mahila Conference of Puri. As a woman, I bow my head in deference to the noble and sincere efforts of the organizers.

The problems that afflict womanhood in this time and age are so unique and strange that it is impossible to imagine what shape they will take in the future. After Independence, the traditional ways of family life have broken down. For the sake of decentralizing

---

* Originally titled 'Mahila Mahal', this essay first appeared in *Asanta Kali*, 11th year, No. 10, October 1961, pp. 177–9. Translated by Chinmay Kumar Hota.

the economy and the administration, women have to face new problems regularly. However, it is difficult to know who has the power to solve these and who will bring about the change.

Our traditional joint families are not seen much these days, and in a socialist system, a joint family has little chance to survive. The joint family system is the backbone of a society. With the crumbling of this system, the foundation of society is shaken. Due to this, it is difficult to find the old ways of thinking and living, as well as cultural traditions. Many of our young girls remain unmarried forever. Not all the educated women of our society succeed in life or achieve economic success to help their families.

Only future will tell how much success will be achieved by those who want to impose the culture of European and American women on us. Just as the crops of warm climates do not grow in cold regions and fruits of cold climates do not sprout in the trees of a hot region, similarly, due to our traditions and natural and geographic limitations, the roots of foreign culture cannot spread in the minds of Indian women....

Our society does not have many organizations devoted to women. Some women's societies have come up in the rural areas with the help of block development officers (BDOs). These societies do not hold much discussion about making women aware and responsible for nation-building. There is no proper system for educating women in villages or even towns to make them good citizens. It is not possible to find solutions to the problems of women by teaching them dance and songs, or by holding handicraft exhibitions.

The main reason why social welfare schemes are not working effectively is that members of the welfare boards meant for improving education, health, and childcare in villages are selected on the basis of party considerations. The job needs educated, sincere, hard-working, high-thinking, and selfless women volunteers. How can such a responsible work be accomplished by public funds and government-nominated women who have half their allegiance to 'democracy' and the other half to the 'Congress'?

The need of the day is unity and cooperation among our conscious women. Women's organizations fail to be effective because members take a backseat after choosing their officials. The officials do not monitor work that does not progress much in any case, after the resolution is passed and noted. There are countless illiterate women in our villages and towns. Many girls pass minor- and matric-level examinations year after year. After that, some continue their study while others drop out and remain at home waiting for marriage. If these young girls could make the adult women of their community literate, it would bring great benefits to the status of women. Be it a woman or man, if someone remains uneducated, they will remain neglected and unwanted in today's world. Are our women not aware of this basic fact of life? If at all the welfare of women and children is anybody's responsibility, it is that of the educated women of our society. Regarding the question of money, it cannot be claimed that they have received education solely with their parents' financial support; society, too, has spent thousands of rupees for their education. Therefore, all educated women have a bounden duty to remove the blindfold from the eyes of other women with their dedicated service. Individuals receive education in order to gain knowledge and to be humane in their attitude towards other fellow beings. If they want to trade their learning for money, the very purpose of their education is defeated. Those who render selfless service to society with hard work and devotion will never face the shortage of money. Society and the nation will take care of that.

From this point of view the different women's clubs of Balasore should each undertake an area of social work. One will take the responsibility of literacy drive; another will work for making new mothers aware of child care, nutrition, and health of their children; and yet another will train young girls in sports and games, music, and dance. While some clubs can take charge of imparting training on household work, cooking, and sewing, some others can inculcate the habit of reading books and newspapers by opening reading rooms and libraries. Members should work in groups on different areas, and they should submit their progress report to the apex body, hold periodical meetings, and celebrate annual functions. If selfless women workers of the district do not function in this manner, their efforts will be restricted only to conferences, rallies, and speeches.

Women have an important role to play in eradicating the dowry system. If they do not come forward collectively to root out this menace, the abnormality which ails the lives of young women can never be reversed. The steady erosion of social values such as honesty, righteousness, and sincerity, which can all be traced to the evils of dowry, will take a more virulent form.

The sale of virgin widows is going on in Ganjam district openly. The police have no power to check that because public opinion can render a law ineffective. I had learnt from some letters from women social workers of Balasore district that aged males of this area were marrying the young widows on sale. Complaints with the police brought no redress. What can authorities do about this if women themselves do not fight with resolve? Women should work to make the government open rehabilitation homes for fellow women who have been victims of the evils of society in each town. Will it not look ridiculous if women dream for emancipation while a section of their sisters cannot protect themselves from touts and immoral traffickers? Women's societies should be formed in each village of Balasore district with the avowed mission of saving women from commercial trafficking.

Women's groups can play a big part in improving the deplorable state of children's health and education. Can the problems be removed only by holding Children's Day, exhibitions, and baby shows? Many of the women are malnourished. Good clothing, a nutritious diet, engaging classrooms, good teachers, gymnasiums, and a pleasant environment for games and entertainment are highly essential for the development of children. However, these facilities do not exist in our society. Parents sell the milk produced at home without letting their children drink it. If children throw tantrums, parents lull them with doses of opium so that they can go to work. Who can check these but the women's groups?

Modern women are bent on adopting *modern ways* forgetting the pious and sacred customs of the past such as *vratas* (fasting), worshipping, festivities, and the allied principles. The culture of Indian and Odia womanhood is under threat because of this. If we do away with our own culture and tradition, and give up our nationalistic feelings, can we expect anything other than disdain from the world?

There is an important contribution of Indian womankind to the civilization of the world, and that is our folk culture. If we abandon our manners, dresses, and speech and keep imitating others, will the distinctiveness of Odia women survive? Is it not essential to keep alive our culture and nationalism if we wish to keep our race thriving? Maharashtra and Gujarat became full-fledged states, so did Andhra, but our province still remains fractured. Saraikela and Kharsawan remain with Bihar. Odia culture has perished in Madhya Pradesh and the Andhra regions. Women should keep alive their own culture. If they do not work unitedly, they will have no place of their own even if the nation survives. That is why it is important that there should be women members in legislative assemblies and in Parliament.

*Sisterhood for Empowerment*

# World Revolutionaries[*]

## Kalpana Dutta

We all have heard of the bravery of Queen Durgabati and Laxmi Bai. We also know of the valour of Joan of Arc. They now figure in books of history. The extraordinary courage displayed by a young woman from Chattagram[1] in Bengal fills us with a sense of wonder. She confronted an army equipped with modern weapons not once or twice but thrice. She escaped like a gust of wind while bullets fell like raindrops around her. She was no stranger to fear. In her heart, there was no room for anything other than love for her motherland and a spirit of self-sacrifice. God had given her not only a big heart but brilliance of mind too.

[*] Originally titled 'Kalpana Dutta', this essay first appeared in Bishwa Biplabini (Cuttack: Orissa Publishing House, 1958), pp. 37–58. Translated by Anuja Khatua.

[1] It is now known as Chittagong and is part of Bangladesh.

She passed her entrance examination at the age of 14, winning a scholarship. She found mathematics as gripping as a work of fiction. She finished her education in the face of terrible odds in a dark prison cell. She was a simple-hearted and genial person. The beautiful eyes of a woman can cast a spell on any man, but she thought that a woman is much more than an object meant to give a man sensual pleasure; she possesses the power to inspire a higher kind of love. Her smiling face charmed everyone. However, that face never appealed to the baser instincts of anyone. Perhaps this was why she could make men as well as women plunge themselves into the revolutionary movement. She was a woman of few words, but whatever she said left a deep impact on everyone. Once a fellow revolutionary, who was a man, told her that women could never become revolutionaries; they could only serve male revolutionaries as assistants. To this, her response was, 'All right. I will prove you wrong.' This, uttered with heartfelt conviction, must have convinced her friend.

This intrepid woman who had ignited the fire of revolution in Chattagram was none other than Kalpana Dutta. She was the granddaughter of Zamindar Durgadas Dutta of the Sripur village in Chattagram. Her father's name was Binod Bihari Dutta. In this family, everyone was a loyal subject of the British empire. Their outlook was reactionary. They were orthodox Hindus and extremely rich. Her mother was a pious woman and was well-read in holy texts. Kalpana's maternal grandparents were extremely fond of her. She loved to listen to stories, especially those about ghosts. She was terribly scared of ghosts though, and to give her courage, her grandmother would always lay a piece of iron near her. She used to listen to the devotional songs at her house every day and partook of the prasad offered to the deities. Her maternal grandfather was a doctor by profession. He had got a large pucca house built in Chattagram and engaged in medical practice there. His was an educated family that encouraged women to get an education. So Kalpana began her studies at home at the age of four. At the age of five, she got enrolled in Class II of Dr Khastagir School, which had been established by her grandfather. In the course of time, she graduated from reading small volumes to poring through large books. When she was 11 years old, she read Sarat Chandra's *Pather Dabi* and the biographies of martyrs such as Kanhai Lal. In 1924, two of her uncles joined the Non-Cooperation Movement led by the Congress. This must have left a deep influence on Kalpana, who was six or seven at the time. As she grew older, her thirst for knowledge grew more. She was very good at mathematics, and science was her favourite subject. She looked upon Acharya Prafulla Chandra Ray as her role model because she wanted to become a scientist. She passed her entrance examination at the age of 14. She had opted for Sanskrit as the second language. She did not devote all her time to studies and did physical exercise too. She taught herself swimming in a pond in Sripur. Although two of her relations had taken part in the Non-Cooperation Movement, her grandfather's family remained loyal to the British. Tea parties for government officials were organized at his residence. In his house in Chattagram, there was a big shop selling foreign clothes. Once Gandhi visited this place. At that time the shop was stocked with clothes from Banga-Laxmi Mill. Kalpana went to meet Gandhi in the company of the other women of the family. The women donated gold jewellery to him, and Kalpana, on her part, offered him two gold bangles. However, Gandhi did not accept her bangles as she was a child. Her uncles, who were participating in the freedom struggle, often talked to her about the Non-Cooperation Movement. People used to say that the whole country would reject foreign goods the day the Dutta family would do so. Kalpana, who belonged to the third generation of the Dutta family, was filled with love of swadeshi. In 1938, a students' conference was held at Chattagram. Her uncle prepared a speech for Kalpana, which she delivered at the conference. She read a lot of books after her examinations were over. A club of revolutionaries was formed around this time in Chattagram. It received inspiration from young revolutionaries such as Surya Sen, Ananta Singh, and Ganesh Ghosh. Purnendu Dastidar, one of those revolutionaries, used to visit her house sometimes. Under Dastidar's influence, she changed her literary preferences and began to read revolutionary texts.

It had been arranged that Kalpana would study science at Bethune College in Kolkata because only boys could opt for science in the college at Chattagram. At that time, the science syllabus included physics, chemistry, and botany. She attended a students' conference in Kolkata. The revolutionary spirit had already seeped into her consciousness. To acquire bodily fitness, she joined Simla gymnasium and a boating club. In addition to studying at college, she took lessons in Hindi and French. The names of relatives who were permitted to visit the boarder of a girls' hostel were recorded in a register. Kalpana added the name of Dastidar to the list of her visitors. This enabled her to obtain and read revolutionary texts. At that time, Dastidar was a student of Sivpur College. She heard about the great revolutionary Bhagat Singh. Countless proscribed revolutionary texts found their way to Kalpana and her associates. She was a devotee of the goddess Kali. She held the Bhagavadgita in high esteem. She was never scared of death and would say that according to the Gita, death was nothing more than discarding old clothes. She wanted to throw herself into the battle for freedom. She wanted to prove that as a revolutionary a woman can display as much heroism as a man. She herself underwent training in wielding sticks and knives and learnt how to ride a bicycle. In 1930, she played a very active role in organizing a strike at Bethune College. The lady principal of the college was very annoyed with the girls and scolded them bitterly. So the girl students stuck to their decision not to appear in the exam, which compelled the principal to apologize to them. In 1931, the revolutionaries launched an attack on the armoury of Chattagram. This attack revealed the revolutionaries' mastery of strategy, their military discipline, and capacity for organization, which created a sense of apprehension in the British. They began fearing for the future.

Time will never be able to erase the memory of this attack. After the strike at Bethune College, Kalpana wanted to go back to Chattagram. However, all the routes were blocked by the police after the attack on the armoury. Many of the revolutionaries involved in the attack had been captured. However, Dastidar managed to escape. By the last week of April, Kalpana reached her village but she was no longer able to remain in touch with the revolutionaries because curfew had been imposed on Chattagram.

She now wanted to study at the college in Chattagram. She wrote to her father saying that she would stop receiving government scholarship if she continued her studies in Kolkata where she would be forced to take part in strikes. In Chattagram, she succeeded in establishing contact with a few revolutionaries with great difficulty. And gradually, more tasks were added to the ones she had already set herself. The authorities of Bethune College were unwilling to issue her a transfer certificate, and the college in Chattagram was reluctant to give admission to a girl. A lot of time was wasted in sorting out these problems with correspondence. So she was obliged to decide against taking her examinations. However, Ananta Singh and others insisted that she appear for the exam. When students went on a strike at Bethune College, Kalpana had stopped receiving her scholarship. In the end, she decided to appear in the examination as a private candidate. A test was held in November in Kolkata and she did very well. Then she returned to Chattagram. She was so keen to take part in revolutionary activities that she felt terribly restless. She spread the message of revolution secretly and read revolutionary literature. She also taught herself how to fire a pistol. Her classmate Miss Surama Dutta was a communist. She talked to Kalpana about capitalism, materialism, and the working class. However, despite being friends, Kalpana maintained a distance from her.

Ananta Singh would ask her if she would kill her own parents without the slightest hesitation for her ideals. Kalpana no longer believed in the sacred scriptures. She now followed a radically different code of conduct. So she said to Ananta Singh, 'I can do everything.' Those accused of the armoury raid were being tried inside the Chattagram jail. Serious charges had been brought against them. They had killed British soldiers. Revolutionaries like Kalpana who had escaped capture planned to blow up the jail with dynamites, and so they used a house near the port as a laboratory.

In February 1932, Surya Sen, the chief of the Indian Republican Army, ordered his associates to procure arms and ammunitions from Kolkata. Kalpana travelled to the city on the pretext of getting her eyes checked up. After purchasing ammunitions, she returned home. The successful execution of this task inspired Surya Sen's confidence in her. He decided to make her a member of the group of revolutionaries. The group had decided to assassinate Mr Simpson. They wanted to perform a spectacular feat on the day Ramkrishna Biswas was to be hanged. Explosives were made. Kalpana's college examination was at hand. The task the revolutionaries had set themselves appeared more important than her examination to Kalpana. However, Ananta Singh persuaded her to appear for the exam. The dynamites were placed under the perimeter walls of the jail. The fuse was kept at a long distance. However, a sepoy chanced upon the fuse and the dynamites were discovered. Dynamites placed in the government office situated on a hill were also found out. Many young revolutionaries were arrested. Dinesh and Ramkrishna were hanged, and the revolutionaries' plan came to nothing. Ananta Singh, Ganesh Ghosh, and Lokanath waited for their death sentence to be pronounced. Passing the exam brought Kalpana no joy at all because the only revolutionary task she had performed led nowhere.

Kalpana took admission in BSc. first year at Chattagram College. At Sripur, there were facilities for her to learn how to fire pistols. So Kalpana often visited Sripur. This young girl, who was once mortally scared of ghosts, now thought nothing of practising shooting in deserted fields infested with poisonous insects at the dead of night. Surya Sen had not been captured yet. So he tried to reorganize his scattered group.

In 1930, the police summoned Kalpana and her father and told them, 'Kalpana is in contact with the revolutionaries. If she gives an undertaking, she would not be arrested.' Kalpana had to undertake that she would not read proscribed books and keep in touch with the revolutionaries.

However, this undertaking could not keep her away from revolutionary activities. On 17 September 1930, she went to the foot of a hill in the guise of a man to meet a fellow revolutionary. The police arrested her on the way and sent her to jail. Seven days later, the revolutionaries performed an extremely courageous feat.

Their attack on the European Club, located at the same foothill
where Kalpana was arrested, left many Englishmen wounded
and one Englishwoman dead. Pritilata Waddedar, a woman
revolutionary, had participated in this attack. To escape arrest, she
consumed potassium cyanide and killed herself. The police tried
to implicate Kalpana in this case because she had been caught
by them seven days before the attack took place. Many of the
revolutionaries were captured but all of them were acquitted as the
police failed to produce reliable witnesses. The government kept
Kalpana in jail for two months and filed a case under Section 109
against her. However, she was released on bail on the condition
that she would stay confined in her house. She now remained
in contact with the revolutionaries through her six-year-old
sister. Surya Sen advised her to leave home and join him. On
20 September 1932, the Dutta family was performing the sraddha
ceremony for Ray Bahadur Durgadas Dutta. Everybody was busy
feeding Brahmins and beggars. The upper story of Kalpana's house
overlooked a hill. She tied the end of her sari tightly around her
waist, climbed out of the window, and made good her escape. No
one in her family got whiff of this.

As two terrorist attacks had already taken place, army camps
were set up in Chattagram. Kalpana spent the first night after her
escape in the house of an acquaintance in the town. The next
day, at night, she took the guise of a bride and went with Surya
Sen to a village 10 miles away. Her daring escape left the police
shocked and amazed. The government now punished her father
for her deeds. He was dismissed from his service and his property
was confiscated. The police combed forests and hills to capture
Kalpana. Surya Sen took all the necessary precautions: At night,
they took all decisions regarding the future courses of action
together, and during daytime, Kalpana stayed in the house of one
of their trusted associates. She spent the day making bullets for
pistols.

It was the January of 1933. There were army camps in every
village. Surya Sen and Kalpana never spent more than a day in
any village. One night, four Gurkha soldiers banged on their door.
Kalpana woke up and, anticipating danger, roused Surya Sen from

sleep. Three other terrorists were also hiding in their room. At this moment of crisis, Kalpana and her associates noticed that one of the exits of the house had not been sealed by the soldiers. So they managed to sneak out and escape. A few days passed. One day Kalpana and her associates had taken shelter in someone's house. It was nine p.m. Surya Sen, Kalpana, Shanti Chakraborty, and three other associates were busy discussing strategies. Gurkha soldiers had camped at the village. One of the terrorists came out of the house. A soldier spotted him and asked him who he was. All the terrorists withdrew into the back garden, and the soldiers opened fire at them. The tracer bullets dispelled the darkness. One of the soldiers tried to capture Kalpana. To escape being shot at, Kalpana threw herself on the ground, got up, and jumped into a ditch. The terrorists now started firing at the soldiers hiding behind a clump of bamboos, for they were not willing to surrender. However, Kalpana realized that if they did not surrender, the soldiers would kill all the members of the family that had given them shelter. The terrorists had also run out of ammunitions. So she shouted that they were going to surrender and asked the soldiers to stop firing. However, they did not trust them. When Kalpana repeated her words, they sent a soldier to get them to handover their weapons. The soldiers tied up the hands of this brave girl. The Jat subedar whipped Kalpana. The soldiers objected saying that no soldier should hit a woman. Then they took Kalpana and one of her friends to the jail. At night the captives were given food but they did not touch it because the death of one of their young associates had filled their hearts with grief. The army officer took Kalpana in a motor boat and asked why she got involved in the attack. Kalpana replied, 'You have robbed us of our freedom. So we are fighting you.' 'What an obstinate girl you are!' was the officer's reply. Everyone lavished praise on this intrepid girl. Even the police joined the chorus of praise.

The police superintendent, Mr Springfield, noticed that Kalpana's hands had been bound very tightly and asked the subedar, 'Don't you know how women should be treated?'

Then he asked Kalpana gently, 'Do you have anything to say?' Kalpana replied, 'No, I have nothing to say.' So she was sent to jail. After spending a month there, Kalpana learnt that the police were preparing to file another case against Surya Sen, Tarakeswar, and Dastidar. A tribunal comprising a Hindu, a Muslim, and an Englishman was formed. The trial went on for two months. Only the relatives of the accused were allowed to attend the trial. The papers that had been seized from the terrorists rendered their acquittal impossible. The three of them waited to be executed. On 14 August, Surya Sen and Tarakeswar were sentenced to death. As Kalpana was a young woman, she was sentenced to deportation for life. Kalpana felt humiliated at being spared because she was a woman. She saw her two associates for the last time in the court. Then she was sent to Hijli jail. The verdict was appealed against at the high court, but the sentence was upheld and Surya Sen and Tarakeswar were hanged.

After three months in Hijli jail, Kalpana was transferred to Rajshahi jail. There she was made to sew and stitch for six months. Then she spent a year and a half in Medinipur jail. She was allowed to read only novels. When some girls who were involved in terrorist activities were brought to this jail, Kalpana was shifted to Dinajpur jail. She was brought back to Medinipur jail after spending 11 months there. When the Congress formed governments in the provinces in 1937, an agitation to reduce the prison term of the terrorists and release women prisoners and political detainees was launched. Kalpana was brought over to Kolkata to arrange a meeting between her and Mahatma Gandhi. She told Gandhi that she no longer believed in terrorism. Then she was brought back to Medinipur jail. The advisory committees set up by the government recommended that women prisoners be released. C.F. Andrews met the representatives of the government of Bengal in this connection, and Kalpana was released on 1 May 1939.

There were more male terrorists in the jail. Kalpana and her fellow prisoners had opportunities to read Marxist literature and exchange ideas. Such facilities were not extended to women prisoners. When Kalpana came out of jail, she found that all her associates were working for the Communist Party. She met her cousin Subodh, who had served a jail term for his role in the

Chattagram Armoury Raid. He told her, 'After giving the matter much thought, I have decided to join the Communist Party. You take your own decision.' Her stay in jail had not made Kalpana deviate from the path of revolution. However, she had come under strong influence of the Upanishads and the Gita while in jail. When anyone mentioned socialism to her, she used to respond spontaneously, saying, 'Yes. That is the way.' The changes which had come over society during the time she was in jail deeply affected her when she was released. No college was willing to take her as a student. So there was no way she could sit for her BSc examination. The political climate in Chattagram had undergone a change. Marxism had replaced terrorism there. Kalpana now read Marxist literature and worked with girls of the communist parties. Shortly afterwards, she was down with typhoid fever; she suffered for 15 days and narrowly escaped death. In 1940, she passed the BA examination with Bengali, Mathematics, and English as her subjects. Her fever had left her with only three months to prepare for the examination. After passing the examination, she was able to decide the course of her life. She realized that her temperament and the communist ideology were in harmony. She had grown apart from her family in Chattagram. So she went to Kolkata to do party work and pursue MA in mathematics. She organized the daily labourers in Kolkata, and the police kept harassing her. In 1940, she was ordered to leave Kolkata and was kept under surveillance in Chattagram. She lived under these restrictions till 1941. Even after the conditions were relaxed, she was not allowed to go beyond the municipality limits. This made it difficult for her to meet and interact with former revolutionaries. However, Kalpana was not someone who would sit quietly. She set up a study circle for women and got them to bring out a handwritten magazine that featured many articles on communism. She formed a women's group for women belonging to all classes, which had 200 members on its rolls. She opened night and day schools for women. These schools were attended by women from untouchable and tribal communities.

In 1942, the government came to know of the communist stand on the war and Kalpana was released since she said she would fight against Japanese fascists. She went down with typhoid again as her health gave way because of hard work. When she learnt that she had been enrolled as a member of the Communist Party, she felt elated. In September, she underwent military training as a member of a team of soldiers to resist the Japanese attack.

She also taught women the art of self-defence through the women's group. In December, she travelled to Bombay [now Mumbai] to learn more about the objectives of her party. She had heard a lot about the abilities of the then secretary of the party, P.C. Joshi. She met him for the first time in Bombay and listened to his lecture. Then she went back to Chattagram. The party now put her in charge of the organization for the whole of Bengal. In 1943, she became the organizing secretary of the party committee. All her family members including her four sisters joined the Communist Party. In June, Kalpana went to Bombay for party work. She met P.C. Joshi again. Although Joshi opposed terrorism, he was full of admiration for the heroic revolutionaries of Bengal who had laid down their lives for the nation, and he believed that the Communist Party in Bengal rested on the solid foundation of their sacrifice. Joshi who adored Kalpana for her bravery proposed to her. Kalpana felt that this marriage could enable her to realize her cherished ideals and accepted the proposal. P.C. Joshi is now the president of the Communist Party of India. As for Kalpana, the women of India would always adore her for her courage and heroism.

# World Revolutionaries

## Sofia Bardina*

M any revolutionaries had lost their lives fighting against the tyranny of the despotic czar. However, like the mythical Raktabirya, they went on multiplying even after being killed. It is true that the hangman's noose broke their necks but their voices kept echoing and inspiring the masses. Death made them immortal. As Victor Hugo memorably said, 'One can resist or repulse the attack of an army but the march of thoughts and ideals can never be resisted.'

Russian women shared the feeling of humiliation that had seeped into the marrow of their oppressed nation and its desire to hold its head high in the world. So they felt obliged to step

* Originally titled 'Sofia Bardina', this essay first appeared in Bishwa Biplabini (Cuttack: Orissa Publishing House, 1958), pp. 23–36. Translated by Anuja Khatua.

into the turbulent world of revolution, leaving behind happy domesticity. When the revolutionaries fighting the tyranny of the czar faced a terrible crisis, a woman from a respectable family came forward to give them leadership. Her name was Sofia Bardina.

Sofia was born in a town called Mersank in 1856. Her father was an extremely oppressive policeman. Her mother was always intimidated by his cruel ways. Sophia's education began in a local government girls' school. She went to Moscow to pursue higher education after successfully completing her schooling. Her interaction with fellow students at the college in Moscow exposed her to nihilist ideas. During this time, she made the acquaintance of two women nihilists. Later they worked with her to spread the message of the revolution and became her companions in jail.

With these two friends, Sofia travelled to Zurich, which was then a centre of women's education. They dedicated themselves to the cause of liberating the downtrodden masses. In those days, a women's group was active in Zurich. The members of this group were under 18 years of age. Sofia made a mark as a member of this group. She always expressed the view that the rich had robbed the poor of food, clothes, and their voice and had reduced them to animals by oppressing them endlessly. The rich had to pay for this. The oppressed must be raised from the gutters of hell and be convinced that they were human beings. The members of the women's group gave up higher studies and resolved to serve the masses. Sofia enrolled in a medical college in order to be able to disseminate the ideology of the secret society because she knew a lady doctor enjoyed unrestricted access to all persons and places. However, she could not escape the evil eye of the government. She and her friends were expelled from Zurich, following which they went to Paris, but even there the Russian government made their lives miserable and they could not pursue their medical studies. Sofia was compelled to leave for Geneva, where she trained as a midwife.

In 1874, Sofia, some young men and women in Zurich, and members of the revolutionary groups of different provinces got together and formed a secret society. This was a bright auspicious moment in the history of not only Russia but the whole world:

the coming together of a small group of dedicated students. They were determined to battle with a mighty enemy. When the desire to assert their rights arose in the hearts of a subjugated race, its struggle for freedom was bound to be crowned with success. Then the race would neither falter nor would it feel any fatigue. This desire in Sofia and her friends led them to become rebels. Though their energies and experiences were limited, they had no doubt that they were fighting for a just cause, and that, eventually, justice would emerge victorious. This faith sustained them through a life of hardship and destitution.

The revolutionaries worked as labourers in factories to convert ordinary Russians into rebels. Hard work and exposure to the elements turned their white complexion copper-dark. Sacrificing all their comforts, they inspired the workers.

Bardina and her associates found work in a factory. The conditions under which they lived beggar description. Half-burnt bread and stale meat were what they lived on. They used to sleep on cramped berths fixed to the walls of the workers' rooms. Their heads often bumped against the berths above them. For mattresses, they had heaps of rubbish. Bundles of straw served as their pillows. Mosquitoes, bed bugs, and other poisonous insects kept the worn-out workers awake all night. In winters, the workers who slept on these berths came close to being suffocated. It was as if they were fated to breathe this trapped, poisoned air. The workers had mutely endured these inhuman conditions for ages. However, the revolutionaries who had grown up in the lap of luxury and comfort willingly embraced this way of life because they wanted to awaken the masses and win their cooperation.

Bardina and her friends found employment in a factory in Moscow adopting fictitious identities. Male and female workers lived in separate quarters. Bardina sought to spread the message of the revolution among female workers, but they led a morally degraded life. They were the victims of the lust of clerks, the manager, and other male workers of the factory. Finding life in the midst of female workers unbearable, Bardina sneaked into the area where the male workers lived at the end of every day in the factory. At last, her sincere and hard work bore fruit. Unfortunately, one day the manager saw her among the male workers. Feeling scared that all her secrets would be found out, she immediately gave up the factory job.

In those days, many revolutionaries had rented houses in St. Petersburg. In fact, these were used as factories where bombs and dynamites were made and as places to hold secret meetings. Escaped convicts also found shelter there and these places provided a meeting point for highly educated young men and women from rich families and those from the poorest background. To escape the notice of the police, Bardina did all the chores uncomplainingly, including cooking, in one such house. During her stay there with her 50 friends, she was arrested by the police based on information provided by one of the women who lived in the house. This happened in 1876.

The trial she and her friends faced is famous as Trials of the Fifty. The show trial went on for two long years. The cruelty of the czarist system took a heavy toll on her health but could not crush her spirit. This 23-year-old young woman fearlessly expressed her ideas and aspirations in the presence of the judge. The judge and the courtiers looked at her wonderstruck. Her tear-filled eyes made the resplendent world of czarist power appear pale. She proudly declared, 'I do not want you to suffer even slightly on my account. I am confident that a time will come when this sleeping nation will awaken. Their feelings of guilt and regret will turn them wild. You have brute strength and you can tyrannize over us in any way you like. God will come to our rescue. History is on our side and we are endowed with invincible mental strength.'

Bardina was sentenced to nine years' rigorous imprisonment. She cheerfully accepted the punishment meted out to her because she knew that the road revolutionaries like her had chosen led to hunger, destitution, prison, and the gallows. However, due to her ill health her sentence was reduced and she was exiled to Siberia.

Far away from home and friends and subjected to inhuman treatment by the police, Bardina's health gave way. Feeling at the end of her tether, she decided to escape. It was almost impossible to escape from Siberia, which was encircled by watchful guards. However, Bardina managed to give them the slip on 25 December

1880 and escaped to Europe. Russian exiles were delighted to have Bardina in their midst, but the Bardina they met was a pale shadow of her former self. She had grown so hideously thin that her appearance caused great pain to her friends.

Then she came back to Russia and, in spite of her failing health, wandered throughout the country incognito to awaken the masses. However, life as a fugitive presented many difficulties. So her friends pleaded with her to leave Russia. Life in hiding was unbearable for her and she began to suffer from nervous debility and anaemia. She felt so drained that she found it difficult to even read a newspaper. Though she remained cheerful and tried to make everyone around her feel happy, this act of self-deception made her friends feel even more miserable. The very act of living from one day to the other appeared to her a long-drawn-out process of expiation. On 13 April 1883, Bardina resolved to put an end to her misery by committing suicide. She tried twice to shoot herself, but her feeble hand failed to press the trigger. In her third attempt, she held the weapon tight and shot herself. She lay writhing in pain in the smoke-filled room for two hours, but she did not let out a cry. Then, at 9 p.m., the landlady found her in this condition and got her sent to the hospital, where she spent 12 days in great pain. She bore all her suffering and agony with extraordinary calm and fortitude and never expressed despair. On 26 April, this woman of great heroism breathed her last.

# World Revolutionaries

## Utkal Bharati Kuntala Kumari*

The extraordinary talent of Kuntala Kumari has found expression through literature. Had she not died so young, she would have enriched Odia literature and inspired Odias with feelings of patriotism and delighted their hearts. She had a deep love for her land and, through her essays and poems, she attempted to establish its superiority among people in the outside world. Her intense love for her motherland made her immortal for us. Born into a Christian family, she had a Western upbringing and was a doctor by profession. She spent her childhood with her parents in Burma [now Myanmar] and received her early education there. She studied at the Cuttack Medical School,

* Originally titled 'Utkala Bharati Kuntala Kumari', this essay first appeared in Bishwa Biplabini (Cuttack: Orissa Publishing House, 1958), pp. 1–9. Translated by Anuja Khatua.

earned her degree at an early age, and was awarded a gold medal. She passed the entrance examination when she was only 13 years old. She began contributing to Odia and Hindi literature rather late in life. She was jailed for three months for participating in the freedom struggle and took to wearing khadi in the years before her death. She had an excellent command of English, Bengali, Hindi, and Odia. She gave Odias leadership in the fields of social, political, and other activities. She longed to see Odisha, which had been dismembered, whole again. She had three children. Her public speeches were distinguished by their energy and eloquence, and her poetry overflowed with powerful emotions.

Let us now turn to her revolutionary poems. Odias will never forget how her collection of poems titled *Sphulinga* fired the imagination of young men and women, inspiring them to plunge into the Satyagraha movement led by Mahatma Gandhi. Since this book stirred anti-British feelings, the government banned it. Although Kuntala Kumari did not participate in the Satyagraha movement directly, she served as its minstrel who inspired the participants of the freedom struggle through her songs. In Delhi, the image of Odisha and Odia women grew brighter due to her efforts. Her willingness to take part without fear in all activities aimed at public welfare set her apart. She rose in rebellion against the religion into which she was born, embraced Arya dharma, and got married according to Hindu customs. She also edited a Hindi monthly. Her writings containing revolutionary messages were very popular in the villages and towns of Odisha. The fact that the artworks created by Odia artists remained unknown outside Odisha greatly upset her. As the president of Utkal Sammilani and Utkalanari Sammilani, she brought glory to Odisha. We still vividly remember the aura that enveloped her. Her writings were spontaneous like a stream. She embodied the spirit of the new age and strove to rouse people from their stupor and inertia. She was a true Odia at heart in every respect: her feelings, her thoughts, and her cultural aspirations.

*Ahwana* and *Sphulinga* were counted among her best revolutionary compositions, which are unique not only in the context of Odisha but also of India. During the freedom struggle in Odisha, these played the role of war songs. That her writings are now out of print is a reflection on our national life.

She filled the hearts of her readers with a pan-Indian consciousness blended with a feeling of pity for Odisha which lay neglected and despised. The suffering of Odias made her write the following lines:

*The fort of Barabati lies in ruins*
*The crest of the temple of Konarka lies on the ground*
*The banner of blue wheel is buried under the sands of Chilika*
*Odia ships no longer dance on the waves of the sea*
*No one now sings the songs of Utkala*
*The glory of the land is lost for ever*
*Gone is the pride of the Odia race.*
*The motherland lies dismembered,*
*Reawakening the land will never be possible.*

The truncated province of Odisha and the threat Odia language and culture were facing caused Kuntala a lot of anguish when she was young. She dreamt of restoring to Odias their lost glory. She longed to see Odias, who were oppressed and humiliated by others, raising their heads proudly and become the equals of the other races of the world. She expressed these feelings in the following lines:

*Let the mouth never utter words of despair*
*Let these words never reach the ears of this race.*
*May the souls of the millions be stirred with new hopes*
*May they rise from stupor with newfound valour.*
*Why should they bury themselves under the earth like the dead*
*Forgetting their manliness?*
*Destiny hasn't decreed an everlasting death for this race.*
*The millions of Odias will certainly rise and march towards immortal glory.*

She was confident that one day the youth in Odisha would be filled with great enthusiasm. She wrote the following lines because she was convinced that the Odia youth would never stray from the path of duty in spite of their ignorance, poverty, and their lack of courage:

*Some say we lack courage.*
*Some say we are ignorant and lazy.*
*Some say Odias lack vitality and energy*
*And they have lost their glory forever.*

The young in Odisha seemed to her to be full of youthful energy, and she addressed the following lines to them:

*This miserable land will one day retrieve its lost glory.*
*This land of the great poet Bhanja will one day dazzle the world.*
*The great heroes like Ananga and Jajati will return to this land.*
*And the glory of Odisha will be proclaimed to the world.*
*The youth have awakened*
*And the waves of the sea greet them with a song.*

In 1930, Kuntala inspired the youth of Odisha through her songs. She wrote revolutionary songs even before the freedom struggle began.

We have lost our independence on account of our inherent weaknesses. Brothers fight brothers and invite the foreigners to rule over them. Whatever we earn through our back-breaking toil is being spent by the foreign rulers on living a life of luxury.

Kuntala expresses her profound sorrow in the following lines:

*O Mother! Why do you have such worthless sons on your lap?*
*Your love for us has blinded you to our faults.*
*Is this why you have filled the fields with golden corn?*
*We are so useless that we lay our own earnings at someone else's feet.*
*Brothers cut each other's throats.*
*All feelings of love have disappeared from our houses*
*And we swim in the blood of our brothers.*
*Hindus and Muslims are your two arms.*

*But they fight each other bitterly.*
*We have invited the foreigners to rule over us.*
*So who can come to our rescue*
*When we have caused ourselves so much harm?*

As long as Indians do not get rid of feelings that cause division among them and foster unity among themselves, our nation will not win liberty and achieve prosperity. She writes:

*Love will unite everyone, all discord will be forgotten.*
*Devotion, not blood, will now drown them.*

Until these conditions are removed, the situation of India will never change for the better. Kuntala's words 'Who will wash away this ink stain of disgrace?' found an echo in every Odia heart. Had Kuntala taken birth in any place other than Odisha, the translations of *Sphulinga* and *Ahwana* would have been published in many languages and reached readers in many parts of the country. Her *Sphulinga* occupies a special place in the history of revolutionary writing in view of the emotion it expresses, in style, and the power of its language. It has the power to make one's heart overflow with courage and fearlessness.

In *Ahwana*, she gives Odias an irresistible call to action after depicting the condition of Odisha vividly. She writes:

*The world wants to know*
*Who will now sacrifice his life with a smile?*
*Who will give everything he owns with a song on his lips?*
*Who will remove the tattered flag and make the flag of victory*
*flutter?*
*Come, you young ascetics, millions of voices beckon you.*

Many of her poems burn with such intense feelings. The dark night of India's suffering had at last come to an end. Odisha, on its part, had achieved progress to a certain extent and some areas which were part of other provinces earlier had now been merged with it. However, Kuntala's dreams had not been fully realized.

Although she was famous as a revolutionary poet, many of her poems such as 'Anjali', 'Prema Chintamani' and 'Uchhwasa' reflected profound feelings of devotion. She was at once a revolutionary and a devout. There was nothing obscure or difficult about her poetry. Her poems move the readers deeply because her words express the voice of her soul. This accounts for the success of Kuntala as a writer. Her writing is like an instrument which can give expression to the rich diversity of life. It brings a delightful shower of sweet feelings to the readers. Words were like playthings to her. Many of her invaluable manuscripts were lost due to her family's negligence. Her daughter, son, and her co-wife made no efforts to bring out her unpublished manuscripts. Since her collected works have not been published, generations to come will not be able to form an idea of the magnitude of her achievement.

Our land lies under a curse. Although Odias have everything— learning, wealth, and industry—lack of intellectual enquiry has led to the decline of Odia culture and it comes as no surprise that the great works of Kuntala Kumari are no longer available in print. Her writings focused on all aspects of life: education, ideas, religion, nationalism, devotion, and revolution. They have transcended time and space and achieved immortality. Kuntala Kumari inspires feelings of reverence in the heart of Odias. The soul of Odisha has found a voice in the writings of this revolutionary poet.

# Women Revolutionaries during the Buddhist Period[*]

G autama Buddha's view of women was similar to the one that prevailed in ancient India. After the age of the *Rig Veda*, the status of women became problematic. Their situation grew worse as time went by. The age of the Upanishads followed the Vedic age. In this age lived great women such as Gargi, Maitreyi, and Biswabara. However, of the two wives of Sage Jajnabalkya, one was extremely learned and wise while the other was uneducated. A sage having two wives indicated the low status of women in that age. Buddha, the great soul, was born in this era. One can detect a trace of hostility and indifference in his attitude towards women. If one goes through the annals of

* Originally titled '*Boudha Jugara Biplabini*', this essay first appeared in *Bishwa Biplabini* (Cuttack: Orissa Publishing House, 1958), pp. 118–28. Translated by Anuja Khatua.

the Buddhist era, one fails to come across women of the stature of Gargi and Maitreyi in the Buddhist monasteries. Visakha was nothing more than a shadow to Buddha. She had no interest in knowledge or wisdom. She was a kind-hearted person and was loyal to Buddha and his sangha.

The *Therigatha* mentions that many women who came to listen to Buddha renounced the world and attained enlightenment. They were called *theries* and included Maya, Sujata, Prajapati, Jasodhara, and Visakha. Maya or Mahamaya was the mother of Buddha and the princess of a kingdom called Debadaha. The princesses belonging to the Sakya dynasty married into the aristocratic families of this kingdom. Both the wives of King Suddhodana, Maya and Prajabati, belonged to Debadaha. Buddha's wife Jasodhara, too, hailed from this place. She was also called Gopa. Among the Kshatriyas, it was customary in those days to marry the daughter of one's maternal uncle. This was considered a part of the Vedic tradition. Suddhodana married his wife's younger sister, Mahaprajapati. Prajapati was the first woman to be admitted into the Buddhist religious order. Before this, women were not allowed to join the order. Prajapati's deep religiosity brought about a revolution in the Buddhist world. In the face of stiff opposition from the Buddha and his associates, she took to *pravrajya*.[1] Considering the time, it was an extremely brave initiative. When Buddha came to visit Kapilavastu, the high-born women of the Sakya clan demanded that they be admitted to the Buddhist order, but Buddha was opposed to this.

In *Atharva Veda*, the birth of a girl is described as a painful experience. The Brahmins also share this view. Damodar Gupta, a learned scholar from Kashmir, expresses the view that a man who has several daughters is like someone carrying a basket of snakes on his head. This attitude towards women prevailed in the period from twelfth century BC to twelfth century AD. Buddha's opposition to the entry of his aunt Prajapati into the Buddhist order reflected this attitude.

---

[1] The act of renouncing the world and adopting an ascetic lifestyle.

However, Prajapati was no ordinary woman. One day she arrived at the lion gate of the city of Srabasti, crossing rivers and streams on her way. Buddhadev refused to meet him, but his chief disciple Ananda persuaded him to meet his aunt. At last Buddha initiated her into the order and she was accepted as a bhikkuni. However, this decision had caused Buddha much regret and anguish because in response to Ananda's request, he allowed something which went against his cherished principles. After this, women were initiated into the Buddhist order and served it as bhikkunis.

Gautama Buddha's wife was the daughter of his maternal uncle. He had married her according to the prevailing customs of his clan. Nowhere in Buddhist scripture does one find the mention of Jasodhara's other name 'Gopa'. She is described as Rahulmata, or the mother of Buddha's son Rahul. Buddha's early life was spent with this beautiful and accomplished woman. Jasodhara was chosen as Buddha's bride by his father to lure him back into the world of human attachment towards which he was developing indifference. Buddha's son was born after 12 years of the marriage. Buddha got married when he was 16 years of age. In Buddhist texts, one comes across several accounts of his married life. It is mentioned that he left the palace in the company of Chhandaka and Kanyaka when Jasodhara was fast asleep, her hand resting on her son's forehead. Abandoned by her husband, Jasodhara cried inconsolably day and night. However, Buddha did not come back and Jasodhara spent her days lamenting her separation from him.

After attaining enlightenment, Buddha returned to his father's palace. His father paid his respects to his son, but Jasodhara did not go out crossing the lion gate of the palace to meet her husband and waited in the inner wings of the palace. She had not imagined that she would meet her husband in the saffron robes of a sanyasi. Accompanied by Moudgalayana Sariputta, Buddha went from house to house in the city begging for alms and also visited the palace. He handed Jasodhara the begging bowl standing outside the palace. With Rahul standing beside her, Jasodhara set her eyes on Buddha. When the begging bowl touched Jasodhara's hand, she felt overwhelmed and said, 'Lord! You have appeared before me as a beggar asking for alms. So I give you my most precious possession, our son Rahul.' Jasodhara picked up Rahul and offered him to Buddha. (This scene has been depicted on the walls of the Ajanta Caves.) Then she did something expected of a woman and urged Rahul to ask his father to give him something that he would dearly like to have. However, this did not unsettle Buddha in the least and he asked Sariputta to initiate Rahul into the order. What else could a beggar like him have done? He had no wealth to offer his son. So he bequeathed on him the right to join the Buddhist order. All the same, the words Jasodhara had uttered had not gone in vain. This incident influenced the course of the subsequent development of Buddhism as a religion. Buddhadev himself decided that no child would be allowed to join the order without the permission of his parents. Buddhist texts tell us that in the end Jasodhara, too, embraced Buddhism and led the life of a bhikkuni. She became aware of the futility of the worldly life and renounced the world.

Sujata was a famous bhikkuni in the Buddhist order. She had a role to play in Buddha attaining enlightenment. While practising meditation on the banks of the river Niranjana, Buddha was reduced to skin and bones and was almost at the door of death. So he thought he would give up meditating and protect his body in order to be able to eliminate human suffering. He wanted to eat something. He took bath in the river and came and sat under a tree. At this time Sujata, the daughter of a merchant, came with a bowl of rice pudding to offer to the tree god. The emaciated figure of Buddha made her think that he was the tree god in disguise. So she offered him the bowl of rice pudding. Buddha felt immensely contented eating the rice pudding and then went and sat under the Bodhi Tree to meditate.

Another incident relating to women in Buddha's life may be mentioned here. Women could not see Buddha but could listen to him. When Buddha was deep in meditation under the Bodhi Tree seeking ways to end the world's misery, a group of dancers from the Uribela village arrived there. The song they sang meant: If you loosen the strings of a veena, it will not produce any sound. This song made Buddha realize the truth he was seeking. He found the middle path between the extremes of luxury and renunciation. To him, this was the foundation on which man's duties rested.

Visakha was a revolutionary in the field of religion in the Buddhist era. Buddhist literature has immortalized her. She devoted all her energies to the spread of Buddhism. She lived in the city of Srabasti and practised Buddhism while leading the life of a householder. She was treated with respect and affection by Buddha and the members of his order. In Buddhist texts, she finds mention as Marabhamata. She requested Buddha to accord approval to a few proposals. These met with opposition from everyone, but in the end, Buddha accepted them. One of the reasons why her proposals aroused so much opposition was that she had criticized the life led by the bhikkuns and bhikkunis. The Buddhist text *Mahabijna* mentions that she had placed the following proposals before Buddha:

(a) Gifts of clothes should be made to the bhikkuns during the rainy season.
(b) Arrangements should be made to provide food to bhikkuns who arrive suddenly in a city.
(c) Food should be provided to bhikkuns leaving a city.
(d) Medicine should be provided to ailing bhikkuns.
(e) Those who nurse ailing bhikkuns should be given food.
(f) Gifts of clothes should be made to bhikkunis.

When Buddha questioned Visakha closely, she explained to him everything in detail. She told him that the bhikkuns underwent a lot of hardship during the rainy season. Bhikkuns who came to a city for the first time often lost their way and failed to receive alms. They would get tired wandering around the city and would not have the energy to beg for alms. If the bhikkuns were given something to eat, they would be able to perform the task of meditating and disseminating the religion more efficiently. If a bhikkun fell ill, he would not be able to go around begging for alms and those who nursed him would not be able to do so. Unless the bhikkunis were given enough clothes to cover themselves, they would be exposed to ridicule.

Her irrefutable arguments convinced Buddha and her request was granted. Buddhist viharas came to be established with support from Buddhist monarchs. Although the Buddha allowed women to enter his order as bhikkunis, the bhikkuns always enjoyed greater importance. Under no circumstances did anyone consider a bhikkuni superior to a bhikkun. No bhikkuni had the good fortune of coming close to the Buddha before he attained *mahanirvana* (the great nirvana) and many important bhikkuns of the order objected to bhikkunis shedding tears on the Buddha's dead body.

However, it is true that the Buddhist order simply could not function without the bhikkunis. The bhikkunis were also joined by thousands of women who were householders. They brought alms for bhikkuns, cooked meals, and took care of them. The women, who were householders, lived a life devoted to the order. Buddha always advised the bhikkuns to maintain distance from women. There is a very interesting story related to this. The Buddha's disciple Ananda once asked him, 'O Lord! What should we do when we come face to face with a woman?' The Buddha said, 'Ananda, you should look away.' Then Ananda asked, 'What if our eyes meet?' The Buddha replied, 'Never talk to her.' Ananda asked again, 'What if one happens to talk to her?' The Buddha said, 'Then you should walk away in some other direction.'

The Buddha did not feel drawn towards women. He lacked sympathy for them. The bhikkunis were united in order to protect themselves. The women in the Buddhist era did not fear obstacles. They rebelled against social conventions, the family, and other constraints to join the order and spread Buddhism. Indian women belonging to this era brought about a revolution in the familial, religious, and social spheres.

*Writing for Children*

# The Magic Horse[*]

I t was the day of the New Year feast at the palace of the king of Persia. All the citizens had joined the celebrations that went on till evening when the king declared the close of the fest. Just at that moment, an Indian horse trader approached the king, bowed to him, and said breathlessly, 'I know I am late. But you must see my magic horse. I am sure that no other horse in your kingdom can compare with it!' The king replied, 'I see only an ordinary imitation of an ordinary horse—nothing impressive.' The Indian merchant responded, 'Your Highness, I know that your remark is based only on the appearance of the horse. But it is a wish-horse. Think of any place you wish to go to, and it will take you there in moments. Try it!'

The king pointed to a mountain 20 miles away and commanded: 'Fine, get me a leaf of one of the trees from the base

---

[*] Originally titled 'Kuhuka Ghoda', this story first appeared in *Maru Kahani* (Cuttack: Self-published, 1953), pp. 1–16. Translated by Priyadarshi Patnaik.

of the mountain.' Before the king could complete the sentence, the merchant twisted a knob below the stirrup of the horse and, with the speed of light, it whizzed away. In a moment he was back. In his hand was a leaf from the tree indicated. The horse came to a stop next to the king's throne.

The king was pleased and said, 'I am happy that you have proved me wrong. Now tell me what is the price of this horse?' The merchant responded, 'O King, your graciousness. When I had this horse made, I had to give my daughter to the craftsman in exchange for this horse. So I will not sell the horse unless I get a similar value for it.' The king interrupted the merchant and said, 'My great kingdom is made up of many smaller kingdoms. Ask for any one of them. You will be its king for life.' The merchant said, 'O Lord, your offer doesn't appeal to me. Unless you give me the hand of your princess, I will not sell it.'

On hearing this, the courtiers burst out in mirth. As the king was in a dilemma—weighing the horse against the princess—the young prince, who was present there, burst out in anger, 'Out of the question! You cannot give the hand of the royal-blooded princess to any lowly scoundrel!' The king said, 'True, but then he will take the horse away and sell it to one of my rivals. I will no longer possess one of the Seven Wonders of the World. Anyway, see if you can haggle with the merchant and reach a solution. But before that, test the horse once.'

The merchant was pleased. 'Now the king will definitely agree,' he thought. He took the prince to the horse and showed him how to press the lever that would make the horse fly, but before he could reveal how to bring it down, the impatient prince had already pressed the flying knob. In a flash, before the entire court, the prince whizzed away into the sky and disappeared into the golden evening. The merchant was scared to death. Trembling, he said, 'It is not my fault, O King. Before I could tell him how to bring the horse down, the prince had already left! If anything goes wrong, please don't punish me.'

The king was furious. He was worried about the prince. He said, 'Why didn't you tell him about the knob when he mounted the horse?' The merchant said, 'He would not listen to me.

But I shouted about the other knob. I think he heard me. He will definitely come down.' The king replied, 'But who knows where he will land if he finds the knob—upon a mountain or in the sea! Oh, he will be torn to pieces!' The merchant said, 'O King, have faith. The horse is designed in such a way that it will never let the prince fall in any of those places.' The king replied, 'I give you three months. If the prince is not back by then, you will be beheaded.' And he instructed the guards to imprison the merchant.

Meanwhile, the prince was having a great time. He soared so high that even the mountains were no longer visible. But then, when he wanted to come down, he realized that he did not know how to do so. This worried him. Now he regretted not listening to the rider, but he did not lose his head. Rather, he began exploring the area under the neck of the horse with his fingers. There was a tiny knob—smaller than the knob used for going up. He began to turn that knob and, to his delight, found that the horse was responding. One twist and it started straight down. It was dark. Midnight. The prince did not know where he was. By then he was very hungry and weak. As he climbed down the horse, he fainted.

When he regained consciousness, he felt a little better. Then he realized that he was on the roof of a huge building—probably a palace. Marble tiles. A tiny, open door. Through it, he could see the stairs leading down. The prince said to himself: 'I don't care who this palace belongs to, but I must go down and find for myself. Since I don't carry any weapons, no one will attempt to kill me.' By now his eyes had adjusted to the darkness. Below the guards were sleeping. From a distance, through a screen, he could see a bright light. He peeped in and found black eunuchs sprawled in sleep and several maids sleeping on sofas all around. On the central bed lay a beautiful lady. Afraid to wake the others, he quietly crawled up to the princess and tugged at her dress. Then he whispered softly to her.

When the princess opened her eyes, in front of her was a handsome young man dressed in royal clothes. She kept staring at him. Looking down, she found him kneeling. She was about to speak, but the prince quietened her and said softly, 'I am the prince of Persia. Due to misfortune, I am now on my knees in front of you asking for asylum. Yesterday I was feasting with my father. But now I am here. Grant me sanctuary.'

The princess was the daughter of the king of Bengal. The king had built a summer palace for his daughter, and the princess was visiting the summer palace for a change of air. She said, 'Bengal is known for its great hospitality. It will be no less in my palace. I will protect you.' She asked her maids to bring food and then arrange a soft bed for the prince in another chamber. A closet full of clothes was also made ready. The maids hurried about their tasks.

The princess sat alone and thought about the prince. When the maids returned, she asked eagerly, 'What does the prince think of me?' The maids responded coyly, 'How should we know? But it is for sure that a more handsome and well-mannered man can never be found in our kingdom.' The princess retorted angrily, 'Don't talk nonsense. Now go and take rest.'

The next morning, after a long period of preening and grooming and having put on her best dress, the princess went to enquire after the prince. The latter was preparing to bid the princess farewell and go back to his own kingdom. When the maid informed him that the princess wished to meet him, he said, 'Her wish is my command. I am her humble servant.' The princess said, 'I had to make arrangements for your stay in one of the outer rooms of the palace as per the norms of our kingdom. My apologies! Now I would like to listen to the story of your fearless adventure and the magic horse. Only after that you may leave. Tell me everything. How did you reach this place?' The prince narrated the entire story. At the end he added, 'It was only because of your kindness that I survived! As per the norms of your kingdom I am your slave. I have no possessions. Since I saw you I have given myself to you!' The princess' face flushed with embarrassment on hearing this. This made her look even more beautiful. She paused for a moment, then responded, 'O Prince, your story has given me great delight. Please accept my gratitude. I marvel at your courage. You are not my slave—the idea itself is ridiculous! You are as free as you were in your own kingdom. You must have given your heart to someone earlier who must have treated you cruelly. I will not

let you experience such pain again.' As the prince was about to
protest, the maids arrived and announced that the banquet was
ready.

The conversation ended and they went for the feast. On
seeing the beautiful decoration of the chamber and hearing the
soft musical lilt of the maids' voices, the prince was delighted.
Later the princess and the prince went to a chamber wrapped in
beautiful casements. The prince looked around and observed, 'I
was under the impression that there was no kingdom like Persia
and no commodities that could compare to Persian goods. But
I see I was wrong.' The princess responded, 'I don't know about
Persia, and I don't mean to demean my palace, but my father's
palace is even more beautiful. If you go to his palace and meet him,
he will be delighted.' The princess was hoping that if the king met
the prince, he would be won over by the latter's good looks and
pleasing manners. However, the prince was against it. He said,
'I am a prince. I cannot go to meet a king without my courtiers,
processions, and gifts. The king will only think less of me!' The
princess responded, 'That is not an issue. All that is mine is yours.
Please take as many of my men as you wish!' The prince thanked
the princess, but said, 'I have been away from home a long time.
My father must be sad and sick, lamenting that I am dead. I will
never be able to forget your care and kindness. But I must first go
back home. Then I will come back to meet your father.'

The princess agreed sadly but pleaded with him to stay back
for a few days before beginning his journey. It was difficult for the
prince to say no. So he stayed back and, occupied in fun, frolic,
games, and festivities, he soon forgot everything. Two months
passed. The prince was again reminded of home. He told the sad
princess, 'Don't think of me as a heartless cheat. I am not like
them. If you wish to be with me, please come back to my kingdom
on the back of the magic horse. I will secretly carry you there.'

The princess felt helpless but agreed. When the palace was dark
and the servants and maids were sleeping, they quietly slipped
away and jumped on to the back of the magic horse. The princess
sat behind the prince and held on tightly to his waist. They were
in the air for only two hours when they reached Persia. The magic

horse descended in a village on the outskirts of the capital. The prince told the princess, 'I will make arrangements for your stay here and will go along to meet the king first. Then I will come for you.' When the king saw the prince, his happiness knew no bounds. The news spread rapidly and there were celebrations all around the city. The prince did not hide the fact that he had brought away the princess of Bengal secretly. The king immediately ordered a team to bring the princess to the palace with due ceremony. The whole kingdom was in high spirits. Prisoners were released, including the merchant. The king said, 'You are lucky. If the prince had not returned, I would have beheaded you. My son has come back. You are free. Take your magic horse and get out!' The merchant immediately rushed to his magic horse, found out where the princess was waiting for the prince, and hurried to the place on his magic horse.

At the gate of the dwelling where the princess was resting stood a guard. The merchant told him, 'The prince has sent me with the horse to take the princess back to the palace.' The guard believed him when he saw the magic horse and informed the princess. The eager princess came out all decked up to go to the palace. She had no suspicion that the merchant, seeking revenge for having been thrown into prison, was abducting her. Up into the sky she flew, and the king and the prince and all the people of the kingdom could see them from below, but they could only watch helplessly. Knowing well that they had no way of catching him, the merchant flew the horse over the palace and then soared away.

The king was devastated, but the prince said, 'Provide me with the disguise of a beggar. I will go in search of my princess.' As soon as the disguise was arranged, the prince set off.

Meanwhile, the princess was tired. The horse had been in the air for a long time and the merchant was making no efforts to come down. She grew suspicious, but what could she do? Finally, the merchant brought the horse down in the kingdom of Kashmir. Hiding the exhausted and tired princess in a shrubby place near the river, he started for the city. The princess wanted to escape, but was so tired and exhausted without food that she could hardly move. After some time, the merchant came back to her with some food.

Only after taking a few bites was she able to speak. The moment she gained a little strength, she began to rebuke the merchant for his misdeeds, but the merchant threatened to kill her. Frightened, the princess cried for help. On hearing her voice, a group of horsemen reached the site. The princess begged them to save her life.

It so happened that the leader of the horsemen was the sultan of Kashmir. He asked the merchant, 'What is the matter?' The merchant replied roughly, 'This woman is my wife. If she cries, it is none of your business! Go away.' However, the sultan did not believe him. The princess said, 'This magician has abducted me. My husband is the prince of Persia. I am the princess of the kingdom of Bengal.' Her voice choked with grief and then she fell silent. The sultan was convinced by her regal dress and her manners. He ordered his attendants to behead the merchant. His order was immediately carried out. On his directions, a horse was brought for the princess. Then they all went to the sultan's palace.

The sultan provided her with everything: maids, eunuchs, and guards. He had her taken to a separate palace and then told her that he would come back the next day to hear her story. The princess thought that on hearing her story, the sultan would keep her in safety for the arrival of the prince. However, fate would have it so that she only escaped from one danger into another greater danger. The sultan, after taking leave of the princess, decided that the very next day he would marry the beautiful princess. He asked his messengers to have this news circulated all around the kingdom.

Meanwhile, the prince had travelled a long time and was now in the outskirts of Kashmir. The next morning, the prince of Persia, disguised as a beggar, heard the news of the sultan's marriage to the princess. He was upset, but what could he do? He could not think of anything.

The next day when the princess was dressed and ready, the sultan announced to her that he would marry her that very day. 'Get ready,' he said and went away. The princess was devastated.

Overwhelmed with grief, she fainted. The maids fanned her and took care of her. Slowly, she revived, but she acted as if she had gone mad and started blabbering and made all kinds of strange gestures. As the day gave way to night, things worsened. The sultan was clueless. In the end, the marriage was postponed and the princess put in charge of trusted maids.

Many days passed. The sultan consulted the best doctors of the kingdom to find a cure for the princess. However, the princess was very intelligent. She realized that if the physicians examined her pulse, they would come to know the truth. So every time a physician came to examine her, she attacked him so ferociously that he had to rush out in fear. However, knowing that their medicines were harmless, the princess took them. Seeing this, the sultan announced in his kingdom that he would reward the physician who would cure the princess. Soon announcers from his kingdom even went to the neighbouring kingdoms to search for good physicians, but none could cure the princess. Meanwhile, the prince was roaming around the kingdom hopelessly.

Since the time the sultan had announced his marriage to the princess, the prince had been staying in a small inn and keeping track of the events. When he heard the announcement of reward for curing the princess, he hatched a plan and put on the disguise of a physician. Then he arrived at the palace. When the attendants took him to the sultan, he announced, 'I have cured much madness. I am confident of curing the princess.' The courtiers eagerly said, 'Yes, you will be amply rewarded if you cure the princess!' However, the sultan said, 'Don't be so confident. Forget about curing her. If you see her once, you will not even attempt to go near her.' Saying so, he took the prince to the princess' chamber.

The sultan strategically took him to a point from where the prince disguised as a physician could see the patient, but the patient could not see him. The prince saw the princess lying on a bare mat and singing the story of her life as a song. The moment he heard the song, he realized that the princess was faking madness. She was actually not ill. His heart began beating faster. He understood that he was the cause of her sorrow and also understood her intelligent ploy. So he came back and told the sultan, 'It is true that the princess is mad, but if I can talk to her, I might be able to cure her.'

The sultan was delighted. He made all the necessary arrangements so that the treatment could take place without any delay. The moment the prince went to the princess, she reacted angrily and began abusing him. The prince disregarded this and went close to the princess. In a soft voice he said, 'O Princess, look up! See who has come! The prince of Persia has come as your doctor—to free you from this bondage.'

The princess started on hearing the prince's voice. Her anger disappeared in a moment. She looked at her physician with intent longing as if her paradise had been given back to her. When the prince found that the princess could not speak even if she wanted to, he slowly recounted all the events of their life. Seeing her helpless state he said, 'I have travelled far and wide in search of you. It is only today that I have been finally able to find you here in this palace.' On hearing his words, the princess told him the entire story of her travel from the kingdom of Persia with the horse merchant. Then she begged him to find a way out of the tyrant sultan's palace.

The prince let out a sigh on hearing this. He was shocked to hear of the indecent behaviour of the sultan who knew all about the prince and the princess. 'If you don't take me out of here, I would rather die, but I will never marry the sultan,' she said. When the prince asked her about the magic horse, she replied that she did not know about it. 'The sultan knows about the value of the horse. It must be with the sultan.' On hearing this, the prince suddenly had an idea for their escape.

He said, 'When the sultan comes to meet you tomorrow, dress well and talk to him nicely.' Then he took leave of her and told the sultan that the princess was improving. The sultan was overjoyed. The next day when the princess spoke nicely with him, the sultan was assured that the new physician would definitely cure her. The sultan came out of the chamber impulsively even without asking the princess how she was. The prince also came out with him and told him, 'I need to find out all about the princess and her past. For that I will have to talk to her in solitude.' The sultan did not suspect anything and replied, 'She came on a magic horse, and I have beheaded the rogue who abducted her. The horse is in the treasury. But I don't know how to make it fly.' The prince said, 'That is wonderful. Now you have told me exactly what I needed to hear. When the horse merchant made the princess mount the horse, the magic of the horse affected her. But I know how to cure her. Bring the horse here. I must know how the princess travelled from Bengal to Persia and then from Persia to Kashmir. Bring the horse in front of the palace. Invite all the people to that spot. Deck the princess in precious ornaments and then bring her to the same spot. Everyone will see how I cure her of the horse's evil magic.'

So the horse was brought to the palace courtyard. A curious crowd gradually gathered around the horse in a roughly rectangular space. Finally, the sultan arrived with his ministers and courtiers. Then the princess slowly stepped out, decorated in beautiful ornaments, and approached the magic horse. She mounted the horse. Immediately, the prince lit a fire using incense, sandal oil, and logs in a circle around the horse. Putting his hand upon his chest, he circled the horse three times chanting magic charms. The fire caused so much smoke that neither the horse nor the princess was visible any longer.

The prince was waiting just for this opportunity. He quickly jumped into the smoke and hopped on to the back of the horse just behind the princess. Then he pressed the knob under the neck of the magic horse. As the horse rose into the air, the prince shouted at the sultan, 'O Sultan, you, who should have protected the princess who sought your protection, tried to exploit her instead. You humiliated and insulted her. If you wish to marry someone, first learn how to seek her permission.' Then the horse rose into the air and disappeared. In a few hours they were back in Persia. The marriage of the prince and the princess was held with great pomp and ceremony. Everyone was delighted. Once the ceremony was over, a messenger from Persia was sent with gifts to the kingdom of Bengal to tell the king of the state of affairs and to seek his friendship. The king was delighted to know that her daughter was safe and agreed to the proposal. The two kingdoms were built on a beautiful relationship.

With this, my story also comes to an end.

# The Fisherman's Wit*

In a certain village lived an old fisherman named Narahari.
He took his net to the sea every day to catch fish from the
shore. He sold his catch at the local market and provided for
his wife and children with great difficulty. He had decided not
to cast the fishing net more than four times a day. One day, as
he pulled the first net he had cast, it felt heavy. He was elated
but when he pulled out the net, he found a dead ass. He threw
the carcass into the sea. He mended the torn net before casting
it again. The second time he fished out a heap of garbage from
the water. Annoyed, he removed the garbage and cleaned the net
before casting it into water again. He prayed, 'Dear God, please
don't torment me like this.' The next time, too, he netted slime,
shells, twigs, and pebbles from the sea. He cleaned his net and

* Originally titled 'Keutara Buddhi', this story first appeared in
Maru Kahani (Cuttack: Self-published, 1953), pp. 51–3. Translated by
Chinmay Kumar Hota.

hurled it into the water again. As the net felt quite heavy, the old man had already began to think about a big catch of fish, which he would sell in the market and take home some fine rice. Lo and behold! This time, too, there was no fish in the net, but a big sealed box. The fisherman thought that if he could restore the box to its owner, he might receive a handsome reward and finish his day on a good note.

The fisherman could not resist his curiosity and opened the lid with a knife after much effort. When nothing came out of the box, he peeped inside. He could see smoke emerging from it and slowly rising to the sky. The scared fisherman moved aside and observed the box from a safe distance. After the smoke subsided, a ghastly giant appeared from the box. The fisherman was scared stiff. The giant said to him, 'You have saved me from the closed box. Tell me how can I serve you?'

The fisherman said, 'First, you tell me how you entered the box and managed to get yourself locked?'

'Talk to me politely, or I will kill you,' the giant hollered.

'Why should you kill me? I saved you from confinement. How can you forget that?' asked the fisherman.

The giant said, 'You cannot escape by making such excuses. I will do you only one favour: Tell me how you would like to die.'

The fisherman asked, 'What wrong have I done to you that you would want to kill me?'

The giant shouted back, 'I will kill you no matter what you say, but before that listen about my past. Since I had rebelled against the king of giants, he shut me inside a clay box and dropped it into the sea. I could not open the lid as I was under a curse. While in confinement I took an oath that whoever frees me in the first 100 years, I will make him a king; even if he were dead, I will bring him from the land of the dead and shower him with riches. Nobody opened the box. After 100 years I again promised to myself that if somebody will free me, I will give him all the wealth of the world. Nobody came. After 200 years I made a vow that I will kill my liberator, but only after hearing from him how he wishes to die.'

The fisherman touched the giant's feet and pleaded earnestly for mercy, but the giant remained adamant. Then an idea struck the fisherman and he said to the giant, 'I have one question: Did you actually stay inside the box? It is impossible to believe that your mountain-like body can be squeezed inside a tiny box.'

Hearing this, the giant produced smoke over the box and vanished into the smoke. Once inside the box, he spoke, 'You suspicious fisherman! Did you find out whether I am truthful or a liar? You believe me now?'

The fisherman did not say anything but quickly closed the lid of the box. Then he said, 'You unfaithful monster, you must suffer for your deed. I freed you, and you wanted to kill me? Now you tell me how you would like to die. I am throwing you back into the sea.' Then he threw the closed box into the water. The voice of the giant emerged from the box, 'I beseech you; I will remain your servant forever, please free me once again.'

The giant tried to open the lid but could not, as it was a cursed lid. The giant appealed for freedom again, but the fisherman replied, 'If I free you like a fool again, I would invite my own doom.'

The fisherman had saved his dear life with his own wit and taught a lesson to the wicked giant. All evil people should be treated this way.

# The Tale of the Persian Merchant*

Once upon a time there lived a merchant in Persia known as Ali Kozia. He was a bachelor. He used to live a contented life with whatever little he earned. His ancestral assets served him in living in comfort. But then, one day he had a dream and he saw the same dream repeatedly for three consecutive nights.

An old man appeared in his dream and warned him that unless he set off on a pilgrimage to Mecca, great harm would befall him. However, Ali was not perturbed. He thought that if he went off to Mecca, his business would collapse. And if all his clients went to other merchants, he would end up on the streets. So he began to give alms to the poor and gave away gifts for religious causes. He felt this would reduce the burden of his guilt, but then he began

* Originally titled 'Parasya Banika Kahani', this story first appeared in Maru Kahani (Cuttack: Self-published, 1953), pp. 17–28. Translated by Priyadarshi Patnaik.

having the same dream repeatedly. In the end, he decided that he had to go on the pilgrimage. He had to visit Mecca.

He sold off his furniture, his house, his merchandise—all the material possessions he had. At the end, he had earned over 1,000 gold coins. Putting aside a little that he would need for his travel, he put the gold coins in an earthen pot and filled its upper part with olives. Then he sealed the pot using clay. He then carried it over his head to one of his merchant friends. Putting it down in front of his shop, Ali said, 'I am going off to Mecca. Please take care of this pot of olives for me. When I come back, I shall collect it from you.'

On hearing this, the merchant extended the keys of the shop to Ali and said, 'Please put it in a corner of the store. When you come back, you can pick it up. Don't worry; it will be safe with me.' After a few days, Ali started off with a group of pilgrims who had camels and were going to Mecca.

It was a long journey. On reaching Mecca, Ali visited all the holy places. Then he took out some of the wares he was still carrying, hoping that he could sell them to other pilgrims. Some merchants who were in Ali's group told him, 'These goods are very valuable. There are few here who can afford them. But if you take them to Cairo, they will sell for a very good price.' Ali followed their advice and started for Cairo with another group of merchants. There he got a very high price for his goods. With the money earned he began buying exotic goods from Cairo in order to sell them at Damascus, but the merchants in his group tarried at Cairo for more than a month and Ali was forced to stay back with them. Since he had a lot of time to spare, he began exploring the many beautiful cities on the bank of the river Nile. When Ali finally reached Damascus, he marvelled at its beauty and soon lost all interest to go back home.

However, after a long time, he began to feel homesick. So he planned to return to his beloved Baghdad through Aleppo. Crossing Euphrates and then the Tigris River, he soon reached the town of Mufsal. There he found some merchants who had come from his own village. As they were going back to Persia, Ali also set off with them.

Now that he was going home, he remembered his gold and began worrying about his pot of olives. He wanted to find out if his merchant friend remembered him, for in the last seven years Ali had never heard any news from home!

Meanwhile, his merchant friend at home had forgotten all about the pot of olives. One day his wife told him, 'I haven't eaten olives since ages. Please get me some olives.' On hearing this, the merchant suddenly remembered Ali's pot of olives. He told his wife, 'My friend had left some olives in a pot. That was seven years ago. Come, give me a light. I will get some for you.' However, his wife reacted sharply, 'This is a breach of faith! If Ali is not back for seven years, it doesn't mean he is dead! What will he think if he finds out that you had opened his pot? My desire for olives was just a whim. Don't take it seriously and please don't do anything wrong. I have a strong hunch that Ali will come back soon. Besides, the fruits must also have gone bad by now. Please forget about this.'

However, the merchant did not heed his wife's words. Taking a candle he went into his store in search of the pot. His wife, outraged by her husband's behaviour, shouted from behind, 'Mark my words. I have already asked you not to do this. Now if any ill befalls you because of this, don't blame me.' However, the merchant did not listen to his wife and went ahead and opened the pot.

The fruits at the top had rotted away. In order to reach the fruits below, the merchant turned the pot over a metal container. The next moment, along with the fruits some coins also rolled away. The merchant could not contain his greed. When he looked into the pot, he discovered the tightly packed gold coins. He immediately shifted the gold coins to another container and quickly filled the pot again with olives. Immediately, he sealed the pot. Then he came back to his wife with a few olives and said, 'You were right, most of the fruits have rotten. So I have put the fruits back into the container and sealed it again.' His wife, who was still anxious, said, 'Thank God you did so. I hope nothing bad will come of it.'

However, that night the merchant could not sleep. He only worried about where to hide the coins. In the morning, he went to a shop and bought some fresh olives. Removing the rotten olives from the pot, he put fresh olives inside and sealed the pot again. Then he took the coins, hid them in a safe place, and very carefully placed the pot back in its original place.

After a month Ali Kozia returned to his village. Since he had sold his house, that night he took shelter in a small inn. The next day he visited his merchant friend. The merchant was shocked to see him. After they exchanged a few polite words, Ali wanted his pot back. The merchant said, 'Your pot is where you had left it. Please take the key and collect it.' Ali took the pot back to the inn and removed the seal. When he opened the pot, there were only olives inside and no gold. He desperately groped around but all in vain. There was not a single coin inside. Ali virtually broke down at this betrayal and said in despair, 'I never thought that my trusted friend would commit such a great sin!'

After a lot of hesitation, Ali went back to the merchant and said, 'Please don't feel bad that I have come back, but there were a thousand gold coins inside the pot along with the fruits. Now they are not there. I think you may have borrowed that money for some business deal. I have no objections to that. Just write a deed for that money and you can return it to me whenever you wish.'

The merchant, however, was prepared for this. He replied instantly, 'This is very offending. When you left, you took the key leaving your pot behind. Today you opened the lock again and collected it from the same place. I have never even touched your pot. Besides, you told me that you were leaving olives with me. What is this talk of gold coins? You may not believe me but this is the truth.' Ali tried to argue and even pleaded with the merchant. In the end, he said in despair, 'You have a reputation to keep. Now if I go to the court of law, what will be the consequence?' The merchant retorted, 'You neither showed me the contents of the pot when you kept it nor when you took it back. Luckily, you are not claiming that you had kept precious stones inside! I beg you, please leave this place; else people will gather around us if they hear you shouting like this.'

Soon some nearby merchants and other buyers gathered around as the two friends argued. Ali narrated the entire story to the people. When they asked the merchant, he responded with feigned outrage, 'Ali is accusing me falsely. I never knew what the pot contained. He told me that he had kept some olives inside.' Then he pleaded with the crowd trying to woo people to his side. When Ali saw this, he angrily gripped the merchant's arm and said, 'I will take you to the Kazi for justice!' The merchant responded, 'Good, let us go. He will judge who is telling the truth and who is lying.'

Soon the accused and the plaintiff reached the Kazi. After listening to them both, the Kazi asked Ali, 'Who was your witness when you kept your pot?' Ali said that he had none. 'He was my friend, and I knew him to be honest. So I kept my goods trusting his honesty,' he added. The merchant retorted, 'Huzoor, he is a liar! I don't even know what he had in his pot! I am willing to swear to prove my innocence.' The Kazi was convinced when the merchant swore on the holy book, and he acquitted the merchant.

Now Ali was really angry. He shouted at the Kazi, 'You did not do justice. Now I will go to the Khalifa!' However, the Kazi replied, 'I did what I felt was just. You may do as you wish.' The merchant went back home happily.

Ali came back to the inn sorrowfully. The next day he wrote a petition and then waited for the Khalifa who was on his way to the mosque. After giving the petition to his official, he followed the Khalifa to his palace. A little later, a courtier came out and reported, 'The Khalifa will consider your case tomorrow. The merchant will also be called here.' Ali went back to the inn.

That evening the Khalifa had gone out with his courtiers in disguise to assess the state of his capital. At one spot he found a group of noisy urchins playing a game. He found that they were actually holding a mock trial of Ali and the merchant's case. He quietly hid in a corner and watched. The game of enquiry into the statements of the victim and the accused was going on. The Khalifa suddenly remembered that the next day a trial for the same two was to be held. He was now curious to see what would happen. The most intelligent of the boys said, 'Ok, I am the Kazi. Now bring Ali to me. Also bring the rogue who has cheated him of 1,000 gold coins.' The others delightedly took up the other parts. The Kazi sat with a solemn face. The attendant brought in Ali and introduced him. Then the merchant was introduced. Ali narrated the whole story and finally requested that his money be returned. The Kazi heard everything, and then said, 'If this is true, why don't you return the money?' The boy playing the merchant took an oath, exactly like the real merchant, that Ali was telling lies. 'If you ask all the merchants of Persia who is lying, they will point at Ali,' he said. Ali also argued the same way.

Next, as the merchant was about to speak, the boy playing the role of Kazi stopped him and said, 'I would like to verify the pot of olives before we proceed. Ali, bring the pot of olives. I will verify it.' Ali brought the imaginary pot of olives. The Kazi then asked, 'Can you identify this as Ali's pot?' When the merchant kept quiet, the Kazi felt that it was Ali's pot. Then he instructed the boys playing attendants to remove the seal. The seal was opened. The Kazi looked into the imaginary pot and exclaimed, 'What beautiful olives. Let me taste one.' Then he said, 'The olives are very tasty, but how could they remain so fresh for seven years? Now bring two olive fruit merchants from the city. Let us take their opinions.' They were called. The Kazi asked them, 'How long do olives remain fresh and sweet?' They responded, 'Even with the best care, not more than three years. Then both their colour and taste will change and they will be only as good as garbage.' The Kazi asked them to check the fruits inside the pot. The merchants looked into the imaginary pot and responded, 'These are fresh and sweet.' However, the Kazi said, 'You must be wrong. Ali has kept the olives for more than seven years!' The merchants responded, 'No, the fruits are very fresh and must have been kept in the pot recently. Any fruit merchant will tell you that.' The Kazi then declared that the merchant should be hanged for his crime. The children clapped, and the game came to an end.

The Khalifa was delighted and instructed his courtiers, 'Bring these boys to my court along with the two merchants.' He continued, 'The boys have judged the case well. I couldn't have done better myself.' The next day when one of the courtiers came to fetch the boy who had played the Kazi, his mother was frightened and said, 'My son is innocent.' However, the courtier told her about the last night's incident and reassured her. The happy mother dressed her child and the other children and sent them to the palace on horseback.

When the boys arrived at the palace, the Khalifa said, 'I liked your game last night very much. Today you will have to play that game here for real.' He then invited the young boy who had played the Kazi to sit next to him and judge the case.

Ali and the merchant were brought in. They bowed to the Khalifa who said, 'Let the session begin. This boy will act as the judge. Only if he does not do well, I will judge the case.' As earlier, the two presented their cases. The boy now asked for the pot of olives. Ali brought the pot and opened it. The Khalifa tasted an olive and then asked the other fruit merchants to taste it. They tasted the fruits and said, 'Huzoor, these fruits are very fresh—this year's crop.' Then the boy who had played the Kazi said, 'How is that possible? These fruits are seven years old.' However, the merchants would not agree.

The guilty merchant was now terrified. Knowing that his life was on the line, he tried to wriggle out of the situation. The intelligent boy then looked at the Khalifa and said, 'O Khalifa, yesterday we were playing a game. But this is no game. It is now for you to decide if he should be hanged. But please do not hang him because I said so during the game. Please do what you feel is wise.' The Khalifa judged the merchant a scoundrel and thief. He then ordered, 'Take this thief away and hang him.' The frightened merchant acknowledged his guilt and revealed the place where he had hidden the gold.

The Khalifa learnt a lesson in law from the young boy: how to bring out the truth through intelligence. He was very pleased with the boy. So he gave the boy 100 gold coins for his wit and bid him farewell.

# The Tale of the Sorcerer's Wife[*]

In the enchanted land of Kamakshya, a king named Chandramouli used to rule a thousand years ago. He was a very just king who took care of the needs of his subjects. The king was very kind and could not tolerate any form of cruelty, including cruelty to animals. He never went out hunting, and all types of game hunting were forbidden in his kingdom. If he ever heard of any cruelty to animals, he had the culprits punished immediately. Horses, elephants, cattle, goats, and sheep—name any animal—all enjoyed security and happiness in his kingdom. However, he did not forbid the killing of wild carnivores such as lions and tigers and mean creatures like snakes. He even rewarded people who killed them.

* Originally titled 'Kuhuki Bharija Katha', this story first appeared in *Maru Kahani* (Cuttack: Self-published, 1953). Translated by Priyadarshi Patnaik.

One day when the king was in the court, a messenger arrived and said, 'O Lord, there is a man who beats his mare every night ruthlessly. This morning, because of such beating, the mare has gone lame. I told the man about your principles, but he did not heed my words and kept on beating the mare.' The king became angry on hearing this and said, 'What audacity! He would not listen to my edicts! Arrest him and bring him here. Tomorrow morning, in front of the palace, he will be impaled to death!'

The messenger immediately read out the sentence to the mare owner. His name was Mohan Singh. The man was immediately arrested, shackled, and thrown into prison without food and water. The next day the announcement of his imminent death was made in the whole kingdom. Everyone came out to see this event. Then the king arrived with his courtiers. The lame mare was also brought to the site and tied to a post. The prison officers then dragged Mohan Singh to the place of punishment.

The king spoke, 'As per my edicts, anyone hurting domestic animals will be punished with death. Disobeying my words, this man has beaten his mare lame. Shouldn't he be put to death? You decide.' The citizens agreed in one voice. Then the king declared, 'Bring Mohan Singh here. Remove his shackles. Let him admit to his crime.'

The moment Mohan Singh was freed, he rushed straight to the king's feet and began sobbing bitterly. Everyone was surprised. The king said, 'Do you not admit that you have mistreated your mare? You must admit your guilt before being punished.' Mohan Singh kept on sobbing as he spoke, 'O King, you are the father of this land. The fate of millions of subjects is in your hands. Before punishing me, assure me of your grace so that I might tell my strange tale. If you consider me guilty even after hearing my story, then please punish me.' The king was a little intrigued, so he said, 'All right. You have my permission to tell your story. Explain why you treat your mare so cruelly.' A little reassured, Mohan Singh began his tale:

O Lord, you know me. I was not so poor earlier. My father and forefathers had held high posts in your army, had collected wealth and acquired landed property. We were rich, and I was their only inheritor. But I never boasted of this to anyone. I had only one wish: a beautiful and talented wife. When my relatives came to know of this, they identified such a maid for me and we were married.

I thought my days would pass in happiness. But appearances are deceptive. Once we were married, my wife showed her true colours. She treated me so badly that my entire life was in a shambles. My days went by in great unhappiness and bitterness. I lost patience. As per our family traditions the bride and the bridegroom do not meet before marriage. They have to accept whatever is written in their fates. But then, unless the wife is terribly bad-tempered or physically deformed, one should never blame her. Even a deformed wife with a good nature is preferable. But my wife, even though beautiful, was so ill-mannered that soon I could only see ugliness in her and nothing else.

When she first arrived, I told myself, 'I am lucky to have such a beautiful wife. She must be equally good-natured.' The day after marriage, as per convention, food was served to both of us in separate rooms. I waited for my wife, then sent my servants to fetch her, but she would not come. I was impatient but did not know what to do. Finally, she arrived. Then I began to eat. But I was shocked when my wife took out two metal needles, picked rice morsels with them, and began nibbling. I turned to her and asked, 'Kaushalya, is this how you eat in your own house? Do you eat so little because you are not hungry? Do you think we do not have enough? God has given us plenty. Don't worry. Eat as much as you want.'

I thought she would respond politely and start eating normally. But then she slowed down further, ignored all the curries, and bit on a little piece of rice cake which would not even satisfy a crow. Her manners were strange and irritating. I still thought that she was feeling shy, or maybe she had been taught to behave like this by her parents. Finally, I thought that probably she liked to eat alone and walked out of the room angrily.

However, this continued. She always ate very little. This intrigued me. I wanted to find out the reason why she ate so little. Even after many days this did not change. One night I pretended to be asleep. I wanted to find out what was going on. Soon I realized that she was waiting for me to sleep. Once she was convinced that I was asleep, she got up quietly as if to go out. I had never imagined she would do that.

I was very curious. Where on earth was she going? When I looked out of the window, I saw her leaving the compound quietly. Quickly but quietly, I started after her. It was a moonlit night, so I kept my distance. After some time she reached the crematorium ground. I hid behind some shrubs at a safe distance. From there I could see her approaching a witch in a ramshackle hut. These witches usually stay in such places and kill unsuspecting travellers and eat them. But on days when living humans are not available, they dig up graves and eat the putrid flesh of the dead. I trembled with horror. My wife and the other witch dug up a grave and began eating the dead. I shrunk further back. Soon they crossed me, but I could not hear their words because of the distance. I quietly came back home, got into bed, and acted as if I were asleep.

After some time my wife entered the room quietly, changed her dress, and lay down in her place. That night I could not sleep. Early in the morning, I came out to inspect my farmland. I told myself, 'How will I live with her unless she changes her ways?' First, I thought of thrashing her into submission. Then I felt that perhaps soft words were better.

When I came back from the field, she instructed the cook to serve us food. When the food was served, Kaushalya began picking rice morsels with her needles. I felt devastated and could not stop myself. I said, 'Kaushalya, any husband would be saddened by this attitude. But I am patiently waiting for you to change. Since our marriage I have instructed our cook to make the choicest dishes and sweets. Doesn't that taste better than carrion?' Kaushalya started and stopped eating. She realized I had discovered her secret. Suddenly she became so violent that I started trembling. Sweat poured out of my body, and I could not stand up. Meanwhile, she rushed out, got some water in a container, and began chanting a spell. Then she came near me and whispered, 'Wretched man! You have transgressed your limits. I curse you to turn into a dog.' Saying so, she sprinkled the magic water over my body.

Had I known that a sprinkle of water could turn one into a dog, I would have run away. But that was not to be. The moment I turned into a dog, she gave me such a thrashing that I wished I were dead. But then good sense prevailed. I realized that if I stayed there a moment longer she would kill me. I rushed out into the street. Now she was not able to beat me in public view, but she managed to twist my tail hard. I now realized what a monster she was. Without any thoughts I scampered away in whichever direction fate would take me. All the way I kept yelping loudly because of the throbbing pain in my tail.

Hearing me yelp the other dogs began attacking me. I ran into a butcher's house and took shelter there. In the beginning he was kind to me. But later he began to shoo me away. The place stank awfully of putrid flesh. Other smelly dogs also hung around the place. However, because my tail had not healed yet, I dug my head into a corner next to the shop and managed to survive. One day the butcher came towards my hole with a stick. I no longer trusted him, and was now smart enough not to wait, so I rushed out.

On the road there was another small sweet shop. The owner was a kind man. Instead of shouting at me, he threw a fried puri at me. Though I was not feeling hungry, I did not want to hurt his feelings. So I nibbled at it. The shop owner understood. I slowly approached him and rubbed against his leg. He realized that I wanted protection. So he made arrangements for me in a corner. He was a very nice man. I had never expected so much kindness from anybody. He would always call me when he had food. Though I had the form of a dog, I was actually a human! So I tried my best to please him and keep him happy. It was the only way to show him gratitude.

Among dogs, as with human beings, there are many wicked ones. They eat and make merry but do nothing for their masters. But I was never like that. Whenever he started from home, I followed him up to the door and rubbed against his ankle. Then he would pat me. If I were sleeping, he would call my name— Ratan, for he called me that. One day a woman gave my master a defaced coin. My master returned the coin to the woman and asked for a good one. The woman got angry and said, 'Yesterday it was good, and today it is out of circulation!' The sweet seller told her jokingly, 'Forget about me, even my dog will not touch your defaced coin!' Then he called me. I rushed towards him. My master pointed towards the coins and told me, 'Separate the good coins from the bad ones.' I immediately separated the defaced coin and showed my master that I could do it. The woman was awed. She again mixed a bad coin with some good coins. Again, I separated them with my paw. My master was delighted and told this to everyone. Soon this news spread. People gathered to see me perform this act. Now the sweet shop was always crowded. My master sold a lot of sweets and became rich.

But the other merchants and shop owners began to envy him. I became their eyesore. Days turned into months. One day an old, kind-looking woman stood before me and threw six coins on the ground. When I separated the good coins from the bad ones, she was delighted. Looking at me, she signalled me to follow her. Her eyes were so hypnotic that I kept on looking at her. As she walked away, I followed her without the knowledge of my master. Soon I reached her house. It was my desire since a very long time to become human again. But there was no scope for that. I always prayed to God, and on this day, God listened to me.

When I waited outside the lady's house, she invited me in. Inside, her daughter was sitting on the bed sewing. The lady told her daughter, 'You wanted to see the dog that could separate the good coins from the bad ones. Look, here he is. Today I saw him doing that in front of my eyes. I think he is a human. Some witch must have turned him into a dog. No dog can have so much intelligence.

The girl looked at me for some time. Then she took some water and muttered, 'O creature, if you are actually human, then by the grace of the goddess Kamakshya's magic, turn human, or else stay a dog forever.' Then she sprinkled the magic water on me. The next moment I returned to my original form.

In deep gratitude I fell at the feet of the beautiful maiden and thanked her for saving my life. The maiden was both surprised and delighted. She asked, 'Who turned you into a dog?' I told her the entire story. On hearing this, she said, 'I know Kaushalya since a long time. She was always an expert witch but a very evil one. She is friends with all kinds of evil witches, gnomes, and ghosts. Apparently, we are friends, but in reality we don't like one another. We have to make her pay for her sins!' Then she brought out a bottle of magic water and gave it to me. 'Go to Kaushalya and, without a moment's delay, throw this water on her. She will turn into a mare,' she said. Mother and daughter allowed me to take rest and then bid me farewell.

In order to take revenge I came back home and acted as if nothing had happened. The moment Kaushalya saw me she was so shocked that she could not even react. She had never thought that I would be able to turn into a man again. But then she quickly collected her wits. Screaming in rage, she charged at me. But I was ready and before she could do anything, I shouted, 'Witch, pay the price for your sins!' and threw the water in the bottle at her. She immediately turned into a mare.

Since that day I whip her regularly for I cannot overcome my anger. She is now lame because of that beating.

⁂

Mohan Singh sighed deeply, looked at the king, and said, 'O Lord, I have told you my sad tale. Now if you think I am guilty, execute me.' There was silence all around. The king said, 'Since you have told me this wonderful but true story, I am pleased. You shall not be executed. From today I appoint you as my chief commander. You will uphold the tradition of your forefathers.'

Then the king unshackled Mohan Singh and placed the commander's headdress upon his head. Then he said, 'You have punished your wife enough. All punishments have a limit. All crimes must at some point be forgiven. Now turn this mare back into a woman or let her go free, but don't beat her anymore. Mohan Singh thanked the king with folded hands. The crowd broke up. Everyone went home.

And with that my story, too, comes to an end.

*The Gandhian Vision*

# Mahatma Gandhi's Message for Indian Women[*]

If someone were to document the process of the awakening of women during the period from 1921 to 1947, he would give Mahatma Gandhi the credit for whatever progress women made in the fields of education and economic development. All the pioneers in the women's movement have been shaped by his inspiring example. At the root of whatever these women do lie Gandhi's thoughts, ideas, and work. For this reason he would always be revered as the great mentor of the women of India. I cannot think of any other leader in the world whose views on women are as liberal and brave as those expressed in Gandhi's

* Originally titled 'Bharatiya Narinku Mahatma Gandhinka Prerana', this piece first appeared in Nababharata, February 1948, pp. 22–4, and later appeared in Early Women's Writings in Orissa, 1898–1950: A Lost Tradition, Sachidananda Mohanty (ed.) (New Delhi: SAGE Publications, 2005), pp. 164–6. Translated by Anil Pradhan.

writings. The solutions he has suggested to women's problems apply not only to women in India, but also to their counterparts all over the world. In responding to his call to take part in the satyagraha, countless unlettered and neglected women languishing in the villages of India came out and brought glory to their country. Even now many women are engaged in carrying out constructive programmes in villages, following Gandhi's instructions. These women have received affection from the masses for their sacrifice and selfless service. Their example has encouraged other women to rouse themselves from centuries-old stupor, reject superstitions, and plunge into a life of action. What great social reformers of the nineteenth and twentieth centuries such as Raja Ram Mohan, Keshub Chandra, Vivekananda, Ishwar Chandra Vidyasagar, and Dayanand Saraswati could not achieve was made possible by the great saint Mahatma Gandhi. It is the women, Harijans, peasants and the oppressed sections of society who have truly benefited from the freedom struggles led by the Congress. To them, who lacked a voice, Gandhi has given the power to speak out against oppression. Gandhi has enabled women to break the shackles of the *harem* and dedicate themselves to the service of the nation. This awakening has nothing to do with the establishment of a Christian order in the nineteenth century by the missionaries and memsahibs from England. Gandhi discovered the power which lay dormant in Indian women, and strove to bring it out in the open.

In a backward and superstition-ridden state like Odisha, Gandhi ushered in an era of awakening. Since girls in our society are economically vulnerable, greedy parents marry off their beloved daughters to old men or to men, marrying for the second or third time. Such marriages are no different from business transactions. These result in the girls getting widowed when very young and in their becoming victims of abuse. Gandhi has fought relentlessly against the evil practice of child marriage.

The number of children who are born and die after birth is higher in our country than in any other country in the world. This is a consequence of poverty. We should therefore make sure that we do not bring to the world millions of children and let them grow up hungry and illiterate. In view of this, Gandhi has urged young men and women of our country to practise *brahmacharya* and self-restraint and thereby control population growth. In his opinion, a woman's virtue is her most precious ornament. He has therefore urged women to give up their jewellery and luxuries and devote themselves to serving the poor. He expected selfless and dedicated service from women. He advocated widow remarriage and inter-caste marriage. Addressing women at a meeting held in Midnapore, he said that women should raise their children in such a way that they would be able to dedicate themselves to the service of their country and countrymen. This would be the greatest contribution women could make to national life. He has not only inspired women in Odisha, but also given strength and courage to women all over the country.

Gandhiji's movement has thrown up women such as Sarojini, Vijayalakshmi, Aruna, Sucheta, and Amrit Kaur who have won recognition for themselves. His ideals have also inspired women in Odisha who are leading a life dedicated to service. At the moment, Gandhi is earnestly appealing to members of the Hindu community to take women violated and abused by Muslims back into their fold and rehabilitate them. We learn that Gandhi's greatness has been enhanced by his appeal to young Hindu men to marry girls in Naukhali and Calcutta, who have been victims of rape. Women should go through Gandhi's books on women. They should shape their lives according to his ideals and sacrifice themselves in the service of the country. We have heard from Gandhi about how life becomes meaningful if we live it for others. We have also heard about his concept of non-violence, the glory of culture and humanity and the importance of truth in the development of human personality. However, we have learnt nothing from all this. It is only by translating this into action that we can truly worship him. No other mode of paying homage to him would do.

Gandhi has always striven to make truth and non-violence the basis of this politics. However, only future historians could say if these will play any decisive role in our lives. The coming century will judge men and women of his country according to his standard. These are not confined to ideology and idealism. When Gandhi's wife died, he set up a Kasturba fund dedicated to the welfare of children and the improvement of health, educational standard, and economic welfare of women in India's villages. This action is without parallel in the world. Maybe because we are too self-centred and mean, we are unable to follow the path shown by Gandhi. We are indifferent to the question of the welfare of women. However, Gandhi was convinced that unless the women of India awakened, the all-round development of India would never be possible. He disapproved of the way young girls in the West were educated, for he thought that the kind of education they received was unnatural and violent. Work aimed at educating and liberating women and ensuring their collective well-being formed an important part of Gandhi's vision of the future, but where are we now? How close are we to this vision?

# Mahatma Gandhi's Role in My Life[*]

I had come across Mahatma Gandhi on several occasions in Odisha and at many other places where the sessions of the Indian National Congress had been held. On his visit to Odisha, he first arrived at the city of Cuttack. From that time onwards, I had offered myself to tread his path as a faithful follower. Inspired by his ideals, and with the firm determination to dedicate my entire life to the noble cause of freeing Mother India from the shackles of bondage, I left home in my prime. Sworn to his magic mantra of service, I abandoned my home and hearth. Gandhiji brought about a total regeneration of myself and infused into me new notions, a new world vision, and new thoughts and actions. He unfolded the hundred petals of the lotus in my heart and lighted the flame of revolution within me.

* Originally titled 'Mo Jibanare Mahatma Gandhinka Abadana', this essay first appeared in Asanta Kali, 9th Year, Puja Edition, October 1959. Translated by Prasanta Kumar Purohit.

Countless people—children, old men and women, the rich and the poor, the weak and the powerful, the lowly and the haloed—had come crowding to that little cottage on the bank of the river Kathajodi. It had suddenly turned into a festive mela ground of the milling crowds. No one came empty-handed. They all came with their hands full of fruits and flowers as offerings. However, did the cottage fill up? With Gandhiji's instructions, I had been giving away all the offerings to the poorly clad women and their children. Gandhiji needed rest, but people came crowding at the threshold and were choking it. I had been entrusted with the duty of guarding the entrance. All were eager to have a glimpse of the Mahatma. I used to go inside frequently and inform the Mahatma of the enthusiastic, aspiring crowd. He would say, 'Won't you let me rest a while?' To this, I would reply, 'What can I do? People care little for either rain or shine to have one glimpse of you. They are going crazy. They don't think about your health and fatigue. I beg them to clear the place, but they don't care. They keep standing for hours in the sun underneath the mango trees.' Gandhiji had to come time and again to the door to wave to the people waiting outside. At last, he said to me, 'You made me rise so many times, thereby giving me pain. Now tell me what arrangement have you made for collection of funds for the Harijans?' I said, 'Mahatmaji, I have called a meeting of the women at the Town Hall at 4 o' clock. You will be going to the city to attend it. Many women would already have gathered there by now. If you make an appeal, they will offer whatever they can on the spot.'

Gandhiji arrived at the appointed venue before dusk. A notice had already been served to the Ramachandra Bhawan for the necessary arrangements. The hall had already filled with women longing to have a glimpse of the Mahatma. Our Congress volunteers were with Gandhiji. No one had risen the ladder of leadership to a high status yet. All of us belonged to the same rank and file. Therefore, all went well without anyone trying to over-dominate. Mahatmaji shared the reason of his visit, narrated the woeful tales of the people of the untouchable community, called the Harijans, explained the duties of the women of the nation addressing them as mothers and sisters and, finally, proposed the setting up of a fund for Harijans. After his speech, I explained in Odia the gist of his speech delivered in Hindi and made an appeal to the mothers and sisters for generously donating all the money and jewellery they could. Many women attending the meeting in Cuttack gave money, but those who had not brought cash poured into the white bed sheet held by two volunteers at its both ends, all the silver and gold ornaments they had been wearing upon their persons, untying them from their necks, fingers, toes, and ankles. Contributions of jewellery amounting to 60/70 *bharis* and a cash amount of 1,000 rupees were raised on the spot.

Mahatmaji saw the women's elevated spirit, their simple heart and untrammelled mind, and was glad to receive the charity. The ornaments and money were kept in the custody of other people. The meeting came to an end. I had been with him since 6 o'clock in the morning. I was greatly surprised to see all the fruits presented to Gandhiji being given away to children before the very eyes of the givers, without Gandhiji tasting any of it; their offerings being distributed among the unknown women and their children. Gandhiji, Kasturba, and Devdas Gandhi had stayed in Swaraj Ashram in 1921 on their first-ever visit to Odisha. On subsequent visits, he had stayed with Annada Ray and the next time at Naba Babu's house. I had been to those places to meet him. He had been cutting thread with a spinning wheel and advising everyone to do so. After his departure from Cuttack, many people from the villages and towns and the Congress leaders had used spinning wheels to prepare thread. Since the Amber spinning wheel had not come into use yet, the women were using the early spinning wheels made of wood. Gandhiji's speech was focused on the welfare of Harijans, spread of the spinning-wheel culture, cutting of thread, using swadeshi goods, and weaving clothes. He put special emphasis on the removal of untouchability and abandonment of liquor-drinking. He encouraged people to engage in these activities after receiving training in Swaraj or self-governance. All have to unite to keep India intact. In order to fight non-violently against the government, one has to give up all comforts and luxuries, be purified, and accept the tenets of truthfulness and non-violence.

I had written four letters to Mahatma Gandhi, in different situations. He had published the reply to my first letter in *Young India*. He had chosen my name as the first from among a list of selected names, who were to give slogans during the Quit India Movement of 1942. I had written to him that I would be the first one to follow satyagraha. Hence, it was my turn first to shout the slogan 'Quit India' in Odisha.

I courted arrest and went to jail after customarily shouting slogans at the Choudhury Bazaar. During my jail terms, I realized that the Congress volunteers were only increasing the number of inmates, but not treading the path of truth and non-violence sincerely. So I wrote letters to Gandhiji narrating the situation in detail and communicating my desire to resign from the Congress, citing reasons thereof. After being freed from the prison in 1940, I tendered my resignation.

The people who joined the Congress used to do so by paying money, but they were not following the tenets as enumerated in the receipts. I wrote similar letters to Rajendra Prasad both in Bengali and English.

Others opposed my move. I had written to Gandhiji that quitting the assembly would be an unjust decision at a time when there was a battle of wits going on in the assembly and people were supporting us. He wrote to me advising me to resign from the assembly, contest the elections, canvass, and come back with people's mandate. Rajendra Prasad, the Congress president, had written to me in this light. I wrote to Gandhiji asking him as to why he did not suggest Rajendra to quit membership. Rajaji, too, wrote in his letter—similar to mine—that Gandhi would not say anything to Rajendra Prasad because the latter was his relation. Rajaji wanted to know how and why Gandhiji had given him the advice to quit the assembly, although the general public did not want him to do so.

Rajaji considered it to be an act of partiality. After some time, Rajendra Babu wrote to me that Gandhiji had written to some people to quit the assembly after listening to my arguments and that I ought to quit. However, it was the time of war and many costly items, food, and clothes were being extorted from villages to be sent to the front for the army. People were put in dire straits with the police forcibly collecting these essential items from their households. I held the opinion that our people would die as an evil consequence of the export of iron and forest produce, paddy, clothes, and other articles. Sharma, the district collector, and L.P. Singh had advised me to tell the villagers to restrict the paddy-filled vehicles from leaving the villages lest they died of drought.

Officials such as the tahsildar, the deputy revenue secretary, and the sub division officer were embezzling a lot of public money collected as contribution to the war fund, without giving the donors any receipts.

The officers stationed at locations having fertile fields such as Khordha, Banki, and Angul were collecting huge contributions. People were being misled into believing that the war was being fought in their interest. They were being duped by way of misinformation being spread through plays, songs, and public speeches in meetings. Women were being lured with the promise of job opportunities arising due to war and spoiled. Girls belonging to distinguished families were mostly getting victimized. The pathetic tale of the ironic fate these girls suffered was later discussed in Parliament. Several women from the rural belt were being transported to war fronts in trucks and buses, to fulfil the carnal desires of the soldiers. This evil crime was being perpetrated by the paid village touts. The families the girls belonged to were being supplied with flour, rice, sugar, kerosene, clothes, and the like. This farce went on in the soldiers' camps set up in Odisha. Quitting the assembly at such a critical juncture was not advisable, especially in Odisha. Many MLAs held this view because that would make the people feel helpless and desperate. I, too, wrote to Gandhiji from this perspective. He opposed the move. However, paying no heed to his words, I kept attending the assembly taking due permission from our leader Swami Bichitrananda.

Several MLAs from the Congress Party had already quit the assembly. However, they used to visit the assembly when they had some special work. I had presented the Hindu Women's Bill in the assembly. Many of the good points enumerated in the bill were being objected to by the Congress leaders themselves. I had the intention to get some good social work, related to women's development, done during the jail terms of these leaders. I had the double motive of availing this opportunity and saving the people during the war conditions. The Congress leaders, who were disciples of Gandhi, looked upon me with envy and used to oppose my initiative and action. I had decided not to quit the assembly so that I could do some good work with the support of the Opposition, in the absence of these people. I had rejected outright the Opposition party leaders' offer of ministership, 200 acres of land, and one lakh rupees in cash.

Although I had differences of opinion with Gandhiji and disagreement with the Congress party decision, the fact remains that I jumped into fire at a very early age for India's struggle for freedom under the inspiring leadership of Gandhiji. I had not abandoned the sanctified ideals and values of a yogic life for the sake of money, status, and position. Guided by Gandhiji's elevated spiritual ideals, I have been saved from many dangerous and difficult situations. I have been able to cross an ocean of hardships and find the bank. I had been left alone, as if in a vast desert, while my husband and my son were in prison. However, I had come out of it unscathed. I had not let the name of my ideal, Gandhiji, and my own name tarnish. My lifeboat did not capsize and drown mid-ocean during such a troubled period due to Gandhiji. That is Gandhiji's direct contribution to me and my life. I shall ever remain indebted to him for this. I have not wavered the least from my path and never ever slipped down as a result of Gandhiji's blessings.

After receiving my letter, he had even written to his relative Rajaji and his disciple K.M. Munshi to visit the assembly. This is the sign of his strong conscience and greatness. He made no distinction between the high and the low, the big leaders and the small ones. He used to judge all as common people having a combination of good and bad qualities.

My son Amitabha Mohapatra had gone to the Swaraj Ashram at the age of 16. The then Congress president of Cuttack district, Pranakrushna Padhiary, saw him wearing mill-spun clothes. He scolded him and directed him to leave the ashram compound and the Congress office. He instructed him not to come inside without wearing khadi clothes. When Amitabha narrated this incident in a sad tone, I immediately wrote to Gandhiji about this: 'You are inspiring the nation's youth to join the Swaraj movement by the use of khadi, purification of the self, and by the spinning of the wheel. However, the Congress leaders here behave badly with them arousing their ire and hatred. How, then, will they wear khadi and join the Congress?' I wrote about Padhiary in detail. Gandhiji replied to me after four days and also sent a copy of his letter to Padhiary. He had written in sadness, condemning Padhiary's bad manners. He had instructed Padhiary to beg forgiveness of Amitabha and me. However, Padhiary was no Mahatma to admit before the whole nation that he had committed a Himalayan blunder. He just wrote a letter to me to convey that he was sorry, but wrote deceivingly to Gandhiji, 'Sarala Devi is the spouse of my friend Bhagirathi Mohapatra. I had said all that not to hurt him, but to advise him.' Gandhiji never ignored an incident considering it trivial. He never sought to protect anyone because the latter was close to him or out of bias against anyone. He never tried to prove a point by mobilizing the majority opinion in its favour. He wrote me another letter of advice. I used to reply to his every letter. I had no fear of him. Rather, I looked upon him as my father. His words were as obligatory for me as the words of the Vedas.

I could not believe in the news of his death. When the vehicle of the All India Radio arrived at my doorstep to pick me up, I went weeping to the broadcasting station. There, too, mine was the first condolence message on Gandhiji's sad demise. I said in that message, 'Today, the father of our nation has left us, leaving tears in our eyes. Now there is no one to look after us. The country has turned fatherless, and so, helpless. Gandhiji left and took along with him truth and non-violence from the national character. His glory and greatness left with him. He left our nation in darkness, leaving behind no wealth for our future.'

A huge number of people had assembled in his *sraddha sabha* (funeral ceremony) at the bank of the river Kathajodi. Unknown to me, tears streamed down my eyes. I learnt about it only later.

In the literary gathering at the Ramachandra Bhawan, I could speak nothing in front of the audience. Tears choked my eyes and throat. I rose to speak but stood dumb. I am one of the unfortunate ones who have now been deprived of the shelter of his feet to which we had once surrendered, and whose tenets of truth and non-violence we have remained faithful to.

# Art and National Life

# Art and Culture in National Life*

A rt and culture are twins, born of the same parents. The two are inseparable; in fact, they are mutually reinforcing. Indian art stands firmly on the edifice of Indian culture. The ancient sculptors and painters whose art blossomed in different parts of the country had strong cultural foundations. The frescoes of Ajanta, the temple murals of South India, the architecture of the Buddhist stupas of Bihar, the expressions of the visual arts in Uttar Pradesh, and the fine arts of our own Utkal, which are so highly prized, are all based on the canons of Indian *kala shastra* (aesthetics). Our dress, ornaments, musical instruments, tools and weapons, postures and body movements, shapes and configurations, and our comic conventions are all born

* Originally titled 'Ama Jatiya Jibanare Kala O Sanskritara Prabhava', this essay first appeared in Asanta Kali, 3rd Year, No. 9, September, and later in Sarala Devi: Lekhika, Sanskarika, Biplabini, Sachidananda Mohanty (ed.) (Cuttack: Agraduta Publications, 2004), pp. 217–20. Translated by Bikram K. Das.

out of the air and soil of this country. Not just the representation of human beings but even that of birds, beasts, trees, plants, and flowers reveals a certain unity that is unmistakably Indian. We have seen many different models of aesthetics reflected in the sculpture and visual art of different countries. The artefacts created by the sculptors of ancient Greece indicate the artistic heights they had attained, but they also bear witness to the uniqueness of Indian art, in its representations of natural forms and display of artistic imagination and design. The stone carvings, clay figurines, and shell ornaments created in primitive times, as well as the metal ornaments crafted in the succeeding ages, represent man's response to the beauty of nature—a paradigm of the human race being born anew after the Apocalypse, through the miracle of 'Nada Brahma' (cosmic sound), like the human voice imitating the call of birds, which first gave expression to the artistic urge. The hunger for beauty, which is enshrined in thousands of years of tradition, has stirred the human spirit in every age and manifested itself in the free creation of artistic forms. This eternal quest, which inspires man to compete with the Creator, has brought glory to the race. The forms, flavours, odours, and sensations of the earth have knocked at the doors of man's consciousness at each moment and aroused him into creative endeavour.

It is not through forms and images alone that he has given shape to his innermost feelings: the doors have opened wide. Through symbols and gestures he has brought the world of fantasy to life on this earth. The human civilization spans centuries. It is man's engagement with art that has pulled him out of the darkness of primitive times on to the path of progress. It is this that has enabled man to overcome his brutish nature and plunge into the ocean of beauty, discovering untold gems, to transcend his own confines and become one with the limitless, to light up the strife-ridden world of everyday realities with the illumination and hope of creativity. His aesthetic aspirations have not been restricted to the mute world of sculpture and the visual arts; they have found expression and resonance in poetry and music. In order to overcome the harsh realities of everyday life, the artist creates garments for the body, ornaments, gardens, palaces, and other artefacts. The demand for the *pran vayu* (the breath of life) is so pressing that it cannot be compared to anything else. Just as life would be totally impossible without the pran vayu, similarly it could not be sustained even for a moment without art. An inalienable bond between life and art, enduring from birth to death, has existed since the beginning of creation. This longing for the beautiful is as inexorable as the Brahma (the all-pervading absolute) and it is for this that the artist has always been placed on the highest pedestal, for it is the artist who first brings the awareness of beauty to ordinary human beings, filling them with the desire to seek beauty in the bosom of nature, giving them a taste of *sat* (truth), *chitta* (consciousness), and ananda.

The artist opens up the first doors to the treasure house of creation, making any further quest unnecessary. The joy which art brings to the ordinary man can be compared to the taste of amrit; his eyes see the abundance of beautiful forms hidden behind ordinary things. He smells the aroma of mango blossoms, the fragrance of the winds; hears the melodious warbling of birds; and feels the touch of silver in the faint moonlight—everything combines to form an endless stream of beauty.

That the creativity of the artist had left a deep imprint on the consciousness of the common people of Odisha is proved by the ruins at Konark and the temples at Ekamra Kanan (Bhubaneswar). It is difficult to imagine that this impoverished state had once been a temple of the arts. Art was worshipped in every Odia home; every life was touched by it. That is why illiterate housewives embellished their huts with exquisite *muruja* patterns—floral and animal motifs drawn on floors and walls. Such was their sense of proportion in design that no scales or compasses were required to draw the lines. What skill and artistry they showed in producing various handicrafts out of metal, wood, grass, or stalks of paddy, enriching their lives with forms, colours, and odours! Men joined their wives in decorating their homes. Gardens lent elegance to ordinary dwellings. The perfume of flowers carried minds to the world of music and thence to poetry. Folk literature thrived; treasures of human creativity were passed on to future generations of Odias.

Meanwhile, in other courtyards the throbbing of drums merged with the tinkling of *nupurs* (bells dancers wear on ankles) and the music of veenas. The changing seasons were celebrated with festivities. Merchants crossed the seas in ships shaped like swans and peacocks by Odia carpenters, to trade with people of distant lands.

However, how long can our people survive only by singing about past glories? Do our artistic traditions still live?

*Literature and Religion/Spirituality*

# Katha Ramayana*

## Adya Kanda

A bove, against the backdrop of the panorama of 'spiritual consciousness', the characters Jeevatma [the spirit of the self] and Mana [the insight] are conversing.

JEEVATMA:

> Behold, my friend,
> How King Dasaratha and Sumantra, his oarsman,
> Are floating across the surging tides
> Clutching at a log of wood.

* Extracted from Katha Ramayana by Sri Sri Sitaram Das Omkarnath and translated from Hindi into Odia by Sarala Devi, this piece first appeared in Sarala Devi: Lekhika, Sanskarika, Biplabini, Sachidananda Mohanty (ed.) (Cuttack: Agraduta Publications, 2004), pp. 162–97. Translated into English by Snehaprava Das.

MANA:

> But who is the person there holding out a casket
> To the jaws of a large whale?

JEEVATMA:

> He is not an ordinary person
> King Ravana he is, the ruler of Lanka
> The demon with faces ten
> The heaven, the earth, and the hell underneath,
> Lord Indra, the moon god, the wind,
> And Death itself tremble in fear
> At the mention of his name—
> He has shut up Kaushalya,
> The princess of Koshala, and held her
> Before the whale's jaws!

MANA: Why did he do that, my friend?

*(In the royal court of Ravana: The subject of discussion is the fate of Dasaratha.)*

JEEVATMA:

> Behold now,
> Down below in the golden domain of Lanka
> The palace of Ravana the demon king
> Settled on the throne in the royal court
> Wait and see what all transpires,
> Soon you will come to know everything.

*(The courtroom in Ravana's palace. Ravana on the throne and the courtiers and Lord Brahma in their respective seats.)*

RAVANA *(to Brahma)*: O Lord Brahma, it is universally accepted that your commandment is inexorable. But I do not agree. I am sure that with virtue, wealth, intense passion, and spiritual enlightenment, one might be able to challenge it.

BRAHMA: You are driveling; no one on earth has the capacity to reverse what I ordain.

RAVANA (*emphatically*): I have the capacity to do that. Ravana makes his own rules and decides his own fate. He does not acknowledge the decrees of destiny.

BRAHMA: Which one of my ordainments were you able to defy? Could you give an instance?

RAVANA: I have told you the other day that I am immortal. No one, be he a demon or an angel, can kill me, let alone the monkeys and men—I feed on them. I have received the boon of immortality from you through deceit. But you presaged that a human being, a prince will be the cause of my death. When I enquired, you revealed that Prince Ramachandra, the son of Dasaratha, the king of Ayodhya, and Kaushalya, the princess of Koshala, will be the one to slay me. I went to Ayodhya and found young Dasaratha boating in the river Saryu. He would marry, I learnt, the princess of Koshala after five days. There was revelry and merrymaking everywhere. The capital city of Ayodhya was rejoicing, all set to celebrate the grand occasion. I declared war on Ayodhya ... many were killed ... Dasaratha drowned in the river Saryu. Reaching Koshala thereafter, I abducted the princess and shut her up in a casket. I put the casket inside the whale's jaws. Haven't I proved your oracle wrong? I tell you, your commandment cannot make any impact on my fate. I am the master and maker of destiny, I am above destiny.

BRAHMA: *Om, punyaham, punyaham, punyaham* (may the day be auspicious).

RAVANA (*in surprise*): Why do you call the day auspicious?

BRAHMA: A marriage is being solemnized through the exchange of garlands.

RAVANA: Where? And who are getting married?

BRAHMA: King Dasaratha and Princess Kaushalya … the marriage is being celebrated inside the casket. I am blessing them.

RAVANA: How is that possible? I have killed both of them.

BRAHMA: You are wrong. No one has perished as you believe. Dasaratha and Sumantra drifted to an island in the middle of the ocean with the help of a log of wood. The casket in which Kaushalya had been shut up had floated there too. As two whales fought over the casket Dasaratha opened the lid and discovered the princess. Their marriage was solemnized inside the casket according to the Gandharva practice, by exchanging garlands. All these events were preordained by me. And now, you will bring the casket here and send them back to Ayodhya. That is what I have decreed.

RAVANA: What are you saying! It is impossible!

BRAHMA: Nothing is impossible. My commandments do not recognize the difference between possible and impossible. You can see the proof for yourself.

RAVANA: All right. (*He turns to look at Nikumbha*) Nikumbha, go to the island immediately and bring the casket here.

NIKUMBHA: As you command, my Lord! (*Leaves.*)

RAVANA: O grand old father Brahma, I find what you say difficult to believe. Dasaratha had drowned in the river Saryu, and the casket carrying Kaushalya was sent floating in the ocean. How could they both come together? How can I accept the truth of this incredible coincidence! I think that old age has unhinged your mind.

BRAHMA: Well, just wait and watch. Very soon all your doubts will be cleared.

(*Nikumbha returns with the casket over his head. He brings down the casket and sets it on the floor.*)

RAVANA (*lifts the lid, finds Dasaratha, Kaushalya, and Sumantra inside, and steps back in shock*): What do I see here! Dasaratha and Kaushalya! I cannot believe my eyes.

(*Dasaratha, Kaushalya, and Sumantra stepped out of the casket and bowed in salutation to Brahma. In a quick movement Ravana pulls out his sword from its sheath and brandishes it threateningly at Dasaratha and others.*)

RAVANA (*ominously*): Who will come to your rescue now?

BRAHMA: Beware, Ravana! The consequences will be disastrous if you touch even the tip of their hair. You had shut one person in the casket and put it in the whale's jaws. But three have come out of it now. Remember, millions will come out of this casket unless you control your impulse. Rama will appear at this very moment and destroy you.

(*Ravana turns pale and returns the sword into the sheath.*)

BRAHMA: Make arrangements to send the newly wed couple to Ayodhya with due honour if you wish to remain alive for some more time.

RAVANA (*to Kumbha*): Take them to Ayodhya respectfully as Lord Brahma says.

KUMBHA: As you command, my Lord! (*To Dasaratha*) Kindly all of you sit inside this casket. I will carry it over my head to Ayodhya.

(*Dasaratha and others bow to Bramha and step into the casket. Kumbha lifts it to his head and strides out.*)

(*The backdrop of the panorama of spiritual consciousness. The characters are Jeevatma and Mana.*)

JEEVATMA:

> Behold, my friend,
> The proud Ravana sits with his head hanging low,
> Pale-faced, eyes brimming with tears.
> The courtiers stand speechless
> And Lord Brahma watches the scene
> With a small smile of amusement.
> The invincible ruler of Lanka
> Has never experienced such humiliation.
> Shocked beyond his wits at the
> Unexpected turn of events.

MANA:

> Strange indeed, my friend,
> How he watches his defeat
> In utter helplessness.
> Now let us proceed, Saketa!

# Tulasi Das: A Play*

## Act One

*Scene One*

(*Prelude.*)
Mahadev, Rama Rama
Bam bam—
Jai Rama, jai Rama!

(*Enter Goddess Durga.*)

DURGA:

> O Lord, the epitome of bliss,
> What is the cause of such great delight?

  * Extracted from '*Pancha Pradipa*', this piece first appeared in *Sarala Devi: Lekhika, Sanskarika, Biplabini*, Sachidananda Mohanty (ed.) (Cuttack: Agraduta Publications, 2004), pp. 162–97. Translated by Snehaprava Das.

> Your wild dance of *Tandava*
> Through Mount Kailash
> Is sending tremors of fright.

SHIVA:

> Tell me, dear,
> When do you find your Shankar cheerless?
> Always happy, free of care,
> Lost in the love of Lord Rama
> He feels so blessed;
> Dwells in the cremation grounds
> Dances with the spirits in delight
> And chants the name of Rama day and night.

FIRST VALET OF SHIVA: My Lord, let me dance once more.

DURGA:

> Something special in all these
> Dancing and singing do I find
> And I guess there must be a strong
> Reason behind ...

SHIVA:

> Goddess Bhabani, you can read everyone's mind
> Nothing happens of which you know not.
> It is true that an event auspicious
> Has filled me with happiness a lot.

DURGA: I am eager to hear the good news from your lips, O my Lord!

SHIVA:

> Dearest mine, listen then,
> To preach and promulgate the glorious name of Lord Rama
> The great sage Valmiki has descended
> On earth once again.

Once again with the chanting of the holy name of the lord
The earth will be flooded with a divine joy
Since the ignorant earthlings
Now under the evil influence of *The Kali*
The original epic they fail to read and enjoy,
Will, in the diction of the common man,
Rewrite the Ramayana, and let all,
Be he a fool or wise one, a Brahmin or a lowbred,
Drink the nectar of the Lord's name
From the fever and fret of the world
It will bring them a blissful respite ...
The world will reverberate with the name of Rama
As long as the sun and the moon shine in the sky
But not just this, there is another occasion
To cause happiness has of late come by....

DURGA:

What is that?

SHIVA:

My Lord 'Vishnu', who, taking a human form,
Has flooded the lands of Banga and Utkala
With the sacred current of the blissful chants of His name,
First in the holy Vrindavan, and finally the Neelachala ...
And after having basked His loved ones in the
Nectar of devotion, is returning to His
Abode permanent
To draw the magic flow of that serene love
Into the arid land of Rajasthan
He has sent a *gopi* (consort).
That gopi, taking a human form, is born
In the royal dynasty of Mewar,

Princess Mirabai, within no time would
Send musical tides of her devotion.
Her songs will travel to reach the far-off corners
Making their melodious way through the aridness
And turn Rajasthan as holy as the Lord's own dwelling
place.
Lord Hari that sojourns the heaven
With the queen of Mewar a love-game will play
Every voice would sing the devotional lyrics
Mirabai versed; her music will ring in the air
And carry the land in its serene sway …
Overwhelmed with the joy the news brought
I am intoning the name of Rama and dancing in this
way …

DURGA:

Great news!
My heart weeps for my children on earth
Passing through difficult times
Under evil Kali's behest,
Chanting of the names of Rama and Krishna
Will bring them peace and rest;
The earth will be transformed to heaven
When the holy songs will be recited,
All pain forgotten, my children will live
Happy and contented.

SHIVA:

There is one thing that worries me
Of Mewar's royal dynasty you are as
The tutelary goddess venerated,
But Mira will ignore you and will dedicate
To Lord Krishna all her love.

DURGA:

> I will be even more delighted
> The pleasure I derive when people worship me
> Grows multifold if my lords Rama and Krishna
> Are worshipped instead.

(*Enter Narayana.*)

NARAYANA:

> I, too, derive joy enormous when
> My mother goddess and my Lord Shiva
> Are held in higher esteem than me,
> A devotee that prays to Shiva and Durga
> To me always dearer than my life will be.

SHIVA:

> O epitome of mercy!
> Your arrival here comes as a great surprise!

DURGA:

> Your arrival here, O Lord
> Is an act of extreme kindness.
> The sight beatific has filled my heart
> With a rare happiness.
> But isn't Kamala there with you?
> My eyes are thirsty to have a glimpse
> Of my goddess.

NARAYANA:

> I am gratified at
> Receiving a darshan of the sire of this earth
> And the mother goddess
> I have hurried here at the Lord's beckoning,
> And had not found occasion to let Goddess Kamala
> Know of my coming.

SHIVA:

> A great devotee is born on earth
> Tulasi Das is his name,
> And to preach and promulgate your name
> Will be his mission divine,
> Hence I dance with my ghost companions here
> Carried away by a joy sublime.

NARAYANA:

> It is with your blessings
> This Tulasi Das has taken birth,
> It is the nectar of your name that
> Has drawn him to this earth.
> By your grace only he'll have the fortune
> To have a glimpse of me,
> In the person of Mahavira I will advise him
> And by his side will always be.

SHIVA:

> How very fortunate am I!
> I shall keep by your devotee
> To listen to your holy name from his lips,
> A priceless treasure of benediction you are
> The Saviour whose grace can be attained
> Only through austere practice.
> How great it is an occasion for me!
> Come my companions, let us sing His name
> And dance around him in glee.

*Scene Two*

(*The street passing by Tulasi Das's house; enter two villagers.*)

FIRST VILLAGER: Brother, whose house is this?

SECOND VILLAGER: Don't you know? Tulasi Das Dubeyji lives here.

FIRST VILLAGER: How would I know? I hardly stay here. But tell me about him.

SECOND VILLAGER: He is the son of an honest man called Atmaram Dubey, who was a royal priest. Strange things are said about this Tulasi Das.

FIRST VILLAGER: Really? What strange things?

SECOND VILLAGER: He was born with two rows of teeth in his mouth, and he came off his mother's womb chanting the name of Rama.

FIRST VILLAGER: What are you saying! This is unheard of! Tell me, what happened next?

SECOND VILLAGER: The midwife in the natal chamber called out loudly when she saw all this.

FIRST VILLAGER: That was quite obvious. And the baby? Did it chant only the name of Rama, or did it say anything else too?

SECOND VILLAGER: He kept saying Rama endlessly. Extremely puzzled, his father consulted some soothsayers. But they, too, did not have an immediate explanation. 'It would take at least three days to find out the reason why the child behaves so strangely,' they said.

FIRST VILLAGER: What happened after that?

SECOND VILLAGER: The poor mother passed away after giving birth to the child. Before her death she had given away all her jewellery to a trusted maid and advised her to leave the place with the baby boy. The maid did as she was told. She left with the baby as soon as its mother died.

FIRST VILLAGER: Didn't the father search for his son?

SECOND VILLAGER: No. He considered the child ominous as his birth had killed his mother.

First villager: And then?

Second villager: The maid brought up the child. But sadly enough, she, too, died when the boy was only five.

First villager: How unfortunate! What happened to the poor baby?

Second villager: The little boy had nowhere to go. He sat forlorn under a tree by the roadside. No one called him or offered him any food. 'He is inauspicious!' they said. 'He would bring bad luck to the home that shelters him.'

First villager: What a pity!

Second villager: It is said that the goddess Durga came down every day to feed the boy.

First villager: That must be true! The mother goddess always takes care of the destitute. Isn't it amazing!

Second villager: A saint came to the village one day. He sought permission of the villagers to take the boy with him. The villagers wanted the inauspicious boy out of the village—the sooner the better, they thought and readily agreed.

First villager: Were not the villagers baser than beasts?

Second villager: They were but instrumental ... after all, it is the will of God!

First villager: And what happened then?

Second villager: I don't remember exactly what happened during all these years. He was a changed man when he came back. A man of wisdom he had become, and unceasingly uttered the holy name of Lord Rama. The villagers, greatly impressed by his wisdom and piety, entreated him to stay in the village. They also got a house built for him. He wanted to keep away from the encumbrances of family life and decided not to marry, but the villagers put a lot of pressure on him and finally he got married after much persuasion.

First villager: And now? Has he settled down happily?

SECOND VILLAGER: Certainly. People are of the opinion that he is an uxorious husband.

FIRST VILLAGER: Well, we will meet this Dubeyji some other day. (*Exit both.*)

(*The front door of Dubeyji's house opens. His wife Ratnamala comes out of the door.*)

TULASI DAS (*calls from inside*): Ratnamala! Ratnamala!

RATNAMALA (*aside*): I shall not answer. Let's see how he reacts.

TULASI DAS (*from inside the house*): Ratnamala! O Ratnamala! There is no sign and sound of her. Where are you, Ratnamala?

(*Ratnamala does not answer. Enter Tulasi Das.*)

TULASI DAS: You are sitting here! Can't you hear me! Why don't you answer?

RATNAMALA: I was with you until some time back! Why do you want to see me again?

TULASI DAS: It's because I haven't seen you for a long time.

RATNAMALA: You call this a long time?

TULASI DAS: Don't you know that my eyes forget to blink when they don't see you? That your absence blinds them?

RATNAMALA: Tell me honestly—don't you feel awkward following me all the time?

TULASI DAS: Not at all. Instead, I feel utterly lost when you are not with me!

RATNAMALA: I have heard that you were a great devotee of Lord Rama before marriage, and always chanted the Lord's name. Where did that devotion vanish?

TULASI DAS: Indeed. I used to utter the Lord's name all the time. I loved the Lord. But marriage has exorcised that obsession. Now you are enthroned in my heart and all my thoughts are about you.

RATNAMALA: I am undoubtedly a fortunate woman to receive so much love from my husband. But won't you agree that there is something called social decorum? The women of the village and the neighbours stay away from me since you never leave my company. They jeer at me and make fun of us behind my back. Don't such things embarrass you?

TULASI DAS: Never mind how the outsiders behave. Let me tell you the inside thing. Instead of Lord Vishnu's name, the name 'Ratnamala' automatically comes to my lips when I say my evening prayers. It is your image that comes to my mind instead of Gayatri when I offer my worship in the morning. I see you when I try to focus my mind on Lord Rama. Day and night, whether awake or asleep, I dream of you. Your name is my prayer (*litany*) … you are the only goddess I worship.

RATNAMALA (*wraps the end of her sari around her neck and bows at Tualsi Das's feet*): Your love has made my life attain fulfillment, but the excess of anything is improper. Are you aware that people look upon you as effeminate?

TULASI DAS: Ratnamala is the world for Tulasi Das. Nothing else matters to him.

RATNAMALA: Suppose I die …?

TULASI DAS: I, too, will die with you!

(*Enter Shivaram. He bows his head to greet the couple.*)

TULASI DAS: Hello, Shivaram. How are you?

SHIVA: I am fine.

RATNA: What about Father and Mother? Are they all right?

SHIVA: Yes, sister, they are fine too.

TULASI: What brought you here so urgently?

SHIVA: Father and Mother are anxious to see sister. She hasn't visited our home since the last four or five years. They have requested you to send her with me for a few days.

TULASI: Now you have put me in a difficult situation. How is that possible? I can't live without your sister even for a moment.

SHIVA: It is just a matter of a few days! I shall bring her back to you myself.

TULASI: How could you realize the pain of separation from wife? You are not married. Leave alone 'a few days', I can't let her part with me even for a few hours!

RATNA: Please allow me to go to my parents for only three days. I long so much to see them! You are not able to experience the intensity of my longing since you have no parents.

TULASI: Three days? I can't let you out of my sight even for an hour!

RATNA: You have always prevented me from visiting my parents on this pretext. I beg of you, please allow me this time.

TULASI: I promise you that I will do anything you ask me other than this. (*Shiva bows to both of them and turns to leave.*)

SHIVA: Okay then. Brother-in-law, I must leave now.

TULASI: Why so much haste? You should leave in the afternoon after taking the midday meal with us.

SHIVA: No, I can't stay that long.

TULASI: Don't be angry! (*To Ratna*) Call your brother inside. (*Shiva enters the house.*)

RATNA: Listen to me, Shiva, come here the day after tomorrow when your brother-in-law is not home. I will steal away with you. Nothing will come off these requests and entreats … Come inside, I will get you some refreshments.

(*Exit.*)

## Scene Three

*(The home of Tulasi Das's parents-in-law; the inner section of the house. Chapala, the wife of Ratnamala's brother, and Ratnamala are talking.)*

CHAPALA: I am so glad to see you after this long. Didn't you ever remember me while you were at your husband's house?

RATNA: Of course I remembered you, but there was nothing I could do about it. My husband never lets me out of his sight. You know Mother has sent people several times to fetch me home. But he always turned down her requests.

CHAPALA: But I must say you are a lucky woman. Men have a fickle mind. They can always be unsteady in their marital love.

RATNA: You can say that, but sometimes I am overburdened with it. He keeps by my side almost all the time. He even follows me to the river when I go to take a bath. No woman in the neighbourhood comes to our home or befriends me due to this. I had to steal away from my home with Shiva while he was out somewhere for some work and was not supposed to return till evening. I knew he would have never allowed me otherwise.

CHAPALA: How do you think he is going to react when he does not find you at home on his return?

RATNA: I think he would somehow spend the night at home and come here in the morning.

CHAPALA: In my opinion you shouldn't have come without his knowledge. He must have felt very bad about it.

RATNA: Let him be ... I haven't come to my parents since the last five years or so. They don't have much time left in this world. I couldn't hold back the desire to meet them any longer. I wouldn't let anyone stop me, be he my husband or anybody else! Anyway, even if it's love, it turns distasteful when it exceeds the limit.

*(A voice was heard at the front yard of the house. Shivaram, Shivaram!)*

CHAPALA: Who is calling?

RATNA: O my God! He has reached here even as I talk about him!

(*Shivaram opens the door and greets Tulasi Das.*)

SHIVA: Come inside, brother-in-law. (*He calls out to his sister.*) Apa, brother-in-law is here.

(*Shivaram leads Tulasi to the inner section of the house.*)

RATNA: I can see that. (*She bows.*)

CHAPALA: Do you recognize me? We haven't met since your marriage.

TULASI: I guess you are the elder sister-in-law. (*He bows to offer his respects.*)

CHAPALA: Stop it, please! You are a saintly Brahmin. You are not supposed to bow to me.

RATNA: Haven't you had your meal?

TULASI (*in an accusing tone*): Meals! Hmm!

RATNA: Just one look at his face tells that he hasn't eaten all day. Get him some refreshment quickly. Shiva, tell Mother that your brother-in-law has come, and get him water to wash himself.

(*Exit both Chapala and Shivaram.*)

TULASI (*to Ratnamala*): A fine person you are!

RATNA: And you? Aren't you a fine person too?

TULASI: How could you leave in this manner when you know I can't live without you even for a moment?

RATNA: When did you reach Rajapur?

TULASI: In the evening; I found the house in total darkness. A graveyard-like silence reigned everywhere. I looked around for you frantically. The maid Gelhi told me that you have left with Shivaram for here. I felt as if I was struck by a thunderbolt. My heart stopped beating and my head began to spin. The world seemed to have disappeared inside a thick black veil. The maid asked me to take food, but who would eat? Tulasi Das was no longer there—whom she asked to eat was only his lifeless body. His soul was not there. I rushed here without even bothering to wash myself or change my clothes. Gelhi tried to stop me, but it was in nobody's power to change my mind. I have walked all the way here from Rajapur uttering your name. How cruel are you!! What an unusually hardened heart do you have! You can't even imagine how desperately I miss you! (*His voice choked*) Did it ever occur to you what I must have gone through when I didn't find you at home? How could you be so indifferent to the feelings of someone who loves you so much? (*He weeps.*)

RATNA: Please ... don't you weep. You are my husband, my lord, and my mentor. I have great respect for you, but I must tell you something today. Why do you have such a great attraction for this body of flesh and blood? After all, it is the body of an ordinary woman—subject to perish in the dust. You have become so mad after it that you have rushed here blindly, without caring if you could survive the strain of the journey? If you had even a hundredth part of such love and attachment for Lord Raghunath, you would have sanctified not only this life of yours but even the afterlife. Shame, shame on you!!

(*Tulasi stood in silence for some time, his arms crossed over his chest.*)

TULASI (*as if awakened from a deep slumber*): How true! What an enigma is this! What a deep stupor has numbed my soul? It was an illusion I have been chasing mindlessly all along. O my Lord Rama, an epitome of mercy you are—your boundless mercy has lifted the curtain of blindness. O Lord, where are you? How can I get a glimpse of you? (*He turns to face Ratnamala*) Goddess mine! You are my guide and mentor— you have pulled me out of the depths of ignorance and shown me the light of wisdom. You have opened my eyes to the truth. I am indebted to you for this great favour of yours. But I have nothing to give you in return except my salutations. (*He bends to bow to Ratnamala.*)

RATNA (*stepping back in surprise*): What is this? What are you doing? I am your wife. Why do you bow to me?

TULASI: No, you are no longer my wife. You are the goddess—a rare, priceless guide you are. You have guided me to the path of truth and wisdom. O goddess mine, accept my respects. (*He looks around like a man under some spell*) Where is Lord Rama? Where? How shall I get a glimpse of the Lord? (*He hurries outside.*)

RATNA (*shocked at her husband's reaction*): O my God! What is the matter with him? Listen to me, please! Where are you going away? Shiva, run after your brother-in-law and stop him. O my dear sister-in-law, what have I done? I have brought ruin upon myself by my own action. I have destroyed my life! Why in the name of devil did I say such things? Let me see where he has gone. (*Leaves in a hurry.*)

## Scene Four

(*The holy land of Kashi. Tulasi Das is seen walking by the side of the river Ganges with a small pot of water in his hand. He is singing a morning hymn.*)

> Arise, O Lord merciful,
> In this auspicious hour of the morning,
> The moonlight has faded and to meet her mate
> The she-swallow has left,
> The birds have begun to sing;
> Wafting fondly the leaves of the trees
> There blows a cool, soft breeze;
> In the eastern sky glows a crimson light

As the rising sun appears
Dispelling the darkness of the nights;
Slowly the lotus opens its petals
The morning to greet
At the music of the bemused bees
That circle around it;
In great joy does Tulasi Das
Gaze at the Lord's lotus face.
The lord benevolent as if invites him
With open arms
And generously showers His grace.

(*Enter two men.*)

FIRST MAN: Tell me, brother, who is this person?

SECOND MAN: He is Tulasi Das, an astute devotee of Lord Rama, and he keeps uttering His name constantly.

FIRST MAN: Where does he live?

SECOND MAN: He always keeps the company of saints and seers. He is a man of extremely calm temperament.

FIRST MAN: How long has he been here in Kashi?

SECOND MAN: For about a year. I have never come across such a mild and decent sadhu. He is never irritated, nor does he grumble like the other sadhus. Most of the reputed pundits of Kashi and other devotees hold him in high esteem.

FIRST MAN: Can you tell me who is regarded as the most knowledgeable sadhu in Kashi these days?

SECOND MAN: Sure, he is Srimad Madhusudan Saraswati, a man of great wisdom and a staunch advocate of the Advaitavada philosophy.

FIRST MAN: Advaitavada? What is that?

SECOND MAN: It is the cult that believes that only the Brahmin is real—the supreme truth—while the mundane world is an illusion. Man, in his ignorance, mistakes the world as real just the way one mistakes a length of rope for a snake in the dark. It is through the study of the shastra that self-illumination is attained. The soul realizes the truth of 'Brahmo-asmi' or 'I am Brahma' and at that state of fulfillment the soul transcends the limitations of its earthly existence. The soul of the one that follows Advaitavada gets redeemed while he is alive and attains quick salvation after death.

FIRST MAN: All these are going above my head. Tell me more about this Advaitavadi sadhu.

SECOND MAN: Anyone who debates with him is vanquished. No one can argue with him and win. Every day hundreds and hundreds of such pundits, humiliated by their defeat, return heartbroken. And at last, Abadhuta Swami Paramahansa—a saint who wandered around nude—came to him. Madhusudan Saraswati greeted him and offered him his humble regards. 'Swamiji,' the nude saint said, 'you have cast off everybody as ignorant and are living in the solitude of your wisdom. I have one question for you; I hope you will answer me honestly. Don't you feel proud of yourself defeating all these seers and savants? (*The first man glances around furtively.*)

SECOND MAN: You are not listening. Why are you so restless?

FIRST MAN: I don't know but something strange is happening to me. My nerves feel frozen.

SECOND MAN: People say a ghost has taken up abode in this tree. Many claim to have seen it.

FIRST MAN: Is it? A ghost in the divine land of Kashi, where every soul is sure to attain salvation!!

SECOND MAN: This ghost is believed to be a sinner as well as virtuous at the same time. It dwells in this southern border of Kashi, perhaps with a hope to attain salvation some day.

FIRST MAN (*in surprise*): How is that possible?

SECOND MAN: It has committed a great sin due to which it has not attained salvation until now, and at the same time it has also committed some noble deeds due to which it has the fortune of living in this holy place.

FIRST MAN: Well, okay. Now tell me what else did the nude saint say to Swami Madhusudan Saraswati.

SECOND MAN: 'I must say that you are committing a sin by hurting their sentiments,' the nude saint said to Swamiji. Had the remark been made by anyone else than Swami Paramahansa, Swamiji probably would have laughed it away. But coming from a great saint like Paramahansa, the remark made a deep impact on him. 'Listen, O brother,' Swami Paramahansa explained, 'scholasticism and arrogant arguments always cast a negative influence on a man. One cannot enjoy the divine bliss unless he destroys these negative instincts by means of austere piety.' Swami Madhusudan Saraswati fell at Swami Paramahansa's feet and entreated him to teach a mantra for invoking God. The latter taught Swami Madhusudan a mantra to worship Lord Krishna. 'You will certainly have the fortune of attaining a glimpse of Lord Krishna in three months' time if you chant the mantra with faith and sincerity, and worship the Lord,' he advised before leaving. Following the advice, Swami Madhusudan worshipped the Lord, but Lord Krishna did not show Himself to Swamiji. Disappointed, Swami Madhusudan left Kashi.

FIRST MAN: Swami Paramahansa must have possessed extraordinary power, otherwise he would not have been able to influence a pundit of Madhusudan Saraswati's stature so easily. Tell me what happened after that.

SECOND MAN: After leaving Kashi, Madhusudan Saraswati went to Kapiladhara and dwelt there. As he was walking along the street, Swamiji met a person who belonged to a lowly class. 'People, even after practising austerity for life after life, fail to attain a glimpse of God,' the man said, 'and you accepted defeat after only three months!!'

FIRST MAN: Strange! How could he learn about Swamiji's endeavours?

SECOND MAN: Swamiji thought exactly the same thing. 'How could this man know about all this?' he wondered. Then he fell at the man's feet. Getting up, he found that the man was none other than his mentor Swami Paramahansa. Paramahansa asked Madhusudan Saraswati to worship the Lord with love. 'You will have a glimpse of the Lord if you worship Him and take His name with love,' he assured. Swamiji returned to Kashi. He practised austerity and worshipped Lord Krishna as he was advised. In the end the Lord showed Himself to Swamiji. He asked the pundit to write the prelude to the sacred text Srimad Bhagavadgita.

SECOND MAN: Where does this pundit live? Let us have a look at him.

*(Exit both. Tulasi Das enters singing the name of Rama. He pours water from a pot at the trunk of a tree; a spirit appears.)*

SPIRIT: A great devotee you are! Every day you offer me water. I am pleased. You may ask me for a boon.

TULASI: Kindly tell me who you really are and why are you wandering in the form of a spirit.

SPIRIT: Listen to me then, O devotee. I will tell you why I am here. In the past I was the royal priest in the kingdom of Vindhya. However, I was an abominable character with many vices. I was greedy, impious, and ignoble. I engaged in acts like offending the saints and degrading people. I stowed away a lion's share of the money and other valuables from what the king gave away to the Brahmins. I spoke harsh words and drove away people who came to my door asking for some water to drink. This is the reason why I have always been thirsty. The water you poured at this tree has finally quenched my great thirst.

TULASI (*curious*): How is it that you are here?

SPIRIT: I had accompanied the king to Kashi with the intention to pinch a sizable part from the charity he would offer to the sadhus and Brahmins here.

TULASI: Well ...

SPIRIT: A snake bit me on the way, and I died. However, Lord Bhima Vinayak stopped the angels of death who came to carry my soul away to hell. 'He may be a great sinner,' the Lord said to the angels, 'but since he has left home with a mind to come to the holy land of Kashi, his soul cannot be taken to hell. Let this sinner dwell in a tree in the outskirts of this holy land and suffer the punishment of insatiable hunger and thirst Lord Kala Bhairava has meted out to him. His soul will attain salvation only if he quells his thirst with the leftover water which a Brahmin devotee of Lord Rama pours from his pot at the base of this tree after performing his ablutions.' The propitious hour has arrived at last. I shall leave for heaven after granting you your wish. So please let me know of your wish.

TULASI: O great soul! Enable me to have a glimpse of Lord Rama.

SPIRIT: I don't have the power to do that, but I can show you the way to achieve your end. (*The spirit points to the spire of a temple in the distance*) Look at the tall temple there. Every day the holy Ramayana is recited there. Hanuman comes there every day in the guise of a leper. He is always the first to come and the last to leave. Pray to him. He can fulfil your wish. Now allow me to leave for heaven.

TULASI: May the blessings of Lord Shankara be with you there!

SPIRIT (*smiling in joy*): Let victory be thine, O great devotee Tulasi Das, let victory be thine. (*The spirit soars up towards the sky.*)


*Scene Five*

(*A Brahmin afflicted with leprosy waddles in, a stick in his hand. He looks about himself. Tulasi Das comes in a hurry and falls at his feet.*)

LEPER: Leave my feet; who in the name of God are you? Let go of my feet. Get off, quickly.

TULASI (*still clutching at the leper's feet*): You must take pity on me and fulfil my wish.

LEPER: I am a leper as you can see. How can I help you?

TULASI: Be kind not to pretend. I know who you really are!

LEPER: Really! Tell me then, who am I?

TULASI: You are Mahavir, the greatest of all devotees.

LEPER: How amusing! How can a leper like me be Mahavir?

TULASI: I will not let go of your feet until you take pity on me.

LEPER: Victory to Lord Rama. (*He leaps forward and takes the form of Mahavir*) Who are you? What do you want from me?

TULASI (*with folded hands*): O Mahavir, I want to have a glimpse of Lord Rama. Be kind to me and fulfil my wish.

MAHAVIR: You are the best among all the Lord's devotees.

TULASI: No, my Lord, I am a reprobate!

MAHAVIR: O good soul! I, too, know who you are! I also know why you have been born. I advise you to go to the mountain of Chitrakuta. Your wish will be fulfilled there. Victory to Lord Rama! Victory to Lord Rama!

TULASI: But where can I find *you*?

MAHAVIR: I shall always be there with you. (*Tulasi Das leaves chanting the name of Rama.*)

To preach the holy name of the Lord once again
And to sing of His glory,
Sage Valmiki has descended on this earth
In the person of Tulasi Das;
The name of Rama uttered endlessly
Will gratify my soul.

*Scene Six*

(*Tulasi Das at the mountain range of Chitrakuta in the forest.*)

TULASI:

Having made a thorough search across the
The forest and the mountain of Chitrakuta
I have reached here at last,
But my labour has been wasted it seems
I couldn't find the lord of my heart;
Several times I have climbed up to the mountain peak
And looked about from there,
But I could not see even a faint glimpse
Of my lord anywhere;
I have looked in the undercurrents of the Godavari
Hidden from the eyes it remains though,
On the slippery crystal rocks a number of times
I have walked along to and fro;
The Lord of whom Hanuman is a great devotee,
Who is Goddess Sita's beloved
My hope to see you is not fulfilled yet
I am so utterly disappointed;
Had the son of the Wind God betrayed my trust
And roused false hopes in me?
But that is impossible—as impossible as
The rising of the sun from the west would be;
His assurance is never to be doubted
O my Lord! Show yourself to this slave,
To catch a momentary look of you
How my poor heart does crave!
Wealth or happiness I do not need

To fix my gaze on your image charming as Kandarpa the
love god
Of a complexion bluish-green
As the freshly sprouted grass, that's what I long for,
Let me enjoy the bliss, O Rama;
O the slayer of pride, O the comforter of the soul;
I am not capable of unwavering devotion,
Nor do I know prayer or practise austerity,
I can only beg you with all my heart
To be merciful to appear before me;
An ocean of mercy you are, O Lord;
The most loved one of my hearts,
Alight, and show yourself, but alas!
I know my hope is belied at last;
He is Rama, the supreme Brahma,
The emperor of the universe whole,
A sinner, a villain, a woman's slave,
A creature disgraceful am I;
Why do I nurture a hope to attain
This impossible goal?
Why did you awaken this passion in me?
If they can't see you,
Of what use are my eyes?
I shall throw myself from this mountain peak
And put an end to my life;
But wait! What is this sound?
It is like the footfall of somebody
Is there someone around?
Perhaps it is the sound of His foot.
To have a look at the 'priceless gem of my heart',

Let me rush—but alas! It was perhaps an illusion,
The mountains and the woodlands around
Lay deserted under the scorching sun …

(*Rama and Lakshmana stride in, each carrying a bow and arrows.*)

RAMA: Where did the deer disappear?

LAKSHMANA (*pointing*): It ran away in this direction. (*Both exit quickly.*)

TULASI (*in wonderment*):

How handsome both the princes were!
They looked almost like Rama and Lakshmana.
I can hear someone singing a melodious tune
Let me see who the singer is …

*Scene Seven*

TULASI: An enchanting act of *Ramlila* is performed on the auspicious occasion of Ram Navami. All the actors who played the parts of Rama, Sita, Lakshmana, Sugriva, and Hanuman looked so real! It was a rare experience; I thought I was witnessing the real characters!

(*Enter a sadhu.*)

TULASI: Did you watch the Ramlila?

SADHU: Did you say Ramlila? Where?

TULASI: On the top of this mountain.

SADHU: How is it that Ramlila is being enacted in the month of Ashwin? Are you out of your mind?

TULASI: Why do you say that? I had just now been there, and I witnessed the act.

SADHU: Is it? Come, show me where the act is being staged.

(*Exit both. Mahavir enters incognito.*)

MAHAVIR: Tulasi Das has had the glimpse of the Lord twice, but he fails to realize it.

(*Enter Tulasi Das with the sadhu.*)

TULASI: I don't understand!

SADHU: You cannot, knave fellow! You are disoriented—you must consult a physician. (*Exit.*)

TULASI: Where are you, O Mahavir? Please appear before me. I am so thoroughly disgruntled. Be kind to help me.

MAHAVIR (*appearing in his huge form*): Why are you so doubtful?

TULASI (*bowing*): I convey my respects to you, my Lord! You know everything. You tell me: Was that which I saw only a trick that my vision played on me? Was it not the real thing—the real Ramlila?

MAHAVIR: You saw the princes Rama and Lakshmana. You again watched Lord Rama and all the others in the Ramlila. Don't you realize until now that you saw the Lord in reality?

TULASI (*extremely surprised*): In the name of God! What do you say? I thought the princes to be two lads playing the role of Rama and Lakshmana. How unfortunate I am! The Lord appeared before me, but I couldn't know. O great devotee of the Lord, it was possible only through your blessings. But a half-fulfilled hope nags me constantly. I could not touch the Lord's feet.

MAHAVIR: You must thank your stars that you could see the Lord twice. And don't you worry, you will have the opportunity of touching His feet. You have to sit at the bathing ghat of the river in Chitrakuta every day with a small bowl of sandalwood paste. You must put a mark of the paste on the forehead of everyone who comes up to the ghat after taking a dip in the river. One day Rama and Lakshmana will come there and you will put the mark of sandalwood paste on their forehead.

TULASI: Could I be fortunate enough to do so?

MAHAVIR: Certainly. But now you must come with me; I have something very important to tell you.

TULASI: As you say, my Lord.

(*Exit both. Enter Lord Shiva and Goddess Durga.*)

TULASI (*entering again*): What do I see! Am I awake or asleep? The father of the world, and the mother, too, have descended here. (*He falls at the feet of the god and the goddess.*)

SHIVA: O devotee Tulasi Das, it is the extraordinary power of your devotion that has brought me here. We have come to listen to the chanting of the holy name of Rama from your lips. You will be blessed to have a glimpse of Lord Rama here. Thereafter, you will return to Ayodhya and write the Ramayana.

TULASI: But, my Lord, I am an ignorant person.

SHIVA: I shall give you my blessings. It will awaken the poet in you. You will write the *Bhasa Ramayana* and the text will be regarded with reverence like the *Sam Veda*, until the end of the world. Every home will procure it and it will bring a spiritual bliss to everyone that reads it. The souls of millions of men and women will be redeemed through the recital of this holy text.

TULASI (*falls at the Lord's feet again*): O Lord, you have gratified me. But the insignificant creature that I am, I have nothing to offer you in return.

SHIVA: Get up, my child! You have to return nothing to me. (*Tulasi Das rises to his feet.*)

DURGA: Tulasi Das, do you recognize me?

TULASI: O Mother! You are the one who fed me when I was a child and saved my life! Victory to Gauri Shankara! Victory to Gauri Shankara!

*Scene Eight*

(*The hermitage of Tulasi Das at Kashi.*)

TULASI (*chants the name of Rama*): It is only because Hanuman had been kind to me that I have received Rama's darshan not once but thrice. Both the gods, Rama and Lakshmana, asked me to put the mark of sandalwood paste at the Ramaghat. My wish has been fulfilled. The moment I touched their foreheads to put the mark, I fainted. Mahavir brought me back to consciousness. After that Goddess Gauri and Lord Shankara, too, appeared before me and asked me to write the Ramayana. Obeying their command, I wrote the Ramayana in Hindi and completed it in two years, seven months, and twenty-six days.

(*Enter Mahavir. Tulasi Das bows before him.*)

MAHAVIR: Where is the Ramayana that you have written?

TULASI: Here it is, my Lord.

MAHAVIR: Won't you recite me some paragraphs?

TULASI (*recites*):
>   I invoke you, O Lord Ganesha and Goddess Saraswati,
>   Auspiciousness epitomized!
>   And offer my prayers to Lord Rama,
>   Enable me to effect in my verse
>   A harmonious and meaningful assemblage of
>   Alphabet for narration, and metrical versification:
>   The name of Rama is the ultimate thing,
>   It is the essence of all elements,
>   Be it the sun, the moon, or fire
>   He dwells in every animate and inanimate being!
>   He is Vishnu, Shiva, too, He is,
>   All the Vedas are contained in Him

Offering my prayers at His feet
That Supreme lord I always worship.
He is 'om';
That one syllable supreme
Holds the gist of all the Vedic wisdom.
He is Vishnu and Shiva
And all sects of human beings, I pray to Him,
The Intangible, Whole, and without a form.
On the lips of Tulasi, which is the door to his heart,
The bejewelled lamp of Rama's name
Burns bright,
The outside of Tulasi and his soul inside
Are illumined with its light,
Hold with care on the
Lamp stand of your tongue
The gem-studded lamp of Rama's name
Its light will illumine the darkness,
Follow Tulasi's words and let that light
Radiate through your body and your soul within shine.

MAHAVIR: Excellent, go on—sing more!

TULASI:

On the right of Lord Rama stands Lakshmana,
Janaki on the left,
Contemplating Him
I offer the holy basil leaves to the Lord
That signifies auspiciousness;
Try to solve the complex sum of 'Rama'
The result comes to zero in the end,
Through total surrender to the Lord

Ten times better result is gained.
Like a wish-granting tree is the Lord's name
In a land where the evil Kali takes his abode
Only one that chants Rama's holy name,
Says Tulasi Das, is fortunate like the basil
And obtains His grace;
Though Tulasi wastes his 'today'
Is lazy to utter the Lord's name,
But one who praises Him constantly
Is sure to attain prosperity and fame;
Even a lowly-born can attain glory
Through his unfailing devotion to the Lord
All evil, be it in a plant or a deity, is consecrated
By taking His name, and becomes famous in the world;
Without chanting the name of Rama
One cannot expect the Supreme Truth to attain,
Like expecting a lightning flash
In the absence of the clouds of rain;
Tulasi Das feels that the name of Rama
Holds all beliefs and all religion inside it
Like the sky holds all constellations
And the earth contains all the seed;
To rid the earth from all that is ominous;
Every day the name of Rama one must chant
Like the study of the Vedas and the Puranas,
For purifying the soul, this, too, is a pious act;
The name stands for love and the path of truth,
It is also the ultimate faith.
The utterance of the name, sings Tulasi Das,
Purges the soul of all defilement;

His deeds benign, His name a symbol of sublime joy,
Raghunath radiates a beatific glow;
Adorned with jewels, attired gracefully
He stands with His younger brother
Who is as charming and graceful too;
Rama, Bharata, Lakshmana and Shatrughana,
Auspicious are these names.
All wishes are fulfilled, everything is sanctified,
Take the name of Dasaratha along with them.

MAHAVIR:

As I listen to Lord Rama's tales of glory
My soul surges with a profound bliss
A long time since I haven't heard
A recital such as this.
O Tulasi Das, the incarnation of
Sage Valmiki you are,
When people writhe under evil Kali's oppression
You have come to rescue them
By flooding the world with
The nectar of the holy name.
The rich, the poor, the wise ones, and the fools
All men and women
Afflicted with the sinister designs of Kali
Will read the Ramayana written in their vernacular,
Will be gratified and a divine bliss will attain
In the majestic palace royal
Or in the hermits' huts.
The Ramayana will be regarded
With love and reverence a lot
Till the sun and the moon will shine in the sky,
Embarking upon this holy barge of

The recital of the Ramayana,
As if they are crossing a tiny pool of water
Across the turbulent ocean of life
The devotees will safely sail by
Day and night people will utter the Lord's name
Listening to that I will gratify myself too.
O great lover of the Lord
It has been possible only because of you.
O Tulasi Das, I am extremely pleased with you,
To the world you have done a great service.
Ask for a reward; tell me what is your wish?

TULASI:

O Lord, I have written the Ramayana
As commanded by you and offer you this gift,
To grant a wish mine to retain the devotion
And love for my lord in my heart.
I beg at your feet
Let the name of the Lord, and the tales
Of the Lord and the songs
Remain forever on my tongue.

MAHAVIR:

Granted! I will always be by your side.
Whenever the wish to see me awakens in you,
Pray to me, and I shall appear.

TULASI:

O' Lord mine, I am anxious to see
The Lord once again.

MAHAVIR: Your wish will be fulfilled at Chitrakuta. (*Disappears.*)

TULASI (*chants*):

>Rama, Rama , Rama,
>How much ambrosia the Creator has infused
>As He molded these two letters in solitude
>An enormous source of nectar
>These two letters are!
>The more I chant, the more the passion intensifies
>Prompting me to sing again and again.
>As I sing more
>Sweeter gets the name (*chants the name of Rama*).
>Hear me everyone,
>All trudging painfully across the desert of this life
>Stricken with heat and thirst, the name of Rama
>Will be your convoy.
>Come sing with me and
>The divine taste of nectar do enjoy;
>Every nook and corner of your heart
>Will be illumined with its light.
>You will forget all pains, rise above your tiny self,
>Sing the sweet songs day and night.
>All fevers and frets of this moribund world
>Crushing under your feet,
>Fill every moment of your life
>With absolute bliss.

(*Someone speaks in the background, 'Rama, Rama! I am a cow-slayer, an abominable sinner I am!' Enter a Brahmin.*)

BRAHMIN: I have slain a cow. I have visited a number of pilgrimage places and performed worships there. But I have not been able to shed the sin off my soul.

TULASI: My child, you are uttering the name of Rama incessantly. All your sin has been absolved. Why do you consider yourself a sinner? You are not.

BRAHMIN (*chants 'Rama, Rama'*): Is it so, O noble saint? Is my sin really absolved?

TULASI: Without any doubt! The shastra *Katyayana Smriti* says, '*Krutaischa kriyamanaischa bhavishydvischa patakaih. Rameti dyokshyaram nama sakrujjaptwavishudhyati.*'

BRAHMIN: What does it mean?

TULASI: All the sins that were committed, or are being committed, or are going to be committed will be absolved by the chanting of the two syllables 'ra' and 'ma'. You have already been redeemed through the continuous chanting of these two syllables. Go take a bath and eat the food offerings made to God with me.

BRAHMIN: Victory to Rama! Do you mean to say I am no longer a sinner?

TULASI: Certainly. Now have your bath. (*The Brahmin leaves.*) How erroneous a thought! The uttering of the name of Rama just once, even lightheartedly, rids man of all evils. This Brahmin chants the name non-stop, yet he believes himself to be a sinner!

(*Enter two Brahmins of Kashi.*)

FIRST BRAHMIN: O saint, all of us love you and hold you in high esteem. Do tell us what was your advice to that cow-slayer?

TULASI: I assured him that he is no longer a sinner. I asked him to come here after a bath and both of us shall eat the food-offerings made to God.

SECOND BRAHMIN: He has not performed any act of expiation. How could his soul be purged of the sin without that? Do you think you have done the right thing by taking a course of action which is not approved and accepted by our shastras?

TULASI: Do both of you respect what the shastras prescribe?

THE BRAHMINS: Of course we do.

TULASI: This is what the shastra *Vashistha Smriti* says, '*Kotishah manujanamjad durita samupasthitam. Rama Rameti sankritya tanmasayati manabah.*' It means that the soul of a man who has committed millions of sin is purged instantly of them by singing and celebrating the name of Lord Rama. The *Nandi Purana* also endorses the same: *Sarbada sarbakaleshu je cha kurbanti patakam. Rama nama japamkritwa janti dhama sanatanam.*

THE BRAHMINS: Tell us what it means.

TULASI: Even the perpetually sinning souls attain heaven by chanting Rama's name. All these sayings are not mine; I am quoting from the shastras.

FIRST BRAHMIN: True. These sayings are from the shastras.

TULASI: Then how can you accuse me of going against the prescription of the shastras? If one's sin is atoned with one single utterance of Rama's name, how can this man who constantly chants the name be considered a sinner?

SECOND BRAHMIN: Look here, O hermit, we do not intend to argue with you. However, we do believe that only by chanting the name of Rama, the sin of this man could not be absolved.

FIRST BRAHMIN: Let him go the temple of Lord Vishwanath and offer grass to the stone bull located at the threshold of the temple. If the bull accepts the grass from his hand, only then will he be believed to have shed the sin that soils his soul.

TULASI: All right. (*The Brahmin comes back after taking a bath.*) Come with me, my child.

(*Exit all. In front of the temple of Lord Vishwanath, the cow-slayer Brahmin is asked to offer a bunch of grass to the stone bull.*)

FIRST BRAHMIN: Let us see. O divine bull, accept the grass from the hands of this man if you consider him innocent! (*The stone bull accepts the grass from the cow-slayer Brahmin's hand and munches it.*)

THE BRAHMINS (*together*): Incredible!! (*To Tulasi Das*) O saint, please forgive us! We bow at your feet. We are ignorant and naïve. Be merciful to us and teach us the right way to sing the glory of Rama.

TULASI: May with the grace of Lord Rama you excel in the chanting of His name. (*Takes the name of Rama.*)

*Scene Nine*

(*The hermitage of Tulasi Das at Kashi.*)

FIRST DEVOTEE: O noble hermit! I am a disgraceful creature; I neither know devotion nor do I love God. What will be my fate?

TULASI: You need not worry about your fate in this age of Kali. Only chant the name of Rama. (*Sings:*)

> The name of Rama is the tree of wish-fulfillment
>
> As sweet as raw sugar is its taste
>
> With palms folded take his name and attain your goal
>
> Experience the bliss ultimate.
>
> The name of Rama is the tree of wish-fulfillment
>
> Precious as the heavenly cow is his devotion,
>
> The dust at the Lord's lotus feet
>
> Renders auspicious everything under the sun.

SECOND DEVOTEE: O noble saint, I neither have love for His name, nor am I capable of devotion. I have no spiritual resources to lean on; what will be my end?

TULASI: It is not very important whether you love the name or not; you can take the name at random—even while you eat or sleep. The Lord will bless you.

THIRD DEVOTEE: Shall we obtain the Lord's blessings even if we take his name sitting on the bare earth? I mean, without spreading a mat to sit on, or without having washed or cleaned ourselves properly?

TULASI: Yes, without any doubt. You don't have to worry about such little things while you chant the Lord's name. Man's soul is gratified by just uttering the sacred name—how and when are not important. Do you recite the Ramayana I wrote regularly?

FOURTH DEVOTEE: Yes, we do.

TULASI: It is enough. The Ramayana will sustain you. It will give you the spiritual support you need to sail across the ocean of mortal life. Recite the evening prayers.

FIRST DEVOTEE: I say the evening prayers whenever I find time.

TULASI: That is very good.

ALL DEVOTEES: We bow our respects to you.

TULASI: Bless you. Come again.

ALL DEVOTEES: Certainly.

(*Enter a Brahmin named Sukhapal.*)

TULASI: My child, where have you come from?

SUKHAPAL: I have come all the way from the kingdom of Mewar.

TULASI: Is that so? What is your name?

SUKHAPAL: Sukhapal Mishra is my name.

TULASI: And what is the purpose of your visit?

SUKHAPAL: I have come here to deliver you a letter from the queen of Mewar.

TULASI: I have heard about Queen Mirabai; a great devotee of the Lord she is. Let me have the letter. (*Sukhapal hands the letter to Tulasi Das.*)

SUKHAPAL: O sir, what does the queen say in her letter?

TULASI: Listen, I will read out. (*Reads the letter aloud.*)

*At the feet of Lord Krishna I surrender myself.*

*I offer my sincere regards at your feet, O noble sage Tulasi Das.*

*O' great soul, you are graced with all virtues and can dispel all evils. I bow my respects several times to you. I beg you to destroy the pain and sorrows of my life. I am being harrowed by my kith and kin because I keep the company of saints, practise austerity, and sing prayers to Lord Krishna. Such conduct on my part sparks their rage and they make me suffer through various means. Giridharilal (Lord Krishna) is the only support I have. My mind rests steadfastly at His lotus feet. I regard you as my father and my mother. You bring peace to the minds of your devotees. Kindly advise me about what my duty should be in such difficult circumstances. I end my letter here.*

*Your slave Mira, who serves at your feet*

SUKHAPAL: Please write a reply to the letter. I will return to Mewar at the earliest.

TULASI: I will write the reply, but why are you in a hurry? Take a bath and have a darshan of Lord Vishwanath and eat some of the 'food offering' made to the Lord. Rest for a couple of days. You may leave thereafter.

SUKHAPAL: I have to return today at any cost.

TULASI: Well, take rest tonight. Tomorrow you may leave for Mewar. (*Looks at one of the disciples*) Would you get me a quill and some ink and a piece of paper?

(*The disciple brings a piece of paper, the inkpot, and a quill. Tulasi Das writes the reply.*)

FIRST DISCIPLE: What did you write in your letter?

TULASI: Listen, I will read out. (*Reads out.*)

*May my soul rest at Sri Rama's feet. My blessings to you, Queen Mirabai. Any one that disrespects God is the enemy of man, and if such a person is even the closest kin of yours, he must be abandoned* forthwith. Did not Prahalad abandon his Vishnu-hater father? Vibhisana had abandoned his brother Ravana because the latter hated Rama. Prince Bharatha, too, left his own mother Kaikeyi for similar reasons. King Vali had ignored the advice of his mentor Shukracharya who derogated the dwarf incarnation of Lord Vishnu. The gopis, maidens of Vrindavan, had deserted their husbands and family members to be with Krishna. Such acts of these devotees have proved beneficial and auspicious for the world. It is a sacrilege to keep company of a person who does not love God. No one applies the kohl that stings his eyes. He who guides and helps you to get closer to God, is a true friend and the real kin. You should love him more than you love yourself.

Wishing you well,
Tulasi Das

(He gives the letter to Sukhapal.)

TULASI: Go, Sukhapal, take a bath.

(Sukhapal leaves; the sound of people talking is heard in the background. 'Ma! Please don't be late. All arrangements have been made,' a voice says. A woman's voice is heard close by: 'I will just pay my respects to the saint.' Enter a Brahmin woman. She bows to Tulasi Das.)

TULASI: May fortune favour you!

BRAHMIN WOMAN: Your blessing is of no use to me, O great saint. My husband has passed away a few hours ago. The funeral pyre is ready. I am going to enter the flames of the pyre and die with my husband.

TULASI: Why, my daughter? Why do you want to do that?

BRAHMIN WIDOW: Of what use this life of mine will be without my husband? I shall go to heaven and experience divine joy if I die with him.

TULASI: The heavenly joy you speak about is not eternal. Your soul will return to the earth and pass through the sufferings of life. Will it not be better to follow a course that will put an end to this cycle of death and rebirth?

BRAHMIN WIDOW: O' noble soul, what must I do?

TULASI: Surrender your soul to God; meditate on Him and chant the name of Rama.

BRAHMIN WIDOW (*chants*): Rama, Rama, Rama. Aha! How sweet the name is! (*She falls at Tulasi Das's feet and clutches them*) O great sage, you have witnessed the real God with your eyes; you are much above the common and ordinary people like us. A great devotee of the Lord you are. Your blessing is sure to bear fruit. You have to breathe life into my dead husband in the same way Yama, the god of death, brought Satyavan back to life.

TULASI: The birth and death of man are only in the hands of Sitaram—the god Rama and the goddess Sita.

BRAHMIN WIDOW: The power of Sitaram is transmitted to the Lord's devotees. They become equally powerful through their faith. Please come with me. (*She entreats Tulasi Das.*)

TULASI: Must I come? All right. (*Addressing his disciples.*) All of you come with me.

*Scene Ten*

(*The royal court of Delhi. Present in the court are Emperor Akbar, Tansen, the emperor's councillor, and a Muslim pilgrim.*)

AKBAR: The devotional song which Queen Mirabai was singing in a temple in the kingdom of Mewar still rings in my ears. How melodious a voice she has! And what a beautiful prayer song she sang! I remember the lines too:

> The moment since my eyes fell on the image of Krishna, Nanda's son,
>
> Neither on this life or the thoughts of the other world I can focus on.

Each word is as if steeped in ambrosia! Divine love expressed in a passionate, mellifluous voice created an indescribable, enthralling impact.

TANSEN: *Jahanpanah* (His Highness)! She does not seem to belong to this earth!

AKBAR: You are right. She is not human. Perhaps some maiden of Braja, inflicted by some divine curse, has descended on this earth in a human form.

TANSEN: People say so.

AKBAR: There is no match to your master's song too.

TANSEN: Neither Mirabai nor my guruji sings for human beings. God Himself is the listener of their songs. Those who sing in a royal court like me can, therefore, never stand a chance to match them.

AKBAR (*addressing the councillor*): Wazir, have you sent a messenger to Kashi?

WAZIR: Yes, huzoor!

AKBAR (*turning to Tansen*): A strange news has reached me. Goswami Tulasi Das has breathed life into a dead man. I have never heard of any such thing happening anywhere. I have sent men to invite him to Delhi.

TANSEN: Will he accept the invitation and come here?

AKBAR: I have sent an appropriate man for the task. It is more than possible that he will accept my invitation.

(*A voice chanting 'Rama, Rama' is heard. Enter Tulasi Das. All rise and bow greetings to him. Tulasi Das joins his palms politely in return.*)

AKBAR: Welcome, sir! I am so glad to have the good fortune of meeting a divine saint like you.

TULASI (*chants the name of Rama*): Jahanpanah, please do not call me a divine saint. I am just a poor, ordinary man.

AKBAR: You have brought a dead man back to life. I have never heard of such a miracle. Should I not believe that you are superhuman?

TULASI: Why have you sent for me, Jahanpanah?

AKBAR: I know you possess superhuman power. You have breathed life into a dead man. You have to perform such a miracle here.

TULASI: O Emperor, I have no super power as you say. The holy name of Rama is the only support I have. That is my only resource.

AKBAR: Well, all right. Show me your Rama.

TULASI: It is not in my hands. It is the Lord's wish whether he would show Himself or not.

AKBAR: Are you not a great devotee of Rama? You can make him appear before me if you wish so. He will be compelled to appear if you pray to him.

TULASI: I do not possess the power to make Lord Rama appear any time at any place.

AKBAR: You must forgive me, but you cannot leave from here until you have made Rama give me a darshan.

TULASI: How can I do something which is beyond my capacity?

AKBAR (calls loudly): Guard! (A sentry hurries in and salutes the emperor.)

SENTRY: Yes, Jahanpanah?

AKBAR: Take away this hermit and keep him in the prison. He will be kept behind bars till he makes his Rama appear in person. (The sentry leads Tulasi Das out.)

TANSEN: The man is a saint and devotee. He has committed no crime. To send him to prison ... (he stops).

AKBAR: Ustadji, I am not doing anything to disgrace the saint. I know God always comes to the rescue of His devotees. He will certainly do something to save the saint. We will have the blissful experience of seeing God performing some miracle to relieve his devotee's suffering. Don't you worry about anything. Lord Rama, to whom he has surrendered himself, will not keep quiet at His devotee's distress. He will soon adopt some measure to save him. Won't you sing a devotional song now?

TANSEN (*plays the violin and sings to its tune*):

O Vishnu, O Krishna

Addressed by many names you are,

Madhava, Madhusudana, the lotus-eyed Keshava.

You roamed the woods of Braja

In the guise of a cowherd boy,

The demon-slayer who sent Kansa to his ruins

With power indomitable all pride you destroy.

As Vishnu you sojourn in heaven

In the gigantic dwarf from

You were immanent,

Brahma offers his prayers to you.

O Lord, you wander across the universe

You are supreme, eternal; in you are

Contained all the elements.

Your tales of glory now sings

This Muslim devotee Tansen,

The 'cowherd boy' god, who had lifted

The Govardhan Mountain.

(*A loud noise of people shouting for help and the screeching and chattering of monkeys is heard outside: 'Help! Help! They are out to kill us …'*)

AKBAR: What is the matter?

(*Enter a sentry.*)

SENTRY: Jahanpanah! There is a commotion in the palace. Monkeys in thousands have flocked in the palace. They are attacking people and stripping the clothes off the begums. They have been hanging from the branches of the trees and the roofs of the houses. They have invaded the city of Delhi like floodwater invades the lands during the rainy season. They are stripping the people bare. (*The angry chatter of monkeys is heard.*)

(*A scream is heard outside: 'Help me! It has bared me!'*)

AKBAR: What is this? What is happening?

TANSEN: Hanumanji has sent his army of monkeys to release Goswami Tulasi Das.

(*Some monkeys chattering angrily barge into the royal court. They begin tearing at Emperor Akbar's apparel. One of them gives a hard push to the councillor, and others lift the violin.*)

AKBAR (*to the monkeys*): Stop, calm down. I will get the Goswami released immediately. (*Addressing the sentry*) Guard! Release the saint and lead him here respectfully.

(*The monkeys keep chattering; some examine the violin and try to play it in a wrong manner.*)

TANSEN: O Lord Mahavir, please do not destroy the violin!

(*The guard returns with Goswami Tulasi Das, and Akbar falls at Tulasi Das's feet.*)

AKBAR: Forgive my offence, O noble saint!

TULASI: I am nothing but a poor mendicant. You must not speak to me in this way.

AKBAR: I have realized what a great devotee of Lord Rama you are!

(*The monkeys keep chattering; they give another push to the councillor.*)

TANSEN (*entreats the monkeys*): Please don't break the instrument.

AKBAR: A huge army of monkeys has invaded Delhi. Please do save us! We will vacate the palace immediately. This palace will be henceforth the property of your Lord Raghunath.

TULASI (*prays to Lord Hanuman with folded palms*):
>My salutations to the son of the wind god
>Who wears the Ramayana's string of gems around his neck
>Like mosquitoes the demons he had crushed:
>And had shrunk the ocean to a small pool of water.
>O son of Anjana,
>You are the destroyer of Janaki's woe,
>The Lord in the form of a monkey
>An indomitable warrior, a terror to His foe:
>Who had slain Akshaya, and challenged
>King Ravana's might,
>And had made the domain of Lanka
>Tremble with fright.

(*Loud angry chatters and growls are heard in the background.*)

## Scene Eleven

(*The hut of Tulasi Das at Chitrakuta. Enter a thief.*)

THIEF: A king has gifted a gold platter and a golden pot to the hermit the other day. I had my eyes on them. For the last three nights I have been coming here to steal the gold utensils. But every night, at whichever hour I came, I found a dusky-complexioned sentry guarding the hut with a bow and an arrow in hand. But how strange that I no longer covet the gold utensils! However, I desperately long to catch a glimpse of that dusky-complexioned boy. I seem to have lost all interest in life other than stealing a glance at him. I will come here in the morning and request the hermit to show me that sentry. (*Exit.*)

(*Enter Rama with a bow and an arrow in hand.*)

RAMA: I do not have to worry much about those who are able to take care of their duties and responsibilities. But I have to bear the burden of the responsibilities of those who cannot do that and surrender themselves to me. I fulfil the needs and protect the resources of those who focus their minds on me. Well, let me see where the thief has gone. (*Leaves.*)

THIEF (*calls aloud standing outside the hut of Tulasi Das*): O noble sir, O great hermit …

TULASI: Who are you? What do you want?

THIEF: Where is that dusky-complexioned sentry who keeps vigil here?

TULASI: I don't understand. Which dusky-complexioned sentry are you talking about?

THIEF: I am a thief. For the last few nights I have been coming here to steal your golden plate and pot. But every time I come here I find a sentry with a bluish-green complexion like freshly sprouted grass, guarding your hut. He carries a bow and an arrow. I do not understand what change has come over me after watching him night after night, but I am no longer interested in the gold utensils. My eyes are thirsting to have a glimpse of the sentry. O' noble saint, I fall at your feet and beg of you— bring him just once before my eyes. (*The thief falls at Tulasi Das's feet.*)

TULASI (*in amazement*): How fortunate you are! You have seen Lord Rama in person! O' merciful Lord! Is it that you keep awake through the nights to keep watch over these petty possessions of mine?! (*He hurries inside the hut and returns with the gold utensils.*)

TULASI (*to the thief*): Do you want these? Take them.

THIEF: O' noble hermit, I am not interested in these things any more. Just let me know where can I find that sentry.

TULASI: My son, I have no power to do that. It was because of the virtues you accumulated in your previous lives that you were able to catch sight of the Lord for three nights. Now take these ı utensils and leave.

THIEF: I don't need them. Give me shelter at your feet. If I keep your company, one day or the other I might catch another glimpse of the dusky-complexioned sentry.

TULASI: Well, we will think about it later.

THIEF (*with childlike obstinacy*): Not later, now. You must do something about it now!

TULASI: All right, come back after taking a bath. (*Both leave.*)

(*Enter Rama.*)

RAMA: My job here is over. Tulasi Das has given shelter to the thief. He has practised austerity in many previous lives. That is how he saw me in person.

(*Enter Mahavir. Dasya and Madhura are accompanying him. Both look imploringly at Rama.*)

MAHAVIR: Now seek the advice of the Lord. He will settle the issue.

RAMA: What issue is to be settled?

MAHAVIR: O Lord, these two are the symbols of two types of devotion—one represents servility and the other, love. They debate to prove their supremacy over each other. One argues that the dominant emotion in Ramlila is servility, that is, the devotee is the slave of the Lord; and the other says that in *Krishnaleela* (the play of Lord Krishna) the emotion that guides the devotee is love. Since I was not able to decide, I have brought them to you.

RAMA: Come to me, both of you. (*They approach Rama and he puts his hand on their heads affectionately.*)

Listen to me, O Dasya! O Madhura!

I am the one and only rasa, the only and the ultimate emotion,

I am 'all emotions epitomized'.

There is no second thing except me;

To experience these emotions contained in me

I am embodied in them,

Servility, tranquility, amicability, love, and filial affection

I dwell in all—the act I eternally perform,

All emotions are different forms of me,

I am the whole immense universe.

I am base, I am excellent,

All pervasive I am, omnipotent.

I live forever in man

Which I intend to worship me with

I enthrone myself in his heart

And make his emotion mine for good.

Remember, I am all rasa—all rasa I hold in myself!!

(*Both bow at Rama's feet. The voice of Tulasi Das is heard.*)

TULASI: O Lord Mahavir, enable me to see Lord Rama once more.

MAHAVIR: Come, come, O great devotee.

(*Enter Tulasi Das. He catches the sight of Rama.*)

TULASI (*in excessive joy*): What do I see! Here is the blue-complexioned Lord Rama! May I die at His feet! (*Falls at Rama's feet*) O my Lord, let me take refuge at your feet!

# The Portrayal of Women in
# Sarala Mahabharata[*]

Sarala Das's Mahabharata is unique among the books written in the Prakrit language of India. Few fifteenth-century works of such enormous range are seen in Prakrit. Sarala's Mahabharata is a completely autonomous work and not a mere translation of Vyasa Dev's original work. If we consider Vyasa's Mahabharata to be a reflection of the contemporary sociopolitical realities, Sarala's work will also have to be viewed as a mirror held up to the Odisha and India of his own times.

In his work, Sarala appears to have depicted the condition of the ordinary Odia society of his time, its customs and traditions, joys and sorrows. It is a pioneering attempt at representing a

* Originally titled 'Sarala Mahabharatare Ketoti Samaja Chitra', this essay first appeared in Sucharita, First Year, No. 9, pp. 21–4, and later in Sarala Devi: Lekhika, Sanskarika, Biplabini, Sachidananda Mohanty (ed.) (Cuttack: Agraduta Publications, 2004), pp. 229–35. Translated by Bikram K. Das.

certain social and moral code. Sarala Das has not forgotten to include, at many places in the book, a depiction of the character of the typical Odia woman, her form and appearance, her political views, the marriage rituals, and dress and ornaments. He exhibits extraordinary insight in his portrayal of various characters, particularly women characters. His women are a blend of virtues and flaws; they represent the conflict between the divinity of woman and the humanity of the ordinary mortal.

The men and women of those times observed many social customs along with their religious practices, vows, fasts, and worship of goddesses. *Pitru tarpan* (oblations to the spirits of ancestors), *daan* (giving away of gifts in charity), puja, *upasana* (meditation), *seva* (serving the poor), bhakti, *vinay* (humility), *veerata* (valour in battle), and *guru gaurava* (honouring teachers and elders) were seen in public conduct. No one ignored scriptural or social rules of conduct in daily life. The lives of all, men as well as women, were regulated by the moral code, and there were rules for the ordinary routines of life. The science of astrology was respected, and wise astrologers and scholars were consulted for all social activities.

General as well as art education was prevalent among women. Women, with their inborn feminine intuitions, were actively involved in all kinds of social activity, including the governance of the kingdom and conduct of war.

## Marriage Customs

Sarala's Mahabharata refers to a wide range of marriage customs, including *kanya haran* (marriage following the abduction of the bride), *yuddha* (marriage following the declaration of war), *gandharva vivah* (marriage through the exchange of vows, without priests or rituals), as well as traditional Vedic marriages. Marriage rites that are observed even today, such as *mangala krutya* (observance of auspicious rituals such as the application of turmeric), *lavana chamari* (sprinkling of salt), *diya mangala* (worship of family gods), sprinkling of kumkum, *taila* (application of perfumed oils), *kaudi khela* (ritual gambling with sea shells), purification of the bride and the groom by seven married women whose husbands were alive, *hasta ganthi* (the tying together of the bride's and the bridegroom's hands), and the like, are depicted. Even practices preceding a marriage, such as the matching of horoscopes, are mentioned. There is reference to the giving of dowry by the bride's father, including cattle, horses, elephants, vessels and utensils, gold, diamonds, and the like.

Odia society, particularly in the villages, has not changed much since Sarala's days. The old traditions still survive. Odia brides in the later half of the nineteenth century and the earlier part of the twentieth century wear the same clothes and the same ornaments that Sarala Das wrote about. Many kinds of ornaments were used.

Girls were given away in marriage only after puberty, but a father whose daughter remained unmarried even after that age was considered a social outcast. There is mention of fathers weeping when daughters left their homes after marriage. Mothers then, as now, wailed songs of parting when daughters left. This is how a mother's wailing is shown in Sarala's Mahabharata:

> Queens and noble ladies came to weep
> Calling out the bride's name in sorrow. (*Madhya Parva*)

The ritual of wailing when bidding farewell to the bride still survives in towns and villages.

## Education of Women

The education of women was common in that age. Had it not been so, Sarala Das would not have shown, while depicting the abduction and marriage of princesses, the singing of songs by women near the wedding *bedi* (ritual platform). In the *Virat Parva* of the Mahabharata, when the Pandavas are shown as living in anonymity in the palace of King Virat, the valiant Arjuna, in the guise of Brihannala, served Princess Uttara and taught her dance and music as well as the fine arts. This incident is not an invention of Sarala Das; it is to be found in the original Mahabharata. Although Vyasa Deva refers to Draupadi as a *vidushi* (a woman of learning), Sarala Das makes no mention of the education she received. However, he does depict her educated and cultured behaviour, her highly developed sense of right and wrong, her rationality and power of judgement. When, after the abduction of Sri Krishna's sister Subhadra, by Arjuna, the kings who were the allies of Kauravas, fought against Arjuna, it was Subhadra who took control of Arjuna's chariot, as his *sarathi*.

# List of Selected Works of Sarala Devi

*Nari Jagata* (1935)
*Utkalara Nari Samasya* (1935)
*Bharatiya Mahila Prasanga* (1935)
*Rabindra Puja* (1941)
*Utkal Bharati Kabi Pratibha* (1940, 1958)
*Sarala Mahabharatare Nari Chitra* (1952)
*Beera Ramani*
*Maru Kahani* (1953)
*Bishwa Biplabini* (1958)
*Rajavamananda* (1963)
*Panchapradipa*
*Gopal Krishna Kabi Pratibha*
*Katha Ramayana*
*Satya Dharma*
*Amulyanidhi*
*Jana Bai*

# Bibliography

Athavale, Parvati. 1930. *My Story: The Autobiography of a Hindu Widow*. New York and London: G.P. Putnam and Sons.

Das, Bikram. 1997. '*Adi Biplabini Sarala Devi*', *The Samaj* (Annual Issue): 67–70.

Devi, Banaj. 1999. *Alibha, Anala Sikha: Sarala*. Bhubaneswar: Paschima Publications.

Devi, Kokila. 1915. '*Bilasini*', *Utkal Sahitya*, 20 (5).

Devi, Haripriya. 1940. '*Bandini Nari*' [Woman, the Prisoner], *Utkal Sahitya*.

Devi, Rama. 1884. 'The Birth of Nationalist Fervor', in *Jeebana Pathe*. Cuttack: Grantha Mandir.

Devi, Sarala. 1934. *Narira Dabi*. Cuttack: Hindustan Granthamala.

———. 1935. *Bharatiya Mahila Prasanga*. Cuttack: Hindustan Granthamala.

———. 1936. *Nari Jagata*. Cuttack: Hindustan Granthamala.

———. 1948. '*Bharatiya Narinku Mahatma Gandhinka Prerana*', *Nababharata*.

———. 1953. *Maru Kahani*. Cuttack: Self-published.

Devi, Sarala. 1958 [1940]. *Kuntala Kumarinka Kabi Pratibha*. Cuttack: Bani Binode Granthalaya.

———. 1958. *Bishwa Biplabini*. Cuttack: Orissa Publishing House.

———. 1986 [1931]. *Basanti*. Cuttack: New Students' Store.

———. 2005. 'A Letter from Prison', in Sachidananda Mohanty (ed.), *Early Women's Writing, 1898–1950: A Lost Tradition*. New Delhi: SAGE Publications.

———. 2006, 'My Idol', Sachidananda Mohanty (tr.), in Jatindra K. Nayak (ed.), *Meeting the Mahatma*. Bhubaneswar: Rupantar.

———. 'A Memorable Event of My Life', in Sasmita Mohapatra (ed.), *Atitara Sabuja Smruti* [*Memorable Vignettes of Yesteryears*]. Bhubaneswar: Siksha Sandhan (forthcoming).

Devi, Shakuntala. 1947. 'Nari', *Shankha*, 8 (Magha): 470–3.

Devi, Sushila. 1947. '*Manisha Semane*' [They Too Are Human], *Shankha* (summer): 702–5.

Devi, Urmila. 1937. '*Nari Swadhinata*' [True Freedom of Women], *Sahakara*, pp. 63–71.

Dhall, Manjushri. 1997. *The British Rule: Missionary Activities in Orissa, 1822–1947*. New Delhi: Har Anand Publications.

Forbes, Geraldine. 1996. *Women in Modern India*, The New Cambridge History of India Series. Cambridge: Cambridge University Press. Published in India by Foundation Press.

———. 2014. 'My Life and Women's Studies', in Rekha Pandey (ed.), *A Journey into Women's Studies: Crossing Interdisciplinary Boundaries*. London: Palgrave Macmillan.

Goyal, Omita. 2012–13. 'Interrogating Women's Leadership and Empowerment', *India International Centre Quarterly*, Special Issue, 39 (winter and spring, 3 and 4).

Jayawardena, Kumari. 1986. *Feminism and Nationalism in the Third World*. London: Zed Books.

J. Nehru to A. Swaminadhan. 2 September 1936. Jawaharlal Nehru Papers, G48. New Delhi: Nehru Memorial Museum & Library.

Jha, Madhu, Manjeet Bhatia, and Shelly Pandey (eds). 2014. *Women's Studies in India: A Journey of 25 Years*. Jaipur and New Delhi: Rawat Publications.

Karlekar, Malavika. 1991. *Voices from Within: Early Personal Narratives of Bengali Women*. New Delhi: Oxford University Press.

Kar, Narmada. 1915. '*Dwanda*' [Dilemma], *Utkal Sahitya*, 18 (10).

Kelly, Mary. 1984. *Private Woman, Public Stage: Literary Domesticity in Nineteenth-Century America*. New York: Oxford University Press.

Kishwar, Madhu and Vanita Ruth. 1984. *In Search of Answers: Indian Women's Voices from Manushi*. London: Zed Press.

Lakshmi, C.S. 1986. *The Face behind the Mask: Women in Tamil Literature*. New Delhi: Shakti Books.

Mallick, Basanta Kumar. 2004. *Paradigms of Dissent and Protest: Social Movements in Eastern India, c. A.D. 1400–1700*. New Delhi: Manohar.

'Memorandum for Women's Education in the University in India', submitted by Smt. Sarala Devi, Senate Member Utkal University, Cuttack, n.d., Estate of Sarala Devi.

Minault, Gail. 1988. 'Urdu Women's Magazines in the Twentieth Century', *Manushi*, 48: 2–9.

Mishra, Ajay Kumar. 2004. *Sarala Devi*. Bhubaneswar: Orissa Sahitya Akademi.

Mishra, Prasanna Kumar (ed.). 1994. *Kabibara Radhanath Granthabali*. Cuttack: Granthamandir.

Mohanty, Chandra Talpade. 1997. 'Under Western Eyes: Feminist Scholarship and Colonial Discourses', in Padmini Mongia (ed.), *Contemporary Postcolonial Theory: A Reader*. New Delhi: Oxford University Press. First published in 1994 in *Boundary*.

Mohanty, Jatindra Mohan. 2006. *History of Oriya Literature*. Bhubaneswar: Vidya.

Mohanty, Nivedita. 1982. *Oriya Nationalism: Quest for a United Orissa, 1866–1936*. New Delhi: Manohar.

Mohanty, Sachidananda. 1994. 'Rebati's Sisters: Search for Identity through Education', *India International Centre Quarterly*, 21 (4): 41–52.

———. 1995. 'Rebati and the Woman Question in Orissa', *Interdisciplinary Journal of the Indian Institute of Advanced Studies*.

———. 2002. *Bismruta Parampara: Oriya Sahityare Nari Pratibha: 1898–1950*. Kolkata: Sahitya Akademi.

———. 2002. 'Kuntala Kumari and the Early Feminist Rhetoric in Orissa', in Malashri Lal and Sukritipaul Kumar (eds), *Women's Studies in India*. Shimla: Indian Institute of Advanced Studies.

———. 2002. 'Language Dialectic and Fakir Mohan's Rhetoric of Progress', in *English and the Indian Short Story*. Hyderabad: Orient Longman.

———. 2002. 'Culture, Ideology, Translation Practice: Early Women's Writing in Orissa', in Anisur Rahman (ed.), *Translation: Poetics and Practice*. New Delhi: Creative Books.

Mohanty, Sachidananda. 2004. 'Female Identity and the Conduct Book Tradition in Orissa: The Virtuous Woman in the Ideal Home', in C. Vijayasree (ed.), *Writing the West: Representations from Indian Languages*. New Delhi: Sahitya Akademi.

———. 2004. 'Shall I Write a Book Mama? Zones of Silence and Female Creativity in 19th Century America', in Uttara Chakraborty and Banimanjara Das (eds), *Women's Education and Politics of Gender*. Kolkata: Bethune College.

———. 2004. 'Women as Cultural Icons', *Confluence*, 3 (July–August, 4).

———. 2004. 'Burden of Shakti: Female Agency and Literary Creativity in Orissa', *Economic and Political Weekly*, 39 (24): 2442–4.

———. 2004. 'Female Identity and Conduct Book Tradition in Orissa', *Economic and Political Weekly*, 39 (4).

——— (ed.). 2004. *Sarala Devi: Lekhika, Sanskarika, Biplabini*. Cuttack: Agraduta Publishers.

——— (ed.). 2005. *Early Women's Writing in Orissa, 1898–1950: A Lost Tradition*. New Delhi: SAGE Publications.

———. 2005. *Sailabala Das*. Cuttack: Agraduta Publishers.

———. 2006. *Literature and Social Reforms in Colonial Orissa: The Legacy of Sailabala Das*. New Delhi: Sahitya Akademi.

———. 2008. 'English in Colonial Orissa: The Missionary Position', *Gender and Cultural Identity in Colonial Orissa*. Hyderabad: Orient Longman, pp. 145–50.

Mohapatra, Bishnu. 1996. 'Ways of Belonging: The Kanchi Kaveri Legend and the Construction of Oriya Identity', *Studies in History*, 12 (2): 203–21.

Mohapatra, Chakradhar. 1972. *Kuntala Kumari Jibana Charita*. Cuttack: Granthamandir.

Orwell, George. 1949. *Nineteen Eighty-Four*, ebook. London: Secker and Warburg; Toronto: S.J. Reginald Saunders.

Pai, Sudha. 2006. 'Region and Regional Consciousness', *The Book Review*, XXX (6).

Panigrahi, Nandini. 1949. 'Chimnira Daka' [The Call of the Chimney], *Sanket*.

Patel, Sujata. 1988. 'Construction and Reconstruction of Woman in Gandhi', *Economic and Political Weekly*, 23 (8): 467–8.

Patnaik, Binayak. 2006. 'Alakashram', in Bholanath Rout (ed.), *Jagatsinghpur: Atitha o Barthaman* [*Jagatsinghpur: Past and Present*]. Jagatsinghpur: Sanskruti Parishad.

Patnaik, Indira. 1991. *Kuntala Kumarinka Sahityika Kruti*. Cuttack: New Publishing Press.

Patra, S.C. 1979. *Formation of the Province of Orissa: The Success of the First Linguistic Movement in Orissa*. Kolkata: Punthi Pustak.

Patnaik, Basanta Kumari. 1981 [1951]. *Amada Bata* [The Untrodden Path]. Cuttack: Gitanjali Press.

Prabha, Bidyut. 1983. 'Pratighat', in *Bidyut Prabha Granthabali*. Cuttack: Friends' Publishers.

Pradhan, Atul Chandra. 1988. 'Educational Uplift of Women in 19th Century Orissa', *Our Documentary Heritage*, Vol. I. Bhubaneswar: Orissa State Archives.

———. 1994. 'The Civil Disobedience Movement in Orissa: The Participation and Awakening of Women', *Our Documentary Heritage*, Vol. II. Bhubaneswar: Orissa State Archives.

Raju, Rajendra. 1995. *Mahiyasai Mahila Sarala*. Berhampur: Bijay Book Store.

Ray, Apurba Ranjan. 1985. *Kuntala Kumari Sabat: Jibani O Pratibha*. Bhubaneswar: Orissa Sahitya Akademi.

Ray, Reba. 1323 (1897). 'Nirabe', *Utkal Sahitya*, 20 (Bhadra, 5): 231–4.

Sabat, Kuntala Kumari. 1969. *Granthamala*, Vols 1 and 2. Cuttack: Cuttack Students' Store.

Sangari, Kumkum and Sudesh Vaid. 1990. *Recasting Women: Essays in Colonial History*. New Delhi: Kali for Women. Originally published in 1989 by Rutgers University Press, New Brunswick.

Satpathy, Nityananda. 1983. *Bidyutprabha Grantabali*, Part I. Cuttack: Friends' Publishers.

Schneir, Miriam. 1970. *Feminism: The Essential Writings*. New York: Vintage.

Senapati, Rabinarayan. 1993. *Vyasa Kavi*. Bhubaneswar: Soujanya Publishers.

Singh, Jagabandhu. [1946] 1940. *Grihalakshmi*, Part 1. Cuttack: Cuttack Trading Company.

Srilatha, K. 2003. *The Other Half of the Coconut: Women Writing Self-Respect History*. New Delhi: Kali for Women.

Tharu, Susie. 1989. 'Tracing Savitri's Pedigree', in Kumkum Sangari and Sudesh Vaid (eds), *Recasting Women: Essays in Colonial History*. New Delhi: Kali for Women, pp. 254–68.

Tharu, Susie and K. Lalitha. 1993. *Women Writing in India: 600 B.C. to the Present*, Vol. 1. New Delhi: Oxford University Press. Vol. 2 published in 1995.

*Utkal Dipika.* 30 September 1871. 6 (38).

————. 5 November 1881. 16 (44).

Walsh, Judith. 1995. 'The Virtuous Wife and the Well-ordered Home: The Reconceptualisation of Bengali Women and their Worlds', in Rajat Kumar Ray (ed.), *Mind, Body and Society: Life and Mentality in Colonial Bengal.* New Delhi: Oxford University Press, pp. 331–63.

# Index

# About the Editor and Translators

## The Editor

**Sachidananda Mohanty** is professor and former head, Department of English, University of Hyderabad, India. Currently, he is vice chancellor, Central University of Orissa, Koraput, India. He is the recipient of numerous national and international recognitions, including the Katha Award and fellowships from the British Council, the Fulbright Foundation, and the Salzburg Seminar. A contributing editor to the literary e-journal *Muse India* (www. museindia.com), which is devoted to translations from Indian languages, he has published extensively in the field of British, comparative, postcolonial, gender, and translation studies at the national and international levels. He has done pioneering work in the fields of archival research and cultural history of nineteenth-century India, and his articles have appeared in *The Toronto South Asian Review*, *Economic and Political Weekly*, and *South Asia Review*, among others.

Mohanty has published widely on the theory and practice of translation, including the Odia translations of T.S. Eliot and Ezra Pound. He has contributed to a volume of translations devoted to medieval Indian poetry in regional languages. His notable works in the field of translated anthologies include *Early Women's Writings in Orissa, 1898–1950: A Lost Tradition* (2005).

## Translators

**Bikram K. Das** is a renowned translator of Odia texts—mainly literary—into English. He was awarded the first Sahitya Akademi prize for translation in 1989, for his English rendering of Gopinath Mohanty's *Paraja* (1987). He was formerly professor of Applied Linguistics at the English and Foreign Languages University, Hyderabad, India, and he has also taught at the National University of Singapore. He lives in Bhubaneswar, Odisha.

**Snehaprava Das**, reader in English, Binayak Acharya College, Berhampur, India, has co-translated into English, along with Paul St. Pierre, the first Odia novel *Padmamali* written by Umesh Chandra Sarkar in 1888; it was published in 2005. Her other major works of translation include *The World Within* (2008) by Baisnaba Charan Das, *Bibasini: A Historical Romance* (2010) by Ramshankar Ray, and *Prison Poems* (2014) by Utkalamani Gopabandhu Das. She has translated into English several long and short stories of reputed Odia writers, such as Manoj Panda, Das Benhur, Paramita Satpathy, and Gayatri Basumallick. She translated excerpts from biographies of eminent personalities such as Godavarish Mishra and Gangadhar Meher. Her English translations have appeared in periodicals such as *The Indian Literature*, *The Little Magazine*, and *Rock Pebbles*, among others.

**Chinmay Kumar Hota** completed his graduation from Ravenshaw College, Cuttack, and master's in English Literature from the University of Delhi. He writes essays, book reviews, and fiction in both English and Odia. He translates both fiction and non-fiction from Odia into English. He is the author of a collection of essays titled *Hits and Misses* (2010). He has reviewed books for various magazines and newspapers, including the *Indian Review of Books*, the *New Indian Express*, and *Political and Business Daily*. Hota's translations have appeared in many reputed publications including *Early Women's Writings in Orissa, 1898–1950: A Lost Tradition* (2005), *The Other Side of Reason: Oriya Stories from the Edge, From Bondage to Freedom* (2006), and *Reminiscences: Excerpts from Oriya and Bangla Autobiographies*, among others. He is based at Bhubaneswar.

**Sangram Jena** is a well-known poet, anthologist, translator, and editor. He has been editing the literary journal *Nishant* since the last 20 years. He has brought out more than 10 thematic collections, which include *Cuttack O Kolkata, Kshudha* (Hunger), *Mahanubhuttire Mahatma* (Reminiscences on Gandhiji), and *Nadinanadi* (River Tales). He has co-translated into English collections of poems by Guruprasad Mohanty and Bhanuji Rao. He has also translated into Odia Gabriel Garcia Marquez's novella *No One Writes to the Colonel* (*Chithi Asena*). He received the Sahitya Akademi Translation Award in 2011 for his Odia translation of the Urdu classic *Nati*. He is the editor of *Marg Asia*, a journal devoted to the study of Asian culture and civilization published by the Centre for Asian Studies, Bhubaneswar, India.

**Akhtar Jamal Khan** presently teaches English at Utkal University, Bhubaneswar. He wrote his doctoral dissertation on the fiction of V.S. Naipaul. Between 2009 and 2011, he was Visiting Faculty at King Khalid University, Kingdom of Saudi Arabia. He has co-translated into English the autobiography of Nisakar Das titled *Kharasuanru Kulabiri* (From Kharasuan to Kulabiri, 2006), an excerpt from which has been included in an anthology of Dalit writing which is to be published soon. He has also translated into English two collections of stories for children by Dash Benhur: *Story of Maita* (2007) and *A Basket of Stories* (2007). He has co-edited *Immortal Words* (2005), an anthology of English poems. His essay on 'Mughal Tamsa' was included in *Imaging Odisha* (2012).

**Anuja Khatua** graduated from Utkal University and is currently pursuing her MPhil at the Department of English, Ravenshaw University, Cuttack, India. Her English translation of Nanda Kishore Bal's classic Odia novel *Kanakalata* will be published soon. She has completed a certificate course in publishing and editing from Jadavpur University, Kolkata, India, and served as guest faculty at the College of Engineering and Technology, Bhubaneswar, and Gandhi Institute of Technology and Management, Bhubaneswar.

**Sachidananda Mohanty** (*See under 'The Editor'.*)

**Himansu S. Mohapatra** is professor of English at Utkal University and is a well-known literary critic. He has published articles in journals such as *International Fiction Review*, *Toronto Review of Contemporary Writing Abroad*, *Wasafiri*, and *Economic and Political Weekly*. He has contributed to books and has published a book of literary journalism titled *Model of the Middle* (2014). He has also published about a dozen reviews of translated works in the *Hindu Literary Review*, including Fakir Mohan Senapati's *Six Acres and a Third* (2005), Umesh Chandra Sarkar's *Padmamali*, Gurajada Appa Rao's *A Girl for Sale*, and the Benjamins-sponsored critical anthology *In Translation*. He has explored the theoretical and methodological issues of translation in scholarly essays in the Canadian journals *META* and *TTR*.

**Jatindra K. Nayak** received his education from Ravenshaw College and Merton College, Oxford, UK. He is currently professor of English, Utkal University. He has won the Hutch Crossword Indian Fiction Translation Award (2004) and Katha Award for translation (1997). He has translated Fakir Mohan Senapati's autobiography *The Story of My Life* (1997) and co-translated Senapati's *Chha Mana Atha Guntha* (*Six Acres and a Third*, 2005). His English translation of Chandrsekhar Rath's Odia novel *Yantrarudha* was published in 2003. He has also translated into English a journal titled *Satirtha*, co-translated Manoranjan Das's play *August Na* (*The Ninth of August*, 2005), his autobiography *Smruti Sanlap* (*A Dialogue with Memory*, 2002), Senapati's novel *Mamu* (The Maternal Uncle, 2006), and J.P. Das's *Desa, Kala, Patra* (*A Time Elsewhere*, 2009). Additionally, he has edited several thematic collections and he was editorial advisor to *Imaging Odisha* (2012).

**Jayaprakash Paramaguru** is presently associate professor of English at the Gandhi Institute of Technology and Management. After completing post-graduation in English literature from Utkal University, he published *Terry Eagleton's plays: A Stylistic Study* (2014) and subsequently received his PhD in Applied Linguistics from the same institution. He has published in national and international journals of repute and translated essays, short stories, and autobiographies of eminent Odia writers such as Krishnachandra Panigrahi, Gaganendranath Dash, Pandit Nilakantha Dash, Sarala Devi, and Fakir Mohan Senapati.

**Priyadarshi Patnaik** is professor, Department of Humanities and Social Sciences, Indian Institute of Technology Kharagpur. His areas of interest include visual art and culture, Indian aesthetics, non-verbal communication, and translation. He has published many papers and edited volumes in related areas. Also a creative writer and artist, he has published several poems, short stories, images, and illustrations in national and international journals. He translates primarily from Odia into English and he has coordinated a number of national-level workshops on translation of medieval Odia texts into English. He is currently translating the philosophical texts of medieval Odisha's Santha poets. He has also translated and illustrated Odia literature for children and the works of Odia women writers of early twentieth century, such as Bidyutprabha Devi and Sarala Devi.

**Anil Pradhan**, a social activist, is presently member-secretary of Siksha Sandhan, a resource centre for education based in Bhubaneswar. He has edited *In Their Own Voices: Stories, Memories, Impressions of Tribals in Orissa* (2010), and *Anubhabamala*, which is an autobiography of eminent educationist and Gandhian Sarat

Chandra Moharana. He has co-translated *On Education* (2003) authored by V. Vasily Sukhomlinsky. His English translations of excerpts from Odia autobiographies have been included in *From Bondage to Freedom*.

**Prasanta Kumar Purohit**, reader in English at Bargarh College, Odisha, has done his research in translation studies from Utkal University and was awarded PhD for his thesis entitled 'The Great Whirl: A Translation of Kanhu Charan Mohanty's Oriya Novel *Jhanjha* into English with a Critical Introduction'. He has completed MA in English with Comparative Literature as a special paper and has translated into English many of the stories and novellas by noted Odia writers such as Gopinath Mohanty, Pratibha Ray, and others, which are under consideration for publication.

**Paul St. Pierre** taught in translation programmes in Canada for more than 25 years and served as president of both the Canadian Association of Translation Studies and the Canadian Association of Schools of Translation. He has worked predominantly in the field of the history of translation and edited special issues of the translation journals *TTR* ('History in Translation' [1993] and 'Languages, Translation and Post-colonialism' [1997]), and *META* ('Translation and Post-colonialism in India' [1997]). He has published books on translation, including *Changing the Terms: Translating in the Postcolonial Era* (2000), which he co-edited with Sherry Simon, and *In Translation: Reflections, Refractions, Transformations* (2007), which was co-edited by Prafulla C. Kar. Since the past 20 years he has been collaborating on translations of literary texts from Odia into English. This has led to many notable publications at the national and international levels.